REDISCOVERING AMERICA!

Growing Up in the 40's

H. L. QUIST

"Rediscovering America! Growing Up in the 40's," by H.L. Quist. ISBN 1-58939-616-2 (electronic), 1-58939-616-2 (hardcover).

Library of Congress information on file with publisher.

Published 2004 by Virtualbookworm.com Publishing Inc., P.O. Box 9949, College Station, TX 77845, US. ©2004, H.L. Quist. All rights reserved. No part of this publication may be reproduced, stored in a retrieval system, or transmitted in any form or by any means, electronic, mechanical, recording or otherwise, without the prior written permission of H.L. Quist

Manufactured in the United States of America.

PREFACE

MOST MEMOIRS ARE WRITTEN by the rich and famous. I am neither. But, that fact does not make this story any less interesting, historical, or memorable. You will be the final judge of that.

Rediscovering America! is a trilogy. There are moments in everyone's life that define who we are and what we will be. Book One traces my family roots and my early years. I was born in the depths of The Great Depression, and viewed the world's greatest conflict through the eyes of a grade schooler who sold seeds for victory gardens as the nation unified and rallied to win World War II. These two catastrophic events, The Depression and the War, were perhaps the two most defining moments in 20th Century America. They unquestionably defined my life, as they did my family's and my contemporaries.'

I am a son of a Swedish immigrant father and an American born Swedish mother. Book One pays tribute to my heritage by tracing my roots from central and western Sweden in the 18th Century to the mid-western United States and eventually to a life-changing move to the enchantment of the culturally diverse and wind-driven plateaus of New Mexico.

Rediscovering America! recalls and preserves an era whose living memories will soon vanish with those who lived and loved in the forties and fifties. This memoir, written mostly in narrative, defines who we were as children, purportedly, of the "greatest generation." We were fascinated with a new entertainment medium that introduced us to Uncle Miltie and a zany red-head by the name of Lucy. And, our value systems were challenged by those iconoclastic rebels Marlon Brando and James Dean. Our awareness of sexual repression was heightened by a curvaceous and vulnerable blonde by the name of Marilyn. And, the sound of rock and roll aroused our senses like no music ever before. Elvis told us to let go while our parents desperately tried to hold us back.

Perhaps the most provocative aspect of this memoir is change — the profound change in the mores of America from the forties to the beginning of the 21st Century. The values, the responsibilities and the sexual restraints taught to us by our parents and teachers took a dramatic paradigm shift as the fifties became an era gone by. What happened? Was it rock and roll that liberated us as teenagers? Or, was it the pill that exorcized our fear of pregnancy? Was it the assassination of JFK that ended the "Age of Innocence?" Or, the seeds of distrust of government and the establishment sown by the duplicity of Vietnam? Was it a new pop drug culture in the sixties that in four decades of abuse has genetically flawed our children? Was it our wealth and power and our ability to want and have it all that changed our lives? What was the casual factor that ultimately manifested itself in the moral, financial and ethical breakdown in America, as a new century began in chaos?

During the last six decades we have witnessed more political, social, economic and technological change than in any period in American, or maybe even world, history. Our generation, born in the thirties, has experienced all of it. These threads of history are woven together within the fabric of this book with an intended introspection into us and our times.

This is also a story about a personal quest. First, to achieve recognition and success as a high school and college athlete and then to be a member of the U.S. Olympic Team, as my value and worth to myself and society were measured in achievements on the athletic field and gold medals, rather than dollars. Ultimately, success would later be determined and measured by income and assets as a businessman. This story reveals a unique personal and business relationship with my father as I try to benefit from the attributes of his success, while at the same time avoiding those flaws that caused his heartache and financial ruin.

Above all, this is a love story. A story about love of country, love of family and the unconditional love of an incredible woman who is the love of my life. It is a real, true-life love story about an unlikely and imponderable relationship given little or no chance to succeed that has endured for more than forty years.

For those readers who are children of the "greatest generation," you will relive those days when we "stepped on a crack to break Hitler's back" and cried when our senior prom marked the end of our "happy days" in high school. To those of you who are the age of our grandchildren and are now getting your first tattoo or your body pierced, you will read about our good old days and you might just say, "Hey dude, you guys were pretty cool!"

CONTENTS

REDISCOVERING AMERICA!
GROWING UP IN THE 40'S
BOOK ONE

DEDICATION

To my ancestors who endured so
much and took the risk of change,

and

To my parents and family whose
love and support made all things
in my life possible.

ACKNOWLEDGMENTS

To *Phil Thompson*, whose professional expertise in literature and knowledge of Green Bay history added immeasurable value to this book. Four years senior to the author, Phil's athletic prowess set a standard for all aspiring athletes, including myself. At East High School in Green Bay he excelled in football. He was selected the Most Valuable Player in the sport at Beloit College, and played professionally for the Racine Raiders. He also excelled in track and field in the sprints and long jump, and was an All-Army Champion in swimming and diving. Phil was Professor of English at the University of Wisconsin at Green Bay for 27, years and now lives in Green Bay, Wisconsin.

To *Helen Ferslev*, my fifth-grade teacher at Elmore School in Green Bay, whose knowledge and love of history inspired me at a very young age to revere my family's past and my city's culture.

To *Larry Ebsch*, whose knowledge and love of Menominee, Michigan, and Marinette, Wisconsin, enabled me to trace my father's formative years.

To *Mary Jane Herber*, whose long tenure at the Brown County Central Library made my research an enjoyable and successful task.

To *Larry Lawrence*, my cousin whose extraordinary will to survive and overcome overwhelming odds allowed him to become an integral part of this story.

To *Karen Markwardt (Jones)*, my first love, whose reappearance after 50 years brought real joy to reliving those good old days.

CHAPTER 1: ROOTS

ONE OF THE IRREPRESSIBLE QUESTS of the human condition is to discover our roots. Mine are deeply embedded in the fertile farmland in central and western Sweden. Both the Quists (my father's side) and the Andersons (my mother's side) emigrated near the turn of the twentieth century from areas in Sweden, remarkably not too remote from each other. The Quists (Qvist in Swedish) are from the Province of Bohuslän near the border with Norway, and the Andersons (Andersson in Swedish) had their roots in the Province of Värmland in central Sweden. Digging deeply for my roots proved to be exciting and rewarding, an experience that can also be shared by almost anyone who believes in the theory of "six degrees of separation."

According to the National Research Center, Inc. (NRC), the Swedish name Qvist is classified as being of ornamental origin. This is a relatively new form of surname whose history normally dated back only a few generations, although I have traced our name back six generations. Ornamental surnames are usually composed of two native words, often describing some pleasant aspects of nature, which do not have a direct connection to the eponymous bearer of the name or his place of residence. In our particular instance, our surname consists of one single element, derived from the Swedish and Norwegian word "KVIST," meaning "a twig of a tree." Variations of our surname Quist include Qvist, Kvist, and Kwist.

In the nineteenth century, Sweden formalized its naming system and each person was required to bear a fixed family name which was to be passed on to succeeding generations. So great was the profusion of last names ending in "son" that the government established a committee which published a list of suggested family names. The results from this process were ornamental names. It is possible that our name began with Nicolaus Qvist, born January 26, 1790. The NRC indicates that our name first appears in 1723 with the marriage of Anders Qvist to Anna Elisabeth Salner in Gäule, Gävelborg County. There does not appear to be any direct connection between Anders and our family.

The Swedes and, for all matters, all Scandinavians, were not aboriginal or native to the area that includes present day Norway, Denmark and Sweden. Some 40,000 years ago this large mass of land was covered by ice several miles thick at the peak of the ice age. Approximately 20,000 years ago, global warming (not induced by greenhouse gases) caused the ice to recede, and migrating hunters, using a landbridge connecting the continents, began to establish settlements on an area in southern Sweden which would be later known as Skåne. A second wave of migration left many settlement remains in western Sweden, presumably near the present day Province of Bohuslän (pronounced *Boosulan*), which is one of the areas of my focus. Who were these people and where did they come from? Lars O. Lagerqvist in his book *A History of Sweden* says:

> We do not know for certain, but currently a number
> of researchers tend to think they were probably the
> ancestors of the present-day Sami of Lapland which
> wave of migration brought the Indo-Europeans, who
> at least linguistically have long made up the majority
> of the Swedish population. This again we cannot
> determine with any certainty.[1]

So, our folks may have been Laps (Finnish) or Indo-Europeans or a mixture of both. Swedes for generations have been the brunt of ethnic jokes depicting us as a little slow on the draw mentally. Maybe it's due to a little congenital "lapse" in memory? (No offense to the Laplanders). Swedes, fortunately, do have the ability to laugh at themselves, as you'll discover. It's in our genes.

Lagerqvist helps to dispel the notion that our ancestors were a little slow when he says:

*The culture that arose during the Bronze Age (1800-
500 b.c.) in southern and central Sweden was
highly developed.*[2]

As evidence, Lagerqvist cites the rock carvings of
Bohuslän "... that symbolize fertility, ships, arms, and
other things ..." that "... bear exciting testimony to the
religion of the Swedes three thousand years ago or more."
Amongst the rock drawings are erotic couples that
indicate that there was time taken out from hunting and
gathering for other activities, but we do not need
historians and researchers to tell us that.

Without much question there is no period in
Scandinavian history that is more fascinating, and has
been open to so many interpretations, than the Viking Age
(800-1500 a.d.). Some recall that the Vikings were simply
marauders and pillagers who terrorized all of western
Europe and the Mediterranean, much like their namesake
tried to accomplish in the Central (Black and Blue)
division of the National Football League (many progeny of
the Vikings settled in Minneapolis, of course). Young
people today might consider the Vikings as goofy
characters depicted in the syndicated cartoon "Haggar the
Horrible." Time and contemporary representations may
have ameliorated the Viking's image but, make no mistake
about it and all jokes aside, they were mean, tough and
brutal in their quest to capture bounty and territory.

"The first known pillaging raid by Nordic Vikings was
recorded when they plundered the monastery of
Lindisfarne on Holy Island off the English Coast in 793,"[3]
says Lagerqvist. Hardly a formidable foe, it seems, but the
raids soon spread to Germany, France, Portugal and
Spanish seaboards and actually widened to the
Mediterranean. Apparently, these excursions in the west
were carried out by the Norwegian and Danish Vikings.
The Swedes conducted their raids in the east and reached
as far as Constantinople and the Black Sea by way of the
great Russian Rivers. What is interesting as far as my
ancestral endeavor is concerned is that the Bohuslän area
was Norwegian not only at the time of the Vikings, but it
was a part of Norway up to the seventeenth century. Geez,

the Qvists may have been on the Norwegian Viking team and were, egad, Norwegians and not Swedes! (An inside ethnic joke.)

Were the "Vikes" successful in their quest for fortune? Apparently so. In 1969 a great silver hoard called the Bronze Treasure was discovered on the Swedish island of Gotland. It consisted of coins of the Viking Age from Germany, England and the Cliphs of the Middle East, as well as silver ingots with old Slavic inscriptions from Russia. As recently as 1999, two discoveries of plundered Viking treasure were also dug up on Gotland, and they were almost eight times larger than the Burge treasure, which was over 10 kilos (22 pounds). Most of the coins were Islamic, an indication that our conflict with Islam could have started centuries before the Crusades.

On the positive side, the Vikings discovered North America via Iceland and Greenland. Since there wasn't anything of value to plunder and no villages to pillage, their motives probably were adventure and discovery caused by a unique circumstance.

According to "Vikings in the New World" web site, in the year 982 Eric the Red was outlawed from Iceland for three years at the Thorness *Thing*, so he decided to explore to the west. (The term *Thing* meant a form of government that became obsolete about the thirteenth century.) A number of settlements were established in Greenland and lasted for approximately 500 years.

Several sagas and archaeological evidence indicated that the Vikings pushed westward and established a Norse community on the northern peninsula of Newfoundland which they called "Vineland." Some historians speculate that the Vikings may have explored the coastline of North America as far south as Virginia, but there is no archaeological evidence beyond Newfoundland.

What part, if any, did the Swedes play in the western Viking adventure? In 1898 a runestone was discovered which has been named the Kensington Rune Stone. Translated in part it says: "... 8 Swedes and 22 Norwegians on an exploration journey from Vineland westward ..."[4] It then goes on to tell how many of their group were slaughtered in the year 1362.

One school of thought says that the stone is a hoax, but an equally vociferous voice says it is authentic. For my purpose here, there seems to be ample evidence to support the fact that the Scandinavians were the first Caucasians and Europeans to discover North America. (You'll note that this is a tacit acknowledgment that Native Americans were already on the North American Continent. Where some migrated from is a recent topic of controversy, however.) The Spanish and the Italians and present history rarely acknowledge the role of the Scandinavians, but if this writing serves to ameliorate the Viking image somewhat, my ancestral reputation has been uplifted. Nine hundred years later my family would become a part of the massive Swedish diaspora to North America, the land their ancestors discovered 500 years before Columbus.

An obvious and interesting question: Were any of my ancient ancestors Vikings? My great, great grandfather Nicolaus Qvist was born in 1790 in the village of Tossene, which is near the west coast of Sweden, directly south of Norway. His wife, Britta Sahlberg, was also born there. My grandfather, Knut Robert Qvist, was born in 1877 in Torsby, which is also on the west coast of Sweden, just north of Göteborg. There is absolutely no way, other than genetically, to trace family back thirty to forty generations to establish whether or not the Qvists were part of Viking lore, but some, due to their proximity to the sea, may have been seafarers of some sort.

As mentioned earlier, the Vikings' reputation for aggressiveness has survived the ages (despite the belief — a myth — that their helmets were adorned with horns). One question that has fascinated me during this research: Is this penchant for aggressive behavior a product of time and circumstance, or is it genetic? Is it a personality trait that can occur in any one individual within a family, or is it familial? The reader will discover later why I have raised the question.

Christianity came to Sweden in the year 830 led by the "Apostle of the North," Ansgan, who was French but who obtained permission from the King to preach the new religion. Prior to this time our forefathers worshiped various divinities, such as Odin, the God of Creation and Wisdom, Thor (thunder), Frigg (Odin's wife), Tyr (war), Frey (fertility), and Baldur (sweetness and light). "Simple magic was practiced at home and various nature spirits were propitiated which gave origin of the fairies, wood nymphs, trolls, and goblins of folklore,"[5] according to Lagerqvist.

According to Lagerqvist, Swedish Christianity was nothing like the European version. The priests were appointed by chieftains or peasant communities rather than the Church infrastructure. Christianity became firmly entrenched in Sweden when Nicholas of Albano became Pope. By the end of the twelfth century, imposing and sturdy rock churches served two purposes, one for services and the other for protection. The Diet of Västerås in 1527 was an event that had a dramatic impact on the lives of all Swedes. This meeting initiated the Reformation in Sweden and introduced Lutheranism to our ancestors. It also gave King Gustav Vasa the opportunity to seize all the existing Catholic Churches' assets for the Crown and *voil*, within a few years, Sweden was out of debt. Ninety years later, in response to a Catholic counter-reformation, all Catholics were required to leave the country within three months and any person converting to Catholicism would lose all rights, "as if deceased." The Church played a dominant role in our ancestors' lives. For over fifty years I've often wondered why Sweden was 99.9% Lutheran. The Reformation in Sweden was a part of our history not fully explored in Sunday school.

The history of Sweden from the early Vasa period (1521-1611) to the time of the immigration of my family to "Amerika" at the beginning of the twentieth century, mirrors the rise and fall of empires throughout all of Europe. Trekking through the Royal Palace in Stockholm and the myriad of museums throughout this magnificent and beautiful country at the beginning of the twenty-first century you can't but marvel at the rich and fascinating history, just as if you were Norwegian, British, German, Spanish, French or Italian and absorbing your culture and roots. But underlying the past grandeur of the rise and fall of all the European empires is the overpowering reality and effect that the divine right and folly of kings had on our ancestors and all of mankind.

Our founding fathers, fearful of the absolutism of King George of England, created a republic where the rights of its citizens were granted by God and not by government or royal decree. Some of our parents and grandparents who felt the oppression and omnipotence of the ruling class in Europe found freedom and opportunity in the new world, and they prospered. As we trace in this memoir three generations of my family, from arrival in America early in the 20th Century 100 years to the beginning of the 21st, we, ironically, witness a deliberate direction to return to the collectivism of our European roots. Change incredibly mirrors change.

Sweden enjoyed its day in the sun as a great world power for approximately one hundred years during the seventeenth century. The Swedes not only controlled all of Scandinavia including Finland, but portions of Russia, Poland and Germany that bordered the Baltic Sea. War after war was fought to control this vital waterway and path to the North Sea. Charles XII's failed Russian campaign, like Napoleon's and Hitler's that would follow, marked the end of Sweden's superpower period in history as it did for the aforementioned despots.

There is perhaps no event in Swedish history that exemplifies both the pinnacle of pride and the folly of kings more than the building of the Vasa while the Swedes were taking their place on the world stage as a growing military power.

King Gustavus II Adophus, anxious to build a Swedish "man-o-war" that would intimidate and impress his country's enemies, personally approved the dimensions of this "royal ship" — the pride of the Swedish Navy. It took three years and over four hundred craftsmen to build this magnificent ship that boasted 64 large cannons and masts more than fifty meters high. On its maiden voyage in the summer of 1628, the Vasa capsized and sank to the bottom of the harbor in Stockholm. This magnificent ship,

7

almost 70 meters (over 200 feet) in length, was top heavy.

Who was to blame? Was it the shipbuilder, who was Dutch? The admiral, who knew from tests that the ship was unstable, but was anxious to please his King? Or, was it the King himself, who approved the plans?

At the hearing that followed the disaster, Ament de Groot, the Dutch shipbuilder, was asked by the interrogator, "Whose fault is it, then?" De Groot replied, "Only God knows."[6] Since God and the King were infallible, the Council of the Realm was obliged to rule that no one was guilty, and no one was punished. The reputation of Swedish engineering remained untarnished and the folly of its King forgotten.

There is redemption to the folly of the Vasa which the Swedes, rightfully so, point to with pride. In 1961, after 333 years lying at the bottom of the Swedish archipelago, the Vasa was raised, almost intact. She, in fact, was able to float on her own and in 1988 took her last voyage to a museum, where I and ten million other awed viewers have seen her. She is preserved as a time machine that witnessed life on board ship and land in the early seventeenth century, and includes the remains of many of the fifty souls who lost their lives in the disaster, along with the ship's cat.

The Age of Freedom (1719-1792) in Sweden also marks the first written records of my family history. The death of King Karl XII in 1718 nearly coincides with the birth of Rasmus Olson, my great, great, great, great grandfather, six generations removed, though I doubt that his death (many years later) was marked by similar notoriety.

Rasmus was the great grandfather of my paternal grandmother, Clara Johansdotter, or daughter of Johan Hanson. From the Lutheran Church records at Sanne in the Province of Bohuslän, which I visited, we know quite a bit about Rasmus, who presumably was named after Erasmus, the sixteenth century Dutch theologian and scholar. Children were often named after notable personalities.

Rasmus was, like most of my ancestors, a farmer. His

first wife, Börta Jonsdotter, died early in life and they had no children. Rasmus met Anna Svensdotter, who worked as a maid in the village of Ed, which was within two miles of the Church at Sanne, and they married. Anna was thirty-one years younger than Rasmus, which probably made him the envy of his contemporaries. They had one child, Christina, who was born in 1792, when the old farmer was seventy-two years of age. Remarkable even in the year 2000. A similar unexpected event would recur in the Quist family 150 years later.

Rasmus's time was not a great moment in history for Sweden. Although King Karl's death marked the end of absolute power of the monarchy it also was a time, as noted by Lagerqvist, that "the country was practically bankrupt, at war with all its neighbors, partially occupied, had lost all of its possessions (gained by war) and was being squeezed by high taxes and inflation."[7] On top of that, "eighteen years of war had claimed the lives of or wounded as many as 200,000 men and even greater numbers who died of starvation and the plague epidemic of 1710."[8]

The most remarkable aspect of this memoir is that I possess the good fortune to be able to write it. Considering the centuries of wars, famine, disease and political repression it is an absolute miracle that our line, or yours, survived. Was it genetic? Toughness and tenacity? Pure luck? Or, all of the above? Only God knows, but whatever it took to preserve our line and yours, we must pay tribute to those who prevailed before us. It's a privilege to attempt to recreate and honor their lives. Without them I wouldn't be me and you wouldn't be you and we may not ever have seen the light of day.

Rasmus died in 1807 and Anna died in 1817, and they both were buried at Sanne. I couldn't locate their graves. According to local historians and the Parish office at Monkedal, those who were poor didn't have gravestones. Also, a number of stones were impossible to read, as time and the elements had eroded their names away (but not their memory, which is preserved here).

Rasmus and Anna's only child, Christina, married

Elias Anderson on May 11, 1810, and they had a total of four children. The last, Sara, was born on October 5, 1833, when Christina was forty-one years of age. Sara would become the mother of my paternal grandmother, Clara.

Traversing the beautiful rolling and still heavily forested countryside near Krokstad and Sanne, I'm taken by what would have been herculean efforts by my ancestors to clear this land in order to till the soil. All the removal of trees, roots and stumps was done by hand, with possibly the aid of oxen and horses. It could have taken years to prepare just a few acres for farming to eke out what must have been a modest income.

Sara, the Andersons' daughter, married Johan Hanson on February 19, 1858, and they had ten children. Clara, their eighth child, who would become my paternal grandmother, was born on March 23, 1874.

Despite the fact that Sweden was suffering from political and economic reversals during the "Age of Freedom," a number of technological innovations improved the Swedes' way of life. Anders Celsius invented the thermometer, which assisted the farmers who had such a short growing season. The ceramic tile stove, which had been used since medieval times, was greatly improved, and Swedish homes were reputed to be the best heated in Europe. These large, sometimes ornate, tile stoves extend from the floor to the ceiling, and the tiles give off and retain heat like no other material. They are still in use today to ward off the frigid winter cold.

Jonas Alströmer, who was an industrialist, is better known for introducing the potato to Sweden. For good, this tuber fed the nation, particularly when famine threatened to devastate the country, as we'll soon learn. Most assuredly, it must have been a product that my ancestors grew as a cash crop, and maintained them through some very severe years of famine.

For bad, the potato was distilled into akvavit, which is better know as schnapps, a powerful alcoholic drink that had a deleterious impact on the nation. The Crown had no interest in promoting sobriety, according to Lagerqvist, because of its monopolistic control of the distilleries. Sweden, during this period, was rife with drunkenness. So much in fact that akvavit and other alcoholic beverages were blamed for the reduction in height in the average Swede of four inches since the days of the Vikings. Today, Sweden has an absolute zero tolerance policy on drinking and driving. While dining in Sweden with one of my newly discovered cousins, he, knowing we would be celebrating during the event of our meeting, "drove" to the hotel on his bicycle so he wouldn't have to return home in his car.

Up to this point I've traced my father's mother's line to Clara, my paternal grandmother whom I knew very well, as I was 32 when she died. Clara's father's line's written record begins with Johan Skiöt, who was born on January 26, 1757, in Svarteborg, which is approximately ten miles southwest of Krokstad. Johan married Ingeborg Henkiksdotter on November 3, 1782. Ingeborg was born in Kville, which is only a few miles from the Skagervak Sea and perhaps five miles due west of Svarteborg. Johan was a soldier in the King's army, but was discharged at age fifty due to illness and died a year later of fever. The family did not fare well, either. Three out of four children died at a young age and Johan was, according to the church records, "miserably poor." The sole survivor was Hans, who carried on the family line when he married Anna Nilsdotter on November 19, 1820. Records pertaining to his mother, Ingeborg, were destroyed in a fire in the vicarage at the church in Kville, although current records indicate that she is buried there.

Hans, who was born in Svarteborg on November 11, 1791, had four children with Anna, who was born on August 21, 1797, in Sanne, which is the principal area of residence for my paternal grandmother's family. Their first son was Johan, who married Sara Eliasdotter. These were the parents of Clara, my paternal grandmother.

One point of interest that I think is noteworthy. Almost all the barns in Sweden are painted a dark, crimson red with white trim. The red paint was first manufactured in Falun in the 1600's as a product of the town's copper mines. The Swedes brought this tradition to

Minnesota and Wisconsin when they immigrated. Almost all the barns there are also red. In Sweden, most of the farmhouses are a goldenrod color, but there's a sprinkling of white and some pretty creative colors on others. In contrast, most of the farmhouses in Minnesota and Wisconsin are white. As you look over the countryside in the "old country" (as my grandparents referred to their homeland), you would think that you were in the upper Midwest. It's absolutely amazing. It's no wonder that my family and the Swedish diaspora felt at home in the Midwest. More on that later.

Nicolaus Qvist, my paternal great, great grandfather was born on January 26, 1790, in the Parish of Tossene, which is near the west coast of Sweden on the Skagerrak Sea in the Province of Bohuslän. He married Britta Lovisa Sahlberg, who was also from Tossene, somewhere around 1818 and they had nine children. One of the six boys was Robert Qvist, who would become my great grandfather.

I was in Karlstad in the neighboring Province of Värmland after an enjoyable day and evening with Lennart Andersson, whose grandmother was a sister to my maternal grandmother, Hulda Anderson, whom I have not yet chronicled. The next day, I was scheduled to embark on a search for my Qvist ancestors. The excitement and drama of the prospect of actually standing on the soil that embraced the roots of my father, and those ancestors of centuries past that preceded him, was overwhelming. I found it difficult to sleep. Pictures and portents of what I would see the next day continually flashed in my mind's eye like programmed subliminal messages on a movie screen.

There was the constant and recurring picture of a pristine white church on a hill with the cross-topped steeple that connected with the sky and heavens above, firmly planted amidst an almost primeval forest. The image flashed over and over again as if I had been there before, but I hadn't even seen a country church at that point on my visit to Sweden. The plethora of images greatly heightened the expectation of the next day.

The narrow, winding road designed for the days of wagons and horses led us to our destination. There it was.

The Parish at Krokstad. The picture so accurately framed in my mind had been developed. It was just as my mind's eye had seen it the night before. Heart racing, I began the search for my past. The priest was on vacation. There was no one to help us discover my roots.

The oldest stones were difficult, and some impossible, to read. Hundreds, if not thousands, of parishioners were buried here. Five minutes, ten, twenty minutes passed. No Quists were located. Maybe they weren't there. Maybe they were so poor there would be no memorial to mark their time on earth. Excitement was about to turn to disappointment when my son called out, "Here's Nicolaus, Dad."

At the edge of the cemetery, sheltered by an old but robust oak tree that may have been there as long as my great, great grandfather, was a headstone with the inscription clearly emblazoned:

	N. Qwist				B. L. Qvist		
FODD	17	<u>26</u>	90	FODD Salberg	17	<u>1</u>	96
		1				5	
DÖD	18	<u>15</u>	70	DÖD	18	<u>5</u>	74
		11				4	

I could rest. The past had been found. But what about the discrepancy in the name on the headstone? Was Nicolaus' surname simply chiseled in error as QWIST instead of QVIST? What is remarkable is that Britta's name, listed directly adjacent to her husband's, is spelled QVIST, but of course her death occurred four years later.

Fresh flowers adorned Nicolaus and Britta's grave, which was evidence that their descendants may still live in the area. As I pondered how I would continue my search for my kin, I took one last reverent moment at Nicolaus' grave. Amidst the bucolic mooing of a cow directly adjacent to the cemetery fence (recorded on video) I thought I heard a faint voice say, "Tack för att nikomener ihoag oss," (thank you for remembering us).

Through the Parish office in Munkedal, I discovered a

distant cousin, Eric Bäcklund, who was maintaining the Qvist grave site. Nicolaus and Britta had nine children. The eighth, Nicolaus Donatus Qvist, was Eric's great grandfather and brother to Robert, my great grandfather.

Nicolaus was a land surveyor who, presumably, was in demand during the "rationalization of land holdings" during his working years. Nicolaus died on November 15, 1872, at the age of 80, and Britta died four years later. Both of them are buriéd in Krokstad in the clearly marked plot cited above.

Knut Robert Qvist, my paternal grandfather, was born on August 17, 1872, in Torsby, and the church records indicate that he moved to Sheppslanda, where he married Clara in 1894. Knut was both a carpenter and a farmer, and may have moved considerable distances. He was traveling when Reinhold Napoleon, their second son, was born in Borgvik, which is in the Province of Värmland. This area is approximately 140 km, or 84 miles, to the northeast of Krokstad, a major move in that day. Knut and Clara's youngest child was Alf Herbert Qvist, my father, who was born on May 10, 1904, in Hedekas.

As mentioned previously, Knut Robert Qvist and Clara (often spelled Klara) Johansdotter Hanson were married April 28, 1894. My grandparents' oldest child, Carl Robert, was born July 19, 1895, in the village of Höga, Göteborg Parish, in the Province of Bohuslän.

Knut was born in the Parish of Torsby, which is only a few miles from the west coast of Sweden and approximately 15 miles north of Göteborg, which was a major seaport and city of considerable size at the turn of the century. My aunt, Frideborg, in a letter written to me in 1979, indicated that Robert was born in the village of Haga. There is a village of Höga which is very close to Knut's birthplace of Torsby, so it's quite possible that her reference to Haga is in fact, Höga. Phonetically in Swedish, Haga could be Höga.

Remarkably, on August 17, 1898, the family moved to Värmland and three years later, Knut and Clara's second son, Reinhold Napoleon, was born in the Parish of Borgvik, which is 245 km, or 147 miles, to the north of Höga. Knut was both a farmer and a carpenter. What was the motivation for them to move such a long distance when, by horse-drawn wagon, it would have taken weeks to get there? Railroads were being built but probably not yet in wide use. The history of families in Sweden in this era indicates that they were born, worked and died within their Parish or close proximity. Was Knut a tenant farmer, whereby he could move on more readily, or was he seeking work as a carpenter? We'll never know. It's one of those questions that should have been asked and recorded but never was.

By the time that Aunt Frideborg (we called her "Fre") was born on December 16, 1901, the Qvist family had moved to the village of Hedekas in the Parish of Krokstad, which reversed their move of a couple of years earlier. This was Clara's birthplace, and the proximity to her family may have figured into this move. My father, Alf Herbert, was also born in Hedekas, on May 10, 1904. He was the last of the four children. One year later, Knut, Clara and their four children would make a decision that would be the most defining moment in not only their lives, but also of their issue. They would abandon their family roots, growing for centuries in the soil of west-central Sweden, for the unknown in a foreign land called Amerika. What possibly could have evoked such a dramatic and life-changing decision? What was Knut and Clara's motivation? Beyond the obvious there are some significant surprises.

The late 1800's and early 1900's were a period of radical change in Sweden, as well as Europe and America. Industrialization, railroads and shipping were changing the world, and while new industry created new jobs in urban settings, Swedish farmers saw the price of grains drop dramatically, primarily due to decreased costs of transportation. Russian and American exports of grain depressed the Swedish domestic market, which was unable to restructure its agricultural system. The Rural Party in Parliament, which consisted mostly of peasant farmers, became split between those who favored protective tariffs and those who didn't, thus reducing the collective power of the farmers. The political terms "right" and "left" appeared for the first time, which would be the origin of a new modern political consciousness that would soon bring "Liberalism" (Socialism) to Sweden. Lagerqvist concludes that emigration approached 50,000 per year in the late 1800's "as the main reasons were economic in nature."[9] Inferred, but not said, it appears that the farmers were those that were most gravely impacted economically.

Many of us may recall seeing the Academy Award-nominated film "The Emigrants," starring Liv Ullman and Max von Sydow, released in 1972. The film depicted farm life in Sweden in the mid-1800's when intolerable conditions initiated the Swedish migration to America. The author, Vilhelm Moberg, focused his attention on repression as a major issue, which isn't discussed by Lagerqvist. Moberg cites the overbearing and controlling rule of government and the Church as a major force in motivating Swedes to disperse. Moberg was roundly criticized by the Swedish government and critics for falsely characterizing a derogatory role of the Church. Today, we do have the Church to thank for keeping the meticulous records of its parishioners. Every birth, death, major event or move to another Parish was duly recorded by the Parish Priest. How invasive was the Church in the everyday life of my family? I have no way of knowing. They always spoke of their religion with great respect and reverence.

In the late 1800's, three factors caused Sweden's population to literally explode, causing a nationwide food shortage. A smallpox vaccine was introduced in 1874, which immediately decreased the mortality rate. In addition, Sweden was at peace with its neighbors and young men, instead of marching off to regions unknown and having legions of them fail to return, stayed home and raised families — large families of five to ten children. Lastly, the potato was introduced to the country and became "the poor man's bread," and starvation greatly decreased. Thomas Malthus, who visited Sweden before his death in 1834, predicted that his theory that the population would grow faster than the food supply proved to be correct. "Peace, vaccine and the potato" not only became a popular slogan of the day, these factors created a dilemma. There simply wasn't enough food to sustain the Swedes.

A subtle but significant motivation to emigrate came from an unsuspecting source. Commission salesmen! Entrepreneurs and capitalists in the U.S., like J.P. Morgan and others, were buying up railroads and ocean liners. They needed customers to fill their ships and trains — their people-movers. With the invention of coal-fired steamships (the birth of the initials *SS* for steam ship) that could make the voyage from England to New York in one week instead of six or more, these entrepreneurs set out to sell America as the land of opportunity. Agents and salesmen combed the Swedish countryside (and all of Europe) selling tickets for a fat commission and getting referrals from relatives who had already taken the oceanic plunge. The Swedes soon learned that they could purchase tickets through their "sponsor" already in the U.S. at a substantial savings. As Karl Oscar says in the film, as he capitulates on trying to eke out a substance from his tiny, rocky patch of nutrient-depleted soil, "the greenest meadows are those farthest away." Karl Oscar found Eden in Minnesota. The Qvists found theirs in Wisconsin and Michigan.

———

"Klara, Klara! Vi skall gä till Nord Amerika!" Knut must have said as he announced to his wife and children that they were going to America. One of Clara's five sisters was already in Wisconsin and was the Qvists' sponsor. Her sister may have purchased the tickets for the long and often arduous trip. The cost was significant but unascertainable. We can only assume that there was a celebration and a party at the Qvist farm in Hedekas for family and friends.

Clara, an excellent cook, would have prepared an extensive, traditional meal, probably a "smörgäsbord" or buffet. Some of the dishes would have undoubtedly included Gravlax, which was salmon or other fish that had been preserved and treated with salt, sugar and spices, plus herring pickled with onions and spices or mustard sauce, or marinated with sour cream. Jansson's Temptation, a strongly spiced baked potato dish with pickled sprats (Swedish anchovies) would have been mandatory at the party, along with smoked eel. The bread of choice in central Sweden was crisp bread served with Roquefort and numerous other cheeses. Clara was particularly adept at making desserts. As a child I remember the "spritzers," which were vanilla sugar cookies, one of the "seven sorts" of coffee cakes or desserts.

Every social occasion featured a "spirituous beverage." Brännvin, better known as schnapps, was the drink of choice. It was made from grain or potatoes, heavily spiced and contained 45% alcohol. It was a tradition to fill the first small champagne glass to the brim and the second only halfway, so the first two drams at the party were known as "the whole" and "the half." Before consuming the drink those at the party would have sung a "snapvisa," or schnapps ditty, in honor of the occasion. The actual words (as best translated) provided by May Werner, one of my present Swedish family, goes like this:

I like the schnapps,
The schnapps like me.
Oh what a thrill,
the schnapps can be.

I want to drink,
with the real elite,
Herr Gards Aquavit (Brand).

Over the mountains
and over the sea,
thousands of schnapps
are waiting for me.

Please put away
the juice and tea,
schnapps is the drink for me.

It was unlikely that a whole and a half were the limit, particularly on this occasion. Research of the church records confirms that several families from the same Parish in Krokstad made the same decision, not only to emigrate to the U.S., but to settle in the exact same community and church in Peshtigo, Wisconsin. Per August and Emma Quick, with a name so similar to my grandparents,' must have been close friends in both the old and new country. They may even have made the voyage together.

It's October 1904. I can visualize the Qvist family in a horse-drawn wagon, making their way on a Sunday morning from their farm near Hekekas a couple miles to the church at Krokstad. It's a special day. Alf Herbert Qvist, my father, who later unofficially changed his name to Herbert A. Quist, was to be baptized. All children were christened at a very early age in this era because so many died shortly after birth. No one wanted their child to die a heathen.

Knut was a man with sad, recessed eyes, a slight build, about 5'9" and 150 pounds, balding and had a trademark, handlebar mustache. Klara was very tall and trim, almost equal in height to her husband, with dark black hair. Remarkably, none of the four children closely resembled their father, and all of the three boys would ultimately exceed his height by three or four inches. My father had a likeness to his mother, which could partially explain her closeness and partiality to her youngest son.

All of the family, as well as all of the other parishioners, were dressed in their Sunday "go to meeting" best. Klara, holding Dad, sat with Fre in a wooden pew reserved for women on one side of the sanctuary. Knut, with the two older boys, sat on the other side, a well established practice in those days.

After the regular service Dad was baptized, which automatically made him a member of the Church of Sweden, which was, of course, Lutheran. I can even imagine that he may have cried a bit when the priest sprinkled the holy water on his tiny head. At the completion of the ceremony, the priest presented Knut and

Klara with a "Christening Candle," a medieval custom where the candle would be lit at each anniversary of Dad's christening. Within a few months, Knut and Klara would return to the church to receive permission to leave not only the Parish, but their beloved country. A difficult and often dangerous trip lay ahead — particularly with a child, my father, barely six months old.

On or about the middle of May 1906, Knut and Klara packed the limited amount of their belongings permitted for the long trip abroad, and on a horse-drawn wagon they and their four children headed south from Hedekas to the port of Göteborg (pronounced Gothenberg), a trip of 125 km, or 75 miles. From the Swedish port they boarded a small ship for the two-day trip to Grimsby on the eastern coast of England. From there it was a two-day train ride to Liverpool, where on May 30, 1905, the Qvist family boarded the *SS Caronia* bound for Amerika and the city of New York.

Their crossing took place just seven years prior to the ill-fated *Titanic* which was to have raised ocean travel to a new level of luxury and safety. The images of opulence and fine dining from photographs and the recent film distort what travel in steerage or third-class must have been like aboard the *SS Caronia*. Accounts of the day[10] indicate that steerage offered cramped and unsanitary conditions deep within the bowels of the ocean liner. Food was limited and basic, with no milk available to the children. Sea sickness and the spread of contagious disease were constant companions.

At last the passengers in steerage could come to the upper deck to breathe the fresh air of the new world and view the icon of freedom and opportunity — the Statue of Liberty. As particular as Klara was, she must have had her family dressed in their Sunday best as they readied themselves for processing through the "Isle of Hope, Isle of Tears" known as Ellis Island. Only those passengers in steerage would face the long lines and onerous ordeal. First and second class matriculated quickly.

Knut, Klara and the kids were each given a number. Massive lines could have made them wait all day to be processed. Twenty percent were detained for a more thorough physical exam if "they were liable to become a public charge and burden on society." Two percent were rejected and returned to the ship that they debarked from. The immigration service was particularly on the lookout for "anarchists," and I suspect that officials weren't too concerned about political correctness and offending someone. Our name was changed from Qvist to Quist, and Klara became Clara. Some families had their names shortened or spindled and mutilated completely at the discretion of a government official. Most didn't care. They and their families were in America — that's all that mattered. Most didn't want foreign-sounding names, anyway.

The "Manifest of Alien Passengers" of the SS *Caronia* lists Knut, Clara and each of the four children. Knut had in his possession, at a minimum, twenty U.S. dollars in gold coin, probably equivalent to approximately $1,000 today. That would have to last for the remainder of the grueling trip to Peshtigo, Wisconsin, and enable him and the family to get settled in the new land.

From New York my family boarded a train (as best I can determine probably part of the J.P. Morgan network) to Buffalo, New York, and then another boat for perhaps another week through the locks at Lake Ontario, Lake Erie, Lake Huron, past "death's door" at the convergence of Lake Michigan and Green Bay, and finally to Peshtigo, Wisconsin — their new home and scene of one of the most incredible and little-known tragedies in American history.

———

Anders Anderson (son of Anders) was born on December 28, 1841, in the Parish of Lungsund in the Province of Värmland, which is located in west central Sweden and is adjacent to Bohuslän, the Province of origin of my father's family just covered. Anders is my maternal great grandfather. Sometime around 1863, Anders met and married Maria Gustafsdotter (daughter of Gustaf), who was born in January 1845. Soon after their marriage in the Parish at Lungsund they leased a farm named Kungsskogstorp, near the town of Hedäs.

A photograph that has survived for more than one hundred years amidst my maternal grandmother's possessions, depicts a relatively large, immaculate, two-story home with a picket fence, blanketed with several feet of freshly fallen snow. A small envelope, which holds this photograph as well as one of my grandmother at age 13, has a notation in my mother's stylistic and perfect handwriting that says, "House mom lived in Sweden." Considering that my grandmother Hulda was one of ten of Anders and Maria's children, the large home seemed appropriate. Our research in Sweden discovered that the home depicted in the photograph wasn't the Anderson house. In fact, it wasn't a home. It was the Kungsskogen school attended by Hulda and all her brothers and sisters and, remarkably, it still exists today directly adjacent to the Kungsskogstorp (Anderson) farm.

On my trip to Sweden in July 2002, I produced this photograph to May Werner, who is the daughter of my grandmother Hulda's niece Sophia, and my great aunt reacted emotionally when she looked at the century-old photo. "Oh my," she said in perfect English. "That's my schoolhouse. That's Kungsskogen School!" obviously fondly recalling her carefree, joyous days at the school seventy years prior.

In the whole scheme of things it's a minor issue, but I pondered. Given Anders and Maria's large family, was the schoolhouse their home in the late 1880's before it became a school? Or, did my mother misunderstand her mother and the word *schoolhouse* morphed into *house*? One thing is certain — Hulda spoke excellent English so nothing was lost in translation. Nevertheless, it was a place where my ancestors trod and that fact is sufficient in itself.

Great grandfather Anders was a farmer during the summer months and trekked north to make charcoal during the winter. Sadly, Maria was critically injured when a coach in which she was a passenger rolled over in 1889. She later died as a result of her injuries. She was only forty-four and my grandmother, her last of ten children, was only four years of age at the time of her mother's death. Obviously, there was danger on the roadways prior to automobiles, which were invented just ten years later.

From Franz Holmgren, the Rector of the Parish of Lungsund, in an official sealed document dated June 19, 1948, as well as from my relatives residing in Sweden, we have considerable information on my grandmother Hulda's extensive family. Just prior to Maria's death in 1889, her two oldest sons, Anders Gustaf and Lars Johan, emigrated to North America in 1887.

Family now living in Sweden attest to the fact that, not only the lack of employment opportunities compelled the oldest children to leave their homeland, the Anderssons simply could not feed and support their ten children — the same conditions that motivated the Qvists to emigrate as mentioned earlier.

Anders and Maria's first daughter, whom they also named Maria, was the first daughter to emigrate to the U.S. in 1896 at the age of 27. Maria, once established in Boston, Massachusetts, would become Hulda's sponsor, and my grandmother embarked for the U.S. on October 12, 1901, at the age of sixteen. I've often reflected on my grandmother making the arduous trip to America on her own at such a young age. But "Gramma" (without the "D"), as we called her, had a steely determination that she exhibited all her life, as you will soon discover. Yet, despite her stoicism and resolve she was warm and affectionate with her grandchildren. Sister Joan, brother Terry, cousin Larry and I all can attest to that.

According to the 1948 date of the Holmgren certification letter, nine of twenty-one in Hulda's immediate family of brothers, sisters and cousins had emigrated to the U.S. at the turn of the century. By the beginning of World War I, one out of six Swedes had left their homeland for North America — roughly sixteen percent of the population, probably the largest percentage of citizens of any European country.

Reflecting on my return from the "old country," I had a dream imagining a conversation with my father, my mother and my grandmothers Quist and Anderson, though they all had passed from their earthly existence over thirty years ago.

"I just returned from Sweden," I said, addressing the four as I did so many times during our family get-togethers at Thanksgiving or Christmas.

"Oh my!" was their collective response. Gramma Quist said, "Tsk, tsk," as she often did.

"Where did you go?" Gramma Anderson asked, her face brightening eagerly in anticipation of my response.

"We first flew to Stockholm and stayed there for three days. What a magnificent city built on fourteen islands. I can understand why Stockholm is called 'the Venice of the North.' The only thing I didn't like was that there were nine McDonald's restaurants in downtown Stockholm."

"McDonald's in Sweden?" Dad asked in wonderment, as all my family looked at each other in disbelief. He recalled that one of the first McDonald's in the U.S. was located near our home in Albuquerque, New Mexico, on the southwest corner of Lomas and San Pedro Boulevards.

"Yeah. To me it just doesn't work. I mean, the gaudy golden arches seem out of character with this classic, European city. And out of character with the Swedes' healthy lifestyle. Obesity has become an epidemic in the U.S., you know. We are exporting 'fast fat' to the entire world. I'm all for global trade, but 'Big Mac' has 'OD'ed' in Sweden," I opined.

"Goodness gracious, can you imagine. Hamburgers in Sweden. My oh my," Gramma Quist remarked as she shook her head from side to side, as was her habit.

"Did you find any of my family, Bus?" Gramma Anderson asked. She always called me "Bus" instead of "Buz." I never knew if she couldn't pronounce the Z or she shortened Buster to Bus. Anyway, it was always Bus.

"We drove from Stockholm to Skeborbruk, which is only about 100 km (60 miles) from Stockholm. That's where your sister Emma Sophia's grandniece, Erica Sophia, lives," I related to Gramma. "She goes by the nickname May, May Werner."

"Oh my goodness. I lost track of Emma when I came to the U.S. Tell me about the family," Gramma Anderson implored as her intensity and interest grew.

"You undoubtedly remember that your sister Emma, who was the seventh out of the ten children, had a daughter, Sophia Elisabet, who was born on April 8, 1899, and who was born out of wedlock before Emma and Gustav Jansson were married."

"Yes, yes. That was quite a scandal until they married," Gramma added.

"And Emma and Gustav had five more children, so everything turned out all right, didn't it?" I asked.

"Yes ... yes it did," she said with a pause.

"Well, Sophia married Teodor Persson, who was born on May 8, 1898, and they had only one child. That was Erica Sophia, or May, as she prefers. May was born on May 18, 1925, and she lived near Hedäs, where you grew up. She went to the same school that you did."

"My goodness," Gramma Anderson sighed as she was undoubtedly visualizing their Kunkskogstorp farm.

"May, your grandniece, married Floyd Lennart Werner, who was born May 14, 1927, and who was employed by the Swedish Forest Service most of his career. They lived in such diverse places as Kenya, India, Ethiopia, and other undeveloped countries. Unfortunately, Floyd died exactly two years ago. What is remarkable is the facial resemblance between you and May," I remarked.

"Oh Bus," Gramma Anderson replied wistfully. "Tak...Oh, thank you," Gramma added as she initially replied in Swedish.

"May and Floyd have three children. Cajsa Eva who was born on March 17, 1956 is single and lives in Stockholm. She lived in New York City for a period of time. We have spoken to her often and by e-mail but haven't met her," I related.

"E-mail? What is e-mail?" Dad asked.

"Oh geez, that would take several days to explain. E means electronic. We mail each other over the phone lines," I informed my family, who unfortunately all died before the tech revolution began. I'm glad I didn't mention the word *computer*. They would have been dumbfounded.

"May also has a son, Floyd Peter Werner, who was

born October 2, 1957, and is married to Ann Kersten Fermas. They have two children, Arvid Patrick and Sofia Kristina. Peter is a civil engineer and also lives in Stockholm. Ann Sofia, who was born May 15, 1964, is their third child and she is married to Peter Lars Holmgren, who works for the Food and Agricultural Organization (FAO). Their family lives in Rome. Ann Sofia works for the National Rural Development Agency. The Holmgrens have three children, Therese Sophia, Joanna Erika, and Pontus Leonard, who as a one-year-old has the calmest disposition of a child that age that you would ever encounter. He's the same age as you were, Dad, when you came to the U.S."

"I knew I was a youngster but I didn't know I was that young," Dad replied.

"Oh heavens, I remember that well," Gramma Qvist replied as she sighed. "That was such a tough trip aboard that ship."

"After we met May at her beautiful home in Skeborbruk, we had lunch with her family at a 400-hundred-year-old road house, which was a mail station in the old days, and the next day we went to their summer cottage a few miles east, on the Baltic Sea. It reminded me so much of Door County in Wisconsin," I related to my family who listened intently.

"Yes, yes. Wisconsin is so much like home," Gramma Qvist (Clara) remarked. "Did you get to Bohuslän?"

"Yes, we did, but when we left the Werners we went to Karlstad on Lake Vänern."

"In Värmland ... where our family came from," Gramma Anderson said excitedly. "Who did you see there?"

"Your sister Emma Sofia's daughter, Anna Lisa, who was born June 10, 1914, married another Andersson, Gustav Walter, just as you married an Anderson (one S instead of two). Gustav and Anna had three children. The youngest, a son, Bo Lennart, born February 28, 1944, has lived all of his life in Karlstad. He is a chemical engineer and is a consultant to the paper and pulp industry. Since you and Lennart's grandmother Emma were sisters, I suppose that we are second cousins."

"Does Lennart have a family?" Gramma asked.

"Yes. He has two children from his first marriage. Bo Sven Michael, born June 5, 1963, and a daughter, Annika Elisabet, born March 30, 1968. Lennart married Marie Helen Johansson in 1991 and they have a son, Erick Ola, who was born on December 3, 1987. I met him when Lennart and I played a round of golf. What a delightful young man."

"They play golf in Sweden?" Dad asked, surprised.

"I'd say so. The best woman golfer in the world is a Swede, Annika Sorenstan."

"My goodness. I didn't know there were any courses in Sweden," Dad said in wonderment.

"Driving through the countryside, you find golf courses everywhere. Lennart invited me to play with him at the Karstad Golfklubb. The head pro there is Annika's coach. We had a delightful round on a beautiful day. We were joined by a Norwegian who was on his holiday."

"What did you shoot, Buster?" Dad asked as he laughed, since we had played many rounds together.

"I had a tough time getting used to the unfamiliar clubs that I rented, but I did shoot a 39 on the back with a double bogey on number 11," I relayed to my Dad, who enjoyed the game enormously. My mind switched from time and place, and I briefly recalled the days as a young boy pulling Dad's golf cart, but I snapped back to the present in my dream.

"After our round Lennart, his son Eric and I had lunch on the porch overlooking the course. He relayed to me an interesting story that greatly impacted his life."

"Tell us, Bus. Tell us," Gramma Anderson said anxiously.

Lennart was working at a paper mill and there was a gas explosion. Two of his friends working close to him were killed. Lennart almost died. He told me that this near-death experience dramatically changed his life. It was his defining moment. Being confronted with our own mortality can have a profound impact on all of us. My near-death experiences were as numerous as they were defining, as you know," I said with a sigh of relief, recalling a few.

"Only too well," Mom said, with that all too familiar look of concern as well as frustration on her face that I will soon share with the reader.

"Gram? (Anderson) Your youngest brother, Axel, was born on October 26, 1883, and married Marta Alvina Johansson, who was born on August 18, 1884. They had two sons and one daughter and lived near Stockholm, in the Parish of Huddinge. Axel, I learned from May, was a gardener and raised magnificent flowers for the train station in Stockholm. May knew Axel and Marta very well, since she lived with them when she went to college in Stockholm. I don't know if you knew that Axel cared for your dad in his home until he died in 1918 at age 77," I relayed to my grandmother.

"Yes, yes. I received a letter from my brother telling me dad had passed away. I hadn't seen him since I left for America," Gramma said wistfully, as I'm sure she was recalling that day in 1901 that she said her last goodbye to her parents. "Damn," I thought to myself, "What a gutwrenching experience for a teenager."

"And then you went from Värmland to Bohuslän?" Gramma Quist asked, somewhat impatiently. I got the feeling that she had heard enough about the Andersons and was getting a little "antsy," as she was prone to do.

"Yes, yes we did. It was a beautiful drive except for all the Big Macs every fifty miles along the interstate," I said jokingly. "We drove to Hedekas in our new rented Volvo and had pizza for lunch. The owner of the little restaurant was Arabic. He didn't speak English. He was about the only person we encountered in Sweden that didn't speak English," I remarked.

"A pizza parlor in Hedekas?" Gramma Quist remarked, surprised. "Where was the restaurant?"

"Right in the town square. It probably looks the same as it did 100 years ago, except the streets are paved," I surmised. "One of the large homes on the square has been turned into a museum and a historical society. We met

Sören Henriksson and Helena Blom in the square and they've helped us get information on the area and your farm."

"My oh my oh my," Gramma Quist exclaimed. She added her usual, "tsk, tsk."

We talked extensively about locating the Qvists at the Krokstad cemetery and Clara's great grandfather at Sanne, and Gramma was visibly overwhelmed. As they faded from my view and I withdrew to the present, I woke from my dream. I marveled at the conversation that I dreamt that I had had, but pained at the reality that it had never happened. It would have brought my grandparents and my parents so much joy, so many fond memories. Time is the enemy of opportunity. Too many words go unsaid, particularly as they involve our relationship with our family. *Rediscovering America!* is an attempt to ameliorate the past and open a dialog in the future.

The fourth and last major limb of the family tree is grandfather Sam Anderson of whom we, unfortunately, know precious little prior to his arrival in America. From *Footprints in the Sands of Time*, written by my second cousin Merlin A. Barlament, I've learned almost as much as I know. Merlin's grandmother, Marie Anderson, was born in 1864 in Holbaek, Denmark, the daughter of Hans Anderson, born in 1828. (Unfortunately, not the Hans Christian Anderson of literary fame.) We do not know who was Hans' wife, nor do we know for certain if she was Danish, but we assume so. We do know, however, that my grandfather Sam was born in Sweden in 1873, and that Hans remarried prior to Sam's birth. Sam and Marie, therefore, are half brother and sister.

There always seemed to be an assumption amongst the three Quists as children that we were part Danish, but that probably is not the case. It's almost certain from the scant clues that we have that Hans' first wife was Danish, but when he returned to Sweden he probably married a Swede who gave birth to Sam; therefore, all four of our grandparents would be Swedish. It's only a supposition but further research might shine a genealogical light on the obscure past. Merlin recalls that Sam, on returning from the "old country" on his last visit, remarked that he had also visited relatives in Germany. Presumably, he and Marie had other siblings (two brothers, according to Sam's obituary) and they possibly were living in Germany.

Sometime prior to 1898, Sam emigrated to America and settled in Boston, Massachusetts. We know for certain that it was prior to 1898, because Sam served in the U.S. Army and fought in the Spanish-American War of that same year. As mentioned earlier, Grandmother Hulda Andersson made the voyage in 1901, and also settled in Boston with her sisters Maria and Elin. I know from reading accounts of emigrants from all parts of Europe that they found their way to various ethnic enclaves where they all spoke their native tongues and were comfortable in a strange land. We can only suppose that Sam met Hulda in the Swedish section of Boston, and after a period of courtship they left Boston and were married on February 10, 1906, in Green Bay, Wisconsin. We can further suppose that it was Sam's half sister Marie who, incredibly, had married another Anderson (Charles J. Anderson) and who was living in Green Bay, Wisconsin, that encouraged Sam in 1906 to relocate to the city of my birth.

From Jon Thunberg, who is Elin Andersson's grandson and my second cousin, I learned that Sam and Hulda were not married in Boston as thought, which means they traveled together to Green Bay unmarried. A rare event in those days. It also has a broader significance. My mother was born on October 21, 1906 — just eight months after Sam and Hulda were married. Was Mom a "preemie" or was she conceived in Boston? Given that we know that sister Marie was a dominating and deeply religious spinster sixteen years older than Hulda, my grandmother's pregnancy would not have been celebrated with a tea party at Maria's home in Boston.

This potentially premature but blessed event made me reflect further. Did my mother's knowledge that she was conceived out of wedlock and her parents' guilt give birth to her rigid and puritanical attitudes on sex that were so dominant in her and her children's lives? An interesting conjecture as you'll see.

From my cousin Jon Thunberg, we know a considerable amount about Elin, Hulda's sister who emigrated to America just two years prior to my grandmother, in 1899. The cost of her trip was 108 Kroner, which is ten in today's (2002) U.S. dollars. Hulda witnessed Elin's marriage to Oscar Carl Thunberg on May 16, 1903, in Cambridge, Massachusetts, which union unfortunately was disastrous. As Elin reported to her grandson Jon, Oscar was a loud, obnoxious alcoholic, but she married him in order to get away from a domineering Maria. The family situation became so severe that social services took custody of their three children, and Jon's father and his two sisters were raised in New Hampshire in foster homes. All three children survived but only Jon's father, Carl Axel, had children to continue Elin's line.

So, by 1906 the Quists and the Andersons as a part of the massive Swedish diaspora were settled in the new land. Knut, Clara and the four Quist children were living in Peshtigo, Wisconsin where Grandpa Quist was probably employed as a carpenter rebuilding the town devastated by the "great fire." Sam and Hulda were settled in Green Bay, Wisconsin, where on October 21, 1906, my mother, Thelma Elizabeth Anderson, was born. Within 22 months, on August 14, 1908, my aunt, Elsie Christine Anderson, was born. We are not certain what occupation Sam held in his early years in Green Bay, but as the reader will soon learn Sam and Hulda's incredible work ethic made them secure and successful in their new land. The great risk of change that had taken place was a change for the good.

1. Lars O. Lagerqvist, *A History of Sweden* (Stockholm, Sweden: The Swedish Institute, 2001), p. 7.
2. Ibid., p. 11.
3. Ibid., p. 18.
4. *"Vikings in the New World"* web site.
5. Lagerqvist, op.cit., p. 21.
6. Taken from the Vasa Museum brochures.
7. Lagerqvist, op. cit., p. 87.
8. Ibid., p. 87.
9. Ibid., p. 155.
10. The House of Immigrants Museum, Vaxjö, Sweden.

CHAPTER 2:
THE IMMIGRANTS IN AMERICA

ALMOST EVERY AMERICAN TODAY with some knowledge of our nation's history can recall the story of Mrs. O'Leary's cow, who kicked over a lantern causing the city of Chicago to burn to the ground on October 8, 1871. What is not known is that there was a fire that occurred on exactly the same day, at almost the same hour as the one that engulfed Chicago and, incredibly, killed five times as many people. Where in the world did this horrific event occur? Peshtigo, Wisconsin — the new home of the Quist family thirty-four years after what was America's greatest fire.

In order to give the reader a sense of the terror and extent of the fire in the language of the day, I've taken an excerpt from Father Peter Pernin's eyewitness account. Fr. Pernin was a parish priest in Peshtigo at the time that the fire occurred.

> *Still, the swiftness with which this hurricane, seemingly composed of wind and fire together, advanced, was in no degree proportioned to its terrible force. By computing the length of time that elapsed between the rising of the tempest in the southwest, and its subsiding in the northeast, it will be easily seen that the rate of motion did not exceed two leagues an hour. The hurricane moved in a circle, advancing slowly, as if to give time to prepare for its coming.*
>
> *Many circumstances tended to prove that the intensity of the heat produced by the fire was in some places extreme, nay unheard of. I have already mentioned that the flames pursued the roots of the trees into the very depths of the earth,*

consuming them to the last inch. I plunged my cane down into these cavities, and convinced myself that nothing had stayed the course of combustion save the utter want of anything to feed on. Hogsheads of nails were found entirely melted though lying outside the direct path of the flames. Immense numbers of fish of all sizes died, and the morning after the storm the river was covered with them. It would be impossible to decide what was the cause of their death. It may have been owing to the intensity of the heat, the want of air necessary to respiration — the air being violently sucked in by the current tending upwards to that fierce focus of flame — or they may have been killed by some poisonous gas.

It is more than probable that for a moment the air was impregnated with an inflammable gas most destructive to human life. I have already mentioned the tiny globules of fire flying about my house at the moment I quitted it. Whilst on my way to the river, I met now and then gusts of an air utterly unfit for respiration, and was obliged on these occasions to throw myself on the ground to regain my breath, unless already prostrated involuntarily by the violence of the wind. Whilst standing in the river I had noticed, as I have already related, on casting my eye upwards, a sea of flame, as it were, the immense waves of which were in a state of violent commotion, rolling tumultuously one over the other, and all at a prodigious height in the sky, and, consequently, far from any combustible material. How can this phenomenon be explained without admitting the supposition that immense quantities of gas were accumulated in the air?

Strange to say there were many corpses found, bearing about them no traces of scars or burns, and yet in the pockets of their habiliments, equally uninjured, watches, cents, and other articles in metal were discovered completely melted. How was it also that many escaped with their lives here and *there on the cleared land as well as in the woods? The problem is a difficult one to solve. The tempest did not rage in all parts with equal fury, but escape from its power was a mere affair of chance. None could boast of having displayed more presence of mind than others. Generally speaking, those who happened to be in low lying lands, especially close to excavations or even freshly ploughed earth with which they could cover themselves, as the Indians do, succeeded in saving their lives. Most frequently the torrent of fire passed at a certain height from the earth, touching only the most elevated portions. Thus no one could meet it standing erect without paying the penalty of almost instantaneous death.*

When the hurricane burst upon us, many, surprised and terrified, ran out to see what was the matter. A number of these persons assert that they then witnessed a phenomenon which may be classed with the marvelous. They saw a large black object, resembling a balloon, which object revolved in the air with great rapidity, advancing above the summits of the trees towards a house which it seemed to single out for destruction. Barely had it touched the latter when the balloon burst with a loud report, like that of a bombshell, and, at the same moment, rivulets of fire streamed out in all directions. With the rapidity of thought, the house thus chosen was enveloped in flames within and without, so that the persons inside had no time for escape.[1]

The Peshtigo fire ravaged 2,400 square miles and killed 1,152 persons according to the *Encyclopedia Brittannica*, although other estimates are as high as 1,500. The fire was so intense that burning embers and debris, carried eastward by winds aloft, started forest fires across the Green Bay — over approximately fifteen miles of water — killing hundreds of persons in Door County, Wisconsin.

Conventional theory is that extremely dry conditions coupled with small fires set by hunters, lumberjacks, railroad workers, locomotives, and farmers burning stumps clearing land, caused the fire. Robert W. Wells, in his book *Embers of October*, concludes that the "convection column (a whirling chimney of super-heated air) generated by the fire suddenly broke through the blanket of heavier, smoke-laden air into the cold air above, thus creating a huge updraft that led to the fire tornado, the whirlwinds and the curious phenomena reported by Fr. Pernin and other eye-witnesses."[2]

A recent theory advanced by certain scientists and supported by Fr. Pernin's report of a "large black object" is that Peshtigo was struck by a meteor, which ricocheted and landed in Chicago only minutes later, thereby explaining the near-exact onset of both fires as well as some of the aerial phenomena. The lack of craters in both locations dispels this theory somewhat. Residents of present-day Peshtigo do not place much credibility in this supposition, but the almost exact concurrence of these two devastating fires defies logic.

Peshtigo is an interesting bit of unknown history, but what does it have to do with the emigration of the Quists to America? Grandpa Knut was a carpenter. Peshtigo, like the mythical Phoenix, was rebuilding and rising from the ashes. It isn't too much of a stretch to assume that there was work for a carpenter in the town that, in fact, completely rebuilt during this period. As mentioned earlier, Gramma Clara's sister was already living in Peshtigo and many Swedes who had emigrated earlier perished in the fire.

Attempting to learn where the family put down new roots proved to be frustrating. Clara and the four children joined the Good Shepherd Lutheran Church in Peshtigo in 1913, but Knut apparently did not. Knut joined the Bethel Lutheran Church in Menominee prior to 1913, but Clara and the children did not. Was Knut employed in Menominee and Clara living in Peshtigo with her sister? Where did the kids go to grade school? And, why was there such a gap in years before joining the two churches? Research of town records failed to provide a clue.

In 1906, the Lloyd Manufacturing Co. was founded in

Menominee, Michigan, which is approximately eight miles north of Peshtigo. The Menominee River separates Marinette, Wisconsin, from Menominee, Michigan, and it also is the dividing line between Wisconsin and the Upper Peninsula of Michigan (U.P.). At some point, Knut, in his mid-thirties, took a job at what would become the largest plant in the U.P. and presumably moved his family of six to Menominee, or was already living there. Knut must have worked extremely hard and saved a considerable sum. He bought an impressive, two-story Victorian home on the corner of Spies Avenue and Chandler Street on July 7, 1920, for $4,500, where he and Clara raised their four children.

Lloyd made reed (now called wicker) baby carriages, doll carts, parasol baby carriages, woven wire doormats, and other products. Two-wheel doll carts sold for the grand total retail price of ten cents apiece in 1907! (My cousin, Lois Jean Quist (Holland), still owns a doll buggy that is 68 years old.) Knut worked for Lloyd in various capacities for the rest of his business career until he died at age 66 on March 23, 1938. There is a family photo of me, my sister, and my cousins, after Knut's funeral, taken when I was just age two that memorializes this event. That's what men sought in those days — employment with a good company — and they would devote their entire career to one employer. Grandfather Sam Anderson worked for the City of Green Bay for 25 years, and Knut worked for Lloyd for 30 years. The next generation of Quists would replicate their fathers' allegiance to one employer throughout the fifties. My uncle, Raynold Quist, quit high school and went to work for the railroad at age 14, and remained with the company his entire career. Then, this tradition and the employer-employee relationship began to dramatically change as a part of a major social and cultural paradigm shift that began in the 1960's.

We know little about these early years in Menominee, but suddenly and unexpectedly my dad became seriously ill when he was (at best guess) fifteen or sixteen years of age. It was rheumatic fever which, after the fever and the inflammation of his joints subsided, left Dad with damage to the valves in his heart. In layman's terms, his heart couldn't effectively pump blood into his system because there was leakage around the valves. A terrible blow to someone who looked forward to an athletic career at Menominee High School (MHS).

On September 23, 1920, the school board, the students and the townspeople of Menominee celebrated the dedication of what was termed "the most wonderful stadium found in the Middle West, The Walton Blesch Athletic Field." A generous gift of $40,000 provided a complete, state-of-the-art facility named after the Blesches' only son, who died while a student at MHS. Dad, who was nick-named "Hubby" by his classmates, never thought he would see the day that he would compete on this magnificent field as he sat in the stands as a non-participant during the "dedicatory exercises."

What made it even more difficult, as Dad recalled to me as we attended the Menominee and Marinette football game in 1948, was that MHS was undefeated and unscored-upon going into the final game against rival Marinette in 1920. A team that he should have been a member of. One of the best teams ever in MHS history. On Armistice Day, 1920 (described in *The Record*, the MHS yearbook), on "one of the coldest days imaginable," the game ended in a scoreless tie. One can only imagine how cold it was if it was one of the coldest days in the U.P. Anyplace else, the game probably would have been postponed.

Unable to participate in sports, Dad focused on school activities. He was elected Junior Class President and played the role of an athlete (Pink Hatcher) in the stage production of "Professor Pepp." He and his sister Friedeberg (nick-named "Fre") were members of the Literary Society, the Glee Club and were on *The Record* staff. Resigned to non-physical activities, Dad was able to be recognized on stage rather than on the athletic field. A break came in the spring of 1921. Dad's doctor said he could participate in track and field. He chose the 100 yard dash, the relays and the broad jump. Blessed with a strong right arm (inherited by his two oldest sons), a voice thirty years in the future should have said, "Dad, throw the javelin." He never did.

I am deeply indebted to Larry Ebsch who, as a sportswriter, covered both high schools for 27 years from 1955 to 1982, and has continued to write about them to the present. He knows the history of Menominee High School probably better than anyone. He dug deep in Maroon lore and provided me with a couple of gems.

In a *Menominee Herald-Leader* story dated June 7, 1921, "Hubby" took third in the 100 yard dash when the winning time was 10.45 seconds. The article further noted that Dad carried the relay team to victory in 1:32 — a race that was probably somewhat less than one half a mile.

The real blue ribbon, however, goes to Larry, who discovered, amongst a collection of ancient trophies, a large silver-coated chalice awarded to the MHS track team for its efforts in the Upper Peninsula Championships. Under Coach Guy W. Houston's name is engraved:

CAPTAIN

HERBERT QUIST

And the names of eight team members.

While marveling at the sight of this eighty-one-year-old trophy somewhat with reverence, I recalled the day perhaps thirty years ago that my wife, bless her heart, sold tons of my trophies at a garage sale. Sadly, the trophies are gone, but the events and the memories are, to her chagrin, preserved here (much later).

Included in the pictures of the track team in *The Record* are four javelin throwers, decked out not in the usual track uniforms but in dress shirts, vests, ties and slacks for the photo shoot. Almost all of the boys throughout the entire yearbook are dressed in suits and ties or sweaters and ties, and girls in calf-length dresses and black stockings. Spectators went to athletic events dressed in their "Sunday best." The mode of dress in the 20's was indicative of the formality and structured environment within the school during those formative years. I can imagine Clara, as meticulous and "fussy" as she was, ironing clean white shirts for each of her three sons every day.

The fall of 1921 was a defining moment in "Hubby's" life. The doctor gave him the green light to participate in all sports for his senior year at MHS. Given the fact that he didn't have the experience of competing his first two years in high school, his success was remarkable.

Unfortunately, statistical data from the games has been erased by the sands of time, but *The Record* makes note of a precious few. Playing East Green Bay on October 22, the Menominee Redmen (later re-named the Maroons) beat "the much talked of Green Bay team 34-6." The yearbook adds, "Passes to Barrett and Quist resulted in long gains for us." Dad played left end and often filled in at tackle.

Perhaps what is most memorable of his high school days is Dad's written summary in *The Record* of the 1921 football season — both for the unusual events that unfolded as well as the prose. Referring to the game at Ironwood, Michigan, Dad wrote:

At a very critical point in the game when F. Kruez had plunged through the center for a touchdown that tied the score 13-13 with a chance left to kick a goal and win the game, the referee ruled the touchdown illegal. As the coach saw it, it was a deliberate steal and rather than accept the penalty he took the team off the field and forfeited the game to Ironwood — Score 1-0.

The term "deliberate steal" could easily be interpreted as being "hometowned," an event that would occur thirty years later in "Hubby's" son's (my) life, but fortunately with different results. Apparently, it was more honorable in those days to walk away from a perceived unjust decision than to accept it. So much of the World War I era, as noted in *The Record*, was about honor.

Writing about the annual rivalry in the "M&M" game with Marinette, Dad wrote, "Marinette really earned their first touchdown but the other two were pure luck ... the backfield, though crippled, worked well as usual but nobody can beat a *team with horseshoes in their football pants.*"

Given the license to toot his own horn (as his son would accomplish later in this memoir) Dad added, "Quist did the punting and with the exception of once, outpunted Borofsky, Marinette's star, every time. He punted an average of 40 yards."

Did the reference to "horseshoes in their football pants" simply mean that lady luck was on Marinette's side, or did the opponents carry iron in their pants with the intent to injure a tackler — a device possibly used in the days where the protective pads were grossly inadequate? Who knows? Certainly it was a lament from a time when you rightfully "earned" everything from hard work. Luck didn't play any part in it. In the 50's we were taught by our coaches, "You make your own breaks." Different times, but a similar philosophy. Dad's forty-yard punting average was excellent given that the ball was rounder and less aerodynamic. Hubby's oldest son would follow in his dad's footsteps as a punter and as an end. His second son would break new ground as a running back.

Again, through the efforts of my newly discovered friend and archivist Larry Ebsch, a feature, four-column article from the October 17, 1921 edition of the *Herald-Leader*, describes, in graphic detail, Menominee High's game against the "Orange and Black" Escanaba team. The unique and colorful prose of the day highlights the drama that must have been a major event in all of the U.P. The tradition and roots of high school football were obviously well established early in the 20th Century.

Stopped from the very first down, Escanaba never had a chance. Bigger, older, more experienced supposedly in the art of football, Menominee was surely to go down, it was said, but they didn't.

Menominee, trained to charge at the first move of the ball, was pulled offsides by feints which cost Menominee 50 yards in penalties before the referee placed the offside blame where it belonged, with the Orange and Black squad of Escanaba.

The generalship of Frank Kreuz at quarterback was something that cannot go without comment, and neither can the story of Flum, Beck and Quist on the right side of the line....

Several interesting observations. According to the writer's account, MHS Coach Houston made no substitutions during the entire game. And, those games were sixty minutes, not forty-eight. Incredibly, the Maroons came out of the game "unscathed" — no injuries.

The above piece indicates that Dad played "on the right side of the line," but the lineup in the paper indicates that he was a left tackle. Immaterial as far as I'm concerned. What is significant is that Dad, in his first season of football after a near-fatal illness, played all sixty minutes. The outcome? MHS 3, Escanaba 0. Not exactly a rout.

The *Herald-Leader* indicates that 400 partisan MHS fans made the trip to Escanaba for the game. It's almost certain that Knut and Clara were there and it's quite possible that brother Robert, who was also working at Lloyd's, and sister Fre also made the trip. Reinhold, who was then age twenty-three, married and starting a family, probably was not in attendance. Thirty years later, Gramma Clara, Uncle Robert and Aunt Fre would witness the biggest high school football game of my career. Why not? It was a well-established tradition in America and the family.

Fast forward to the year 1948. I am twelve years old, my brother is ten. Dad has returned to Lauerman Field in Marinette, for the annual "M&M" game. THE game. Maybe it's because Dad filmed the game and I've seen the old, flickery frames a number of times, or maybe it's because we went into the locker room after the game to meet the player who is regarded as "The most notable sports celebrity in Menominee's history," according to Larry Ebsch, but I remember that day well despite the fact that it was fifty-four years ago.

Billy Wells was truly a star. Undoubtedly the first that I ever met up close and personal. I remember how polite he was to Dad and to me and my brother. I had been to the Packer games and saw the likes of Don Hutson and Tony Canadeo but they were a football field away. Here I was in the inner sanctum of the locker room. That's different. Who knows where youngsters get an inspiration to try to do what their heroes have done. Maybe, just maybe, mine, in part, came on that cold but sunny November day in 1948 in Marinette, Wisconsin.

As a postscript, Billy Wells went on to become a star at Michigan State under Coach Biggie Munn's famous "Pony Backfield" in the early 1950's. He was the most valuable player in the 1954 Rose Bowl, and followed that with great success in the National Football League with four teams. It's particularly important to kids at the age that I was then, to attach themselves to a rising star. One that doesn't fall. Billy's star kept on rising. He's gone now, but Larry, who was a classmate of Billy, continues to faithfully illuminate his distant but brilliant celestial body.

Despite the fact that Dad didn't have any competitive basketball playing experience his first two years at MHS, he was elected captain of the team. At 6'0" he was one of the tallest players and must have been popular and respected by his teammates. Although the team had only a .500 season, winning six games and losing six, this was the first team in MHS history to place in the Upper Peninsula Tournament.

One game in that tournament was remarkable. MHS beat Ironwood 7 to 3, which would have to be a near record for scoring futility in a thirty-two minute game. Defense, needless to say, must have been the principal strategy at the time.

I vividly recall shooting hoops with my Dad at the YMCA in Green Bay quite often in the late 40's, and marveling at Dad's set shot. He held the ball waist high and sort of flipped it semi-underhanded at the basket. It was a pretty easy shot to block. Maybe that's why the scores were so low. No one apparently drove to the basket or used a jump shot since players were limited to a maximum amount of "dribbles." What a revolutionary idea. An overhead jump shot. That technique caught on in the 50's.

Dad's teammate, Bob Kruez, must have been an outstanding athlete. He was MHS's star in every sport, including track and field where he threw the javelin a record 134'6" in one of the large meets. Thirty years later, thirty feet more would be a competitive javelin throw in high school, which event will become a focus of this memoir. According to *The Record*, Dad finished third in the broad jump, where the winning distance was 20'2-7/8." He probably leaped about the same distance that his oldest son did in high school (both marks unremarkable in their respective days).

After graduation from MHS in 1922, it is presumed that "Hubby" worked for a period of time at Lloyd's joining Knut, his dad, and brother Robert at the company. Supporting this assumption is a large, untarnished photograph, dated 1922, of the Lloyd's Manufacturing baseball team decked out in their New York Yankee-style pin stripes, with Dad as a member of the team. Industrial leagues in all sports were popular in the Midwest, and though employee records from the era have long been discarded, it's safe to assume Dad worked at Lloyd's since he was on their team. Not long however. He headed south, to Green Bay, in search of greener pastures.

From various sources, it appears that Dad found a job at Northwest Engineering, a heavy equipment manufacturer, working in administration. Soon after getting situated, he would meet a very attractive, strawberry blonde Swede by the name of Thelma Anderson. What could be more perfect for two immigrant families than to be joined by marriage in the new land? There were great expectations and synergism. But an earthshaking event occurred during their courtship. The marriage of my future parents almost ended before it happened. I was nearly not me.

Sam and Hulda Anderson must have arrived in Green Bay from Boston in 1906. Sam, who was only about 5'8" tall but was, according to my cousin Larry, "very stout and very strong," bought a small farm west of town. By 1915, probably after working for the City of Green Bay for some time, he became the tender of the Walnut Street Bridge spanning the Fox River. For 25 years, the bridge was the longest single-span bascule in the world. (A bascule is a bridge that is counterbalanced so that when one end is lowered the other is raised.)

Considerable commercial boat traffic from the Great Lakes passed through Green Bay and required that the bridge be raised for the larger craft. I can remember as a child both riding in my parents' car and walking, waiting for the concrete and steel structure, standing like a massive sentry guarding a gate, to lower so that we could continue our course. Sam's job was important to keep one of the commercial lifelines of the city open. Technology has long since replaced Sam's job, but when I pass that way I can almost see him perched in the tender's lookout, now empty, high above the river. Today, Sam's picture graces the wall at the Titletown Restaurant not far from where he toiled.

Like Dad, very little is known about Mom's early childhood and school years. From Merlin Barlament's (my second cousin) collection there are several precious photographs. One is of Sam and Hulda, with Thelma and Elsie, taken in front of a two-story, frame house when the girls were about three or four years old. The number 221 appears on the side of the house. There is a wooden walkway which together with the number indicates that the home was in the city, but no other homes are in the background.

Another series of photographs, in which Mom has a very large, conspicuous white bow in her hair, portrays Thelma and Elsie, probably ages ten and eleven, with the Anderson and Barlament families. One snapshot with everyone dressed in their Sunday best is aboard an early Model T Ford. Another has a picture of Aunt Elsie in her teens, along with her father and Walter and Patra Barlament, enjoying a picnic lunch with a much-more upscale touring car in the background. Despite what could have been a "muggy" hot and humid day in Wisconsin, Sam and Walter are dressed in white shirts, vests and ties. How did Merlin know it was hot? The men had shed their coats. Pretty formal attire for a picnic but expected in a time when even everyday occasions were formal.

I made the assumption earlier that it probably was Marie Anderson, Sam's half-sister, that encouraged Sam and Hulda to move from Boston to Green Bay, and it was Marie that married Charles Anderson, another Swede whose roots date back to his great grandfather, Swen Anderson, born in 1786, and Anders Swenson, born in 1826 in Sweden.

The marriage of Marie and Charles produced five children: Anna, Patra, Soloman, Arthur and Mathilda, whom we knew as "Tillie." As evidenced by the recitations above and the photographs, the two Anderson families bonded together in their new land. As an aside, what are the odds that each of the Anderson grandparents would marry an Anderson?

It was through Patra, born in 1891 in Green Bay, that the Anderson clan acquired their "French connection." Patra married Walter R. Barlament in 1909 and settled in Duck Creek, which was inhabited mostly by French and a few Belgians. Our Barlament cousins (actually second cousins) were Merlin (born 1920), Doris (1923) and Gerald (1927). Merlin was prominent to me as a small child because he was the closest family member to enlist in the army in World War II. Later, he became the first family historian, for which I am forever grateful.

By the time Thelma and Elsie were attending Fort Howard Elementary School (then called Dousman School), the Anderson family was living at 509 Hubbard Street, only a block from the school. I can recall that Gramma and I, in the 1970's, reviewed her records of the house after it was sold. Sam, amongst his multiple talents, had built their home at a cost (including the lot) for $2,000 around the time of World War I. Upscale condominiums now occupy the lot.

In 1918 Mom enrolled at McCartney Junior High School. One of her teachers was Margaret C. McMahon, a short, stocky, iron-fisted woman who later would become the principal at McCartney and ultimately, in 1928, the principal and commandant of Franklin Junior High. You might consider the military inference somewhat questionable, unless, of course, you were a student while she was in charge. Thelma remembered her with intimidation. Miss McMahon, referred to secretly by her students as "Mickey," was a legendary character in the West Green Bay school system from 1913 to 1953, retiring at age 66. Her dominating presence as an authoritative figure had a profound impact on every (without exception) student she came in contact with. I was one of them. The stories I will relate later will be difficult for most readers to believe but, incredibly, they are true.

One of the few treasures that have survived the sands of time is Mom's 1924 West High School Yearbook *Snapshots*, from her junior year. There are only a limited number of signatories to Mom's yearbook but they are particularly telling. Two of her teachers wrote:

May you bring as much joy to others as you brought to me. — Mrs. Icks

Never get discouraged with the little things. — Miss Ley

These words were prophetic. Mom, as an extremely caring woman, did bring joy to others but, unfortunately, she did make mountains out of molehills, which you will discover.

It does not appear that Thelma Anderson participated in any women's sports or activities, and did not make the honor role. Her sister, Elsie, was active in drama and had one of the leads in *Much Ado About Something*. Mom was introverted and Elsie was an exact opposite. Thelma was tall and blonde. Elsie was shorter with dark black hair. Neither of them seemed to resemble their parents.

One of the most memorable and enjoyable moments that occurred during Mom's life was a summer job as a waitress at the famous and luxurious Grand Hotel on Mackinac Island. The island is located at the northern tip of Michigan that connects the Upper Peninsula through the straits of Mackinac. Thelma probably made the journey by boat across Lake Michigan. I can recall looking at pictures of this magnificent alabaster white hotel, with its long row of statuesque columns gracing the grand porch overlooking an immaculately groomed flower garden. Years after Mom's death an experience occurred that brought me back to this magnificent place. Ironically, it was a movie entitled *Somewhere in Time* that has literally haunted me since.

Christopher Reeve, playing the role of a contemporary playwright, becomes intrigued and fascinated by a photograph of a beautiful actress (played by Jane Seymour) at his theater. So smitten is Reeve with the actress from the early 1900's that he, through magical means, is able to transport himself back in time to the actress's hey day. Where does Chris awake and find himself in the presence of the gorgeous Jane? The Grand Hotel, of course. The movie is a powerful love story and has a mystical aura, but it pursues a dream that is embodied in just about all of us. It takes us back in time. Just as a memoir does.

In my case it took me back to a place and time that freed my mother from the rigid confines of an uncompromising and demanding father who smothered her desire to experience the joys of life. As I watched the film I could see her seated with girlfriends, giggling, on a swing on that well-recognized porch, watching the young men in their three-piece suits and bowlers walking by. Mom wistfully spoke of Mackinac often.

Other than her stint at Mackinac Island, Mom worked at Sheffer's Photography Studio on West Walnut after school and on Saturdays. I believe that she was employed by Sid Sheffer after graduation when she met my father. I suspect, although I don't know for certain, that both girls worked during their high school days and didn't have much time for extracurricular activities. Sam was a tough, uncompromising taskmaster working the farm, tending the bridge and assisting Gramma when they owned the boarding house and restaurant. He expected no less from his two daughters.

During the courtship of my mother and father, an unexpected event occurred that almost derailed my parents' wedding. A young woman called on Gramma Anderson at their home on Hubbard Street. She was holding a young baby. She told Gramma that "Hubby" was the father!

Today, such an event would hardly raise an eyebrow. In the 1920's, having sex outside of marriage was *verboten*. Having an illegitimate child was socially unacceptable. Mom was, in her words, "beside myself." I still do not know exactly what the term means but it must have meant the worst possible feeling.

To this day, no one in our family knows if the young lady's claim was true or false, or the purpose of her claim. Similarly, the Quist siblings do not know if we have a half sister or brother out there somewhere. But we do know that somehow or someway "Hubby" was able to quiet the uproar and Mom relented. Herbert A. Quist and Thelma E. Anderson were married (as best can be determined) in 1928. An event that Mom, much later in life, would lament, saying, "I should never have married your father after that 'floozie' showed up with Hub's baby."

The "Roaring 20's" ended with a resounding thud on October 29, 1929. The rapid rise of consumer spending for autos, household appliances and homes stimulated by a newly created banking tool called "consumer credit," mixed with a "flapper" devil-may-care attitude created a euphoria in America never before experienced by this nation. A capitalistic system, driven in part by hard working immigrants, flourished, but it also provided the helium for a gigantic, speculative bubble on Wall Street.

The Federal Reserve Bank of the U.S., which had just been formed in 1913, had as one of its primary goals to convert a savings-minded populace to spending-conscious consumers. By 1929 it had accomplished what it had intended to do, but now that the credit and spending train was speeding down the tracks at breakneck speed, the Fed was compelled to slow it down.

Credit, also on Wall Street, added fuel to the fire. Speculators bought stock on margin with only twenty percent cash, and as stock prices ballooned they borrowed more and bought more. The Fed governors, bankers and shrewd investors knew the bubble would burst and took appropriate defensive measures. Some seized an opportunity and "shorted" the market, but I would opine that not one of them would have remotely considered that the crash would not only stop the speculative mania, it would derail the economic train for eleven years. In 1930 the Dow Jones Industrial Average fell 34%. In 1931, 52%. In 1932, 23%. The most defining moment in the lives of our parents and our grandparents was at hand. [*The parallels to the mania and stock market crash in the year 2000 are both ominous and instructive.*]

Sam and Hulda were fortunate. Grandpa's job with the City of Green Bay as the bridge tender continued unabated throughout the dark days of The Depression. In addition, the Andersons had the farm, which undoubtedly provided them almost all of the sustenance they required. I suspect that Mom and Dad lived with Sam and Hulda for a short period of time when Dad lost his job at Northwest Engineering when it closed around 1931. It appears that the only significant setback for the Andersons was that their small restaurant on West Main Street, near the present-day West Theater, closed.

Despite the gloom and doom that began to envelop the nation and the City by the Bay, Joan Dorothy Quist was born on August 20, 1931. Dad, out of necessity, had to find work, and began a new career as an insurance agent, which he would maintain for the rest of his life. He went to work for the Old Line Life Insurance Co., which was headquartered in Milwaukee, Wisconsin. An unexpected and tragic event occurred that would cause the Quist family of three to find a new home to raise their family.

Elsie, Mom's sister, married Lloyd "Larry" Lawrence in 1929 just prior to the crash. They had a son, Larry, who was born on July 29, 1930. Lloyd was in partnership with his brother Glen and they operated the B. F. Goodrich Tire Shop on East Main Street. Grandpa Lawrence was also in the auto repair and used car business, and operated a store near the Greyhound Bus Station in downtown Green Bay.

Suddenly and without warning Lloyd contracted spinal meningitis. Apparently doctors were baffled by a disease so rare and Lloyd, only thirty-three years of age, died. My Aunt Elsie was a widow at the age of twenty-six and my cousin Larry was only three. But, unfortunately, that wasn't the worst of it. "Little Lollie," as my mother referred to her nephew, was a very sick child.

Shortly after birth Larry developed severe eczema, a non-contagious inflammation of the skin marked by redness, itching and the outbreak of lesions that discharged serous matter that became encrusted and scaly. Tormented by the constant itching all over his body and infections in the open sores, it was extremely difficult for Larry to sleep. But that wasn't the limit of his problems.

Larry also had asthma complicated by hay fever. He contracted pneumonia several times and doctors told Elsie, "Larry probably won't make it." Apparently doctors advised Elsie to discontinue her breast feeding soon after Larry was born, and the severe health problems began when a formula was substituted for mother's milk. Incredibly, Larry also developed rickets, a vitamin D deficiency, affecting bone growth. Not a promising future for a three-year-old, fatherless child in the midst of a Depression that was gaining a stranglehold on not only Green Bay, but the entire U.S.

It could have been the dire economic conditions, the constant care and vigilance of a sick child, or the innate restlessness of a young widow reared in a rigid home environment (or all of the above) that led Elsie to abandon her son and head for the town that never slept — Chicago. She shed her responsibilities as well as her name (Elsie was the talking cow on Borden's milk advertisements), adopting *Laurie Lawrence* as more cosmopolitan, befitting a Chicago "party girl." Chicago was the wide open town then controlled by Al Capone and his ilk. Thelma, my mom, devoted to the health, well being and education of her children, understandably never forgave her sister for her selfish, irresponsible act of abandoning her child.

Raising and caring for "Little Lollie" would fall either upon the Lawrence family, who were "Eastsiders" (they lived on the east side of Fox River) or Gramma and Grandpa Anderson. Elsie's preference was that Larry remain with her parents and not her in-laws. And so it was, Sam and Hulda Anderson nurtured "Little Lollie" to health and he, defying the doctors' dire predictions, survived.

It wouldn't have happened that way had Larry not been a boy. Grandpa Sam, it seemed, always rued the day that he never had a son. Thelma, my mom, and Elsie suffered the consequences of his frustration. Coming from Sweden before the turn of the century, emigrating from a land and time of kings, many fathers seemed to have a crowning need for a male heir. The absence of a male son was Larry's good fortune. He became Sam's son.

The Anderson home on Hubbard Street was a two-bedroom, one-bath bungalow that could hardly accommodate Sam and Hulda, "Hub," Thelma, two-year-old Joanie and three-year-old "Lollie." (Dad's nickname by this time had evolved from "Hubby" of high school days to a more sophisticated "Hub.") Somehow, in the midst of the gut-wrenching Depression, Dad purchased a home at 1209 Grignon Street, between the Fox and East Rivers. Yes, Joanie and I were born on the east side, which means very little except to Bayites. Present-day neighbors recall a small house set back from Grignon, but it no longer exists.

Building a clientele of insurance clients when there was over 20% unemployment, and people were scavenging for food to eat, must have been an incredible challenge. Dad, to his credit, persisted and was able to find dollars for premiums when people were afraid to put their money in banks or any financial institution. I can recall, with wonderment, reviewing sales results published by Old Line Life from the thirties where a $1,000 life insurance policy with a premium of $5.00/month was noteworthy. A $5,000 life sale was outstanding. An article with Dad's picture appeared in the *Green Bay Press-Gazette* in 1941, acknowledging his success. He produced for his company and provided for his family during the worst of times, when despair was everywhere.

I've often wondered how my parents could possibly afford another mouth to feed, but they, fortunately, wanted another child. I wasn't an "accident." I was born on one of the most memorable days of the year — April 1,

1936. Prophetically, an April Fool. A miniature invoice the size of a register tape from Bellin Memorial Hospital is a classic exhibit of those perilous and difficult days. The room and board cost for my delivery was an unbelievable five dollars per day for a total of $20.00. Sixty years later my confinement at St. Joseph's Hospital in Phoenix, Arizona, would cost $10,000/day! Possibly the largest percentage increase in any product or service that we have consumed in our lifetime.

My birth certificate lists my full legal name as Herbert Larry Quist, Jr. The father is listed as Herbert A. Quist, when actually Dad was christened as Alf Herbert. So, how could I possibly be a "junior?" Technically, I couldn't be and I haven't used the designation. More interesting, perhaps, how did I get the moniker "Buster?"

I like to tell audiences during speaking engagements that since Herbert (Hoover) was guilty (not really) of causing The Depression, Dad didn't want to associate me with the ex-president. The truth is that when I (at a robust ten pounds) finally made my appearance, Mom said, "This boy is a buster!" So, I began life as "Buster" right from the start and I've never been able to shake the name.

So, what was happening on this day when I first saw the light of day? On the front page of the *New York Times*, a true barometer of the era, Bruno Richard Hauptmann, the convicted killer of the Lindbergh baby, got a 48-hour stay of execution. (Charles Lindbergh was the most celebrated Swede in America.) The Russians warned the Japanese to cease its incursion into Outer Mongolia, and at the same time Adolf Hitler pledged not to increase the amount of German troops as the winds of war began to blow stronger. Getting anxious, as was all of Europe, the Swedish parliament approved $34 million (in dollar equivalent) for military spending. The most defining moment in American history was about to unfold as I entered the world.

Saks Fifth Avenue was offering an evening gown for $29.85 and an Easter bonnet for $5.00. Gimbels advertised a man's suit for $29.95, and for anyone who could buy a car a Buick could be purchased for as low as

$765.

On Broadway, *The Great Ziegfeld* was playing at the Astor Theater, starring William Powell and Myrna Loy. Tickets were $.50, $.75 and $1.00. The "boys of summer" were still in spring training and Lou Gehrig had not yet been diagnosed with the disease that bears his name. To the dismay of baseball fans everywhere the "Babe" had retired in 1935, but he had hit three home runs in his last game. Bobby Cruickshank shocked the golf world by shooting a 29 on the first nine at the Masters and led the odds-on favorite, Bobby Jones, by five shots after the first round.

In the financial world, the markets were attempting to rally from the disastrous 90% drop in the Dow Jones Industrial Average. The Dow reached 120 on my birthday, up almost 100% from 1932. The *New York Times* reported that profits in 1935 were the highest since 1930; it had taken a full three months to calculate what now would have been calculated in a matter of one day. Wheat was $1.10, and corn $.78 a bushel as the plight of the farmers, those that were able to hang onto their farms, was horrible. Oil was $1.04/barrel and gold, which was fixed (and confiscated by the Federal Government by President Roosevelt's edict) at $35/oz., was not even listed in the commodity section of the *Times*.

On April Fool's Day 1936 everything ostensibly was looking up. Optimism was in the air. But, true to the day's reputation, it was a fool trick. Despite Franklin D. Roosevelt's re-election in November, the economy and the financial markets headed lower again. The War five years later not only changed the world as we knew it, everyone who was able went to war or to work. The Great Depression was over.

A picture taken on the steps of Knut and Clara Quist's home in Menominee, Michigan, in March 1938 (cited earlier), records a major event in the Quist family that brought the clan together in one of their rare moments. Grandfather Knut passed away on March 23rd. Huddled together dressed in winter wraps, with snow banks adjacent, are cousins Raynold Quist, born October 15, 1922; Ernest Norman, born June 28, 1925; Keith Oscar, born June 17, 1928; and Lois Jean, born December 7, 1932. My sister Joan is sitting next to Lois, and I'm standing decked out in a snowsuit directly behind the two of them, pointing at the cameraman, mouth wide open, giving instructions.

Joanie and my cousins, being considerably older at the time of Knut's death, recall the passing of the patriarch who brought the Qvist family to Amerika thirty-three years earlier. A picture probably taken circa 1924 portrays the four Quist children as adults before offspring. Raynold (who changed the spelling from Reinhold) Quist, my uncle, and his wife, Valberg Johnson (the two were married in 1921), are the only married couple. Raynold and Robert, the two oldest brothers, are already sans hair. Dad's hairline is definitely receding, and within a couple of years he would continue the family tradition of baldness that would be passed on to all of his sons.

This snapshot is further evidence that Dad was probably living in Menominee during the mid-20's and had not yet made his move to Green Bay. Aunt Fre, an extremely attractive young woman, then about age 23, had not yet married Melville King.

Uncle Raynold left Menominee while employed by the railroad. He and Valberg, who was also of Swedish descent, settled in Consol, Iowa, and he began a career with the Chicago & Northwestern Railroad that would continue for a remarkable forty-five years. All four of my Quist cousins were born and raised in Iowa, and I can recall one trip, while I was in junior high, visiting Uncle Ray and Aunt Val in What Cheer, Iowa. I often wondered then, as I do today, how the town ever got that strange name.

The town, founded in 1865, was first named Petersburg, but since there were so many post offices with the same name, the postal authorities in Iowa took on the name *What Cheer* to distinguish it from the others. What Cheer, it seems, was an old English salutation used with the Indians in the early settlements in the east. I'll bet my cousins didn't know that!

My cousins recalled their visits to Menominee. Raynold knew that when he was at the Quist home "he had to behave himself," a common expression we all remember to this day. He thought Grandpa was "very particular with his garden and the yard." He recalls, "everything was just so." Raynold never experienced or required stern discipline, but the Quist house was not an ideal place for a young boy to play.

Lois Jean reinforced her brother's impressions. After Grandpa Knut died, "Grandma and Uncle Bob were so particular. Didn't like to stay there. Uncle Bob always told me that I had ants in my pants because I couldn't sit still, especially at meal times." Lois Jean added, "Grandma always set the table very fancy, drank water out of goblets. Was always afraid I'd spill something."

All cousins agree. Grandma Quist was "fussy." She was proud of her house and it was substantially upscale for the day. Grandpa and Grandma must have, and rightfully so, been proud of their home and what they, as immigrants, had accomplished. Sister Joanie had a very hurtful, memorable experience.

During the summer when Joanie was about ten, she went to Grandma's house to spend a week. She was only there a day when she became ill, which "annoyed" Grandma. The family doctor was called to the Quist home. The diagnosis was the dreaded mumps. The doctor was livid! "Child? Do you know what you have done? You've brought this contagion into my community. You must leave immediately!" She did, and she didn't ever want to come back. Of course she did, but with trepidation.

My recollections? Not as negative as my sister's, fortunately for me. Gramma (I still used the term without the "d") had gobs of "trinkets and doodads" on the coffee tables with fancy doilies. I wasn't curious, but my little brother Terry couldn't keep his hands off of the little figurines. Gramma would slap his hands and say, "Don't touch," adding her usual, "tsk, tsk."

Gramma and Uncle Bob maintained Knut's garden after his death. I remember the old chicken house out in the back yard, that was then void of the feathered friends.

Thanksgiving and Christmas dinners were formal and we were expected to eat all that we were served. On one occasion, I had a second helping of home-made ice cream. Then a third. I was "stuffed" as Mom used to say. I got a bellyache but not much sympathy from Gramma. She said "my eyes were bigger than my stomach." An old cliché of course, but conversations in those days were full of clichés. Observe the dialog of movies from the thirties and forties. Conversation was superficial even amongst the hoi polloi of Hollywood.

Probably the most memorable incident occurred in the mid-thirties, when my cousin Raynold was thirteen years old. Dad, who was living in Green Bay, was visiting his family in Menominee while Raynold was there for a short visit. Dad had a sporty car. He took his young nephew for a spin downtown. He took a sharp left turn. The right passenger door opened. Ray flew out the door bouncing and rolling across the pavement! Dad was horrified! Leaving his car in the middle of the street he ran back to find Raynold sitting up and shaking the cobwebs from his head. Aside from a few scratches and a bump on his head, Ray wasn't injured seriously. It cured Dad's recklessness behind the wheel.

One thing I find interesting about the incident is that Dad had sufficient income to buy a new car. Had his insurance business (that he started in 1931) progressed to the point that he could buy a new automobile for $600 or $800? Or, did his dad assist him? How affluent was Grandpa Quist? Did Lloyd Manufacturing close down during The Depression as a large majority of plants did? I simply don't know, but I think it's safe to say that Grandpa and Gramma Quist were very frugal, and they weathered comfortably the economic storm that threatened almost everyone during the thirties. Uncle Raynold, with his good, secure job, may have assisted his parents.

By the late twenties all of the Quists were married and raising families save Uncle Robert. Robert worked, along with his dad, at Lloyd's in Menominee and continued to live with Clara, his mother, after Knut died. Robert was "fussy" like his mother, and as I grew older I thought that my uncle was a little "strange." He was always very solicitous and kind but I wondered if my uncle wasn't a little "slow on the draw."

On August 22, 1938, Joanie and I had a brand new baby brother, Terry Lloyd, whose middle name was probably in honor of cousin Larry's dad, who died five years earlier. Terry wasn't a planned addition. Mom and Dad were not, according to Mom's confession to me much later in life, "getting along." Thelma didn't want another baby but when Terry arrived, the joy of a third healthy child seemingly mended the rift between our parents. There was a logistical problem though. The house on Grignon was too small for a family of five and sister Joanie, now seven, desperately wanted her own private bedroom.

Mom and Dad purchased a larger home at 1140 Dousman Street, in a more upscale neighborhood, on December 9, 1938, according to the Brown County records. As my brother and sister and I spent most of our formative years on Dousman Street, all of us remember every nook and cranny.

You could decipher quickly that our house was the oldest in the neighborhood. It was brown stucco with red brick trim and a small garage designed for a Model T-sized car from the twenties. Most of the other homes had wood siding, which was the building material of choice just prior to World War II. As near as I can determine our home was built in 1927.

Joanie made claim to her own private bedroom upstairs that had a neat, secret-like closet where Santa hid our Christmas presents and we could sequester ourselves during hide-and-seek. The master bedroom faced the street and we could watch what was happening up and down Dousman on rainy or freezing days which were quite frequent.

Terry and I shared our bedroom in the back of the house, overlooking the vacant lots to the north where we dug our trenches and fought our make-believe wars. We called the unoccupied expanse "fields." I don't know why, but to all of us in the neighborhood they were "fields." We had bunk beds and a large cabinet where we stuffed our clothes and toys.

Directly ahead of the upstairs was a door that led to a pint-sized porch overlooking the backyard. I thought I might fall off the balcony and die. It was kind of useless, really. I didn't go out there much because it was scary. And there was another, more intimidating reason that I will reveal to you in a jiffy.

Also at the head of the stairs was the "master" bath. It was the only bath, so it served many masters. There was another bathroom down in the basement, but it was always cold and musty-smelling so we didn't want to go down there in our bare feet.

The predominant feature of every home in Green Bay and in fact, all of the Mid-west, was the furnace. Making certain that the fire never went out in the winter was everyone's sworn duty, particularly when Dad was gone. Removing the "clinkers" and taking them out to the curb for pick-up was every boy's job. I didn't mind. I thought the hot cinders, glowing red on black like miniature asteroids, were pretty darn intriguing.

On cold, wintery days Mom would hang her washing up in the basement hoping the sheets and our clothes would dry by the heat from the furnace. I remember how those sheets would freeze stiff like plates of ice when Mom hung them outside and the temperature took a dip. It was always dipping, it seemed. And if we didn't get the milk that the milkman left on the back porch inside quickly the milk would freeze and push the top off the bottle.

On the first floor there was a large living room with a rock fireplace on the west end, and a dining room on the east. We could seat ten of us at Thanksgiving dinner, and the table and chair legs served as the forest when Terry and I lined up our toy soldiers for another battle. We had a fourth bedroom at the bottom of the stairs; it served first as Dad's office and then as a card room. It always "smelled to high heaven" after one of Dad's poker games took place. A smoky haze was still there in the morning and the smell was icky, I always thought.

To me, as a child, our house was large and roomy and most importantly, we were warm and secure. But, houses always seem large when you're small. They shrink when you re-visit them when you're bigger. One exception, even as a small kid I knew that our kitchen was small. How small? Very, but that's only an estimate.

Our kitchen table was attached to the wall and hinged so that we could raise the table up and latch it to the wall. We had two benches, like those you use at a picnic, that we moved around so you didn't have to squeeze between the table and the stove and get hot buns. There was limited cabinet space, so Mom stored groceries in the basement. Somehow, all five of us ate most of our meals in our mini-kitchen. Mom ate hers standing up as she served us. We all loved our house and our neighborhood. In the late thirties and forties it was described as an area of "up and coming young professionals." A predominantly Catholic neighborhood with "oodles" of kids to play with, as you'll discover.

At this point in this memoir I have taken the liberty to tell the remaining story primarily through the means of a narrative. Given that the facts and events from this point forward were gathered firsthand from those who experienced them and are still living, I've attempted to create dialog that not only breathes life into all the characters, but, I believe, will be much more interesting and digestible to the reader.

As the decade of the 40's began, cousin Larry Lawrence was nine and he and Grandpa Sam were real chums. Sam took Larry out to his farm every Saturday morning in his Model T Ford that he had purchased from Grandpa Lawrence for $500 in the late 20's, just prior to The Depression. Larry vividly recalls that there was a long hill on the way out to the farm and the old Model T just barely made it each time. It's a good thing that it was downhill when they brought their harvest into the farmer's market. The "T" wouldn't have made it uphill.

"You can go get Grandpa at the bridge," Gramma

suggested, as Larry had been waiting seemingly for hours to hear. With Gramma's approval Larry, having mostly recovered from his incredibly bad health, walked briskly to the Walnut Street Bridge (avoiding the cracks in the sidewalk, as we all did superstitiously).

"Would you like to see how I make the bridge work when a boat comes down the river?" Sam asked the wide-eyed nine-year-old in his Swedish-Northern Wisconsin accent.

"Gee whiz, yeah," Larry replied, as Grandpa showed Larry all the levers that raised and lowered the massive concrete and steel bridge.

"Now, let's go down below and I'll show you how the bridge goes up and down," Sam said as his shift ended. They descended into the depths of the tower to see the massive machinery that could lift such a monstrous load to an incredible height.

"Geez Grandpa. What if these wheels broke? Will the bridge come falling down?" Larry asked.

"It's my job to make sure it don't," Sam replied. "Time's up. Let's go to Bramey's. Your Grandpa needs a beer."

Bramey's was a popular "tavern" — as it was called in those days. All the hard-working men stopped off at their favorite tavern after work. Grandpa said it was a tradition kept from the "old country."

Grandpa ordered his usual large schooner of beer. The bartender slid the mug all the way down the bar. Sam lifted Larry up and placed him on the edge of the bar. There weren't any stools. All the patrons stood at the bar with one foot on a brass rail on the floor.

"Kin I lick the foam off, Grandpa?" Larry asked (this was his accustomed treat).

"Sure. Take off the 'ole head," Sam said.

Larry, after sipping the foam, hopped off the bar and down to the floor.

"Watch out fer tha' spittoons," the bartender said to Larry, not too pleased to have a little kid in his tavern.

Often, on the way home, Grandpa would stop at

Farah's (a grocery store) and buy a case of beer and a few things for dinner.

He and Larry were buddies. Larry was the son that Sam never had, and Larry had a dad to replace the one he never knew. As warm as their relationship was, Thelma and Elsie never saw this side of their father. To them, he was cold, uncompromising as concrete, intimidating and impossible to please. Often, grandparents get a second chance with their grandchildren. Maybe Sam, given time to reflect, regretted his withdrawn and distant relationship with his two daughters.

"Larry? Go Down in the basement and get your Grandpa. Breakfast is ready. I guess he can't hear me calling," Gramma said to Larry as he walked into the kitchen wiping the "sleep" from his eyes.

Larry, still in his pajamas on a Sunday morning, hopped down the rickety, old wooden stairway to the damp, musty-smelling basement where Sam went to stoke the furnace and shovel more coal onto the fire. Even though it was June, a "cold spell" had hit northern Wisconsin.

"Gramma! Gramma!" Larry shouted excitedly and anxiously. "Grandpa is lying in the coal bin and he's not moving," Larry added, sensing something was wrong and fearing the worst.

"Oh my Lord," Gramma said as she stood at the top of the basement steps. "Stay with Grandpa. I'll call Doctor Kuhls," Gramma said as she headed to the dining room and the telephone on her little work desk with the "accordion" rollback cover.

"Mabel," Gramma said to the operator, "Get me Doctor Kuhls ... Hurry ... I think Sam has had a heart attack." In those days you placed your calls through operators and you knew them all by name.

Dr. Milton Kuhls came to the house immediately. He gave Sam a shot and called for an ambulance. They took Sam to St. Mary's Hospital. He had suffered a stroke. He lingered in a coma for three days, but died June 11, 1940, without ever regaining consciousness. Hulda had lost her husband at age 67, Larry had lost his second "father" in a period of seven years, and the three of us had lost a grandfather that we didn't have time to enjoy. Joanie, age nine at the time, remembers Sam's passing. Being four, I did not recall the event. Billy Magaurn was one of Larry's playmates and close friends. Billy's dad was the funeral director at Schauer and Schumacher Funeral Home, and Mr. Magaurn conducted the services at the Westside Moravian Church.

Sam was buried in the family plot at the Aswaubenon Moravian Cemetery. Ninety-eight percent of all Swedes were Lutherans at this point in time. Why, then, was Sam a member of the Moravian Church? And, who were the Moravians? It's an interesting story.

The name *Moravian* identifies the fact that this historic church had its origin in ancient Bohemia and Moravia, in what is the present-day Czech Republic. Jan Hus protested the ecclesiastical jurisdiction of the Roman Catholic Church. He was found guilty of heresy and burned at the stake in 1415. The Czechs formed their own church in 1457, which was sixty years before Martin Luther began his reformation. Moravians began to immigrate to America in 1735 and established a settlement in Bethlehem, Pennsylvania, in 1741. In the summer of 1850, Niels Otto Tank (in Norwegian pronounced *Tunk*), a Moravian pastor and missionary, settled in Green Bay. Having the good fortune of being married to a wealthy Dutch woman, Caroline van der Meulen, Otto Tank purchased "upwards of 800 acres" on the west side of the Fox River, reportedly for $6 to $8 per acre. Tank's dream was to build a Norwegian community in America, combining religious service with agricultural activity and higher education. Tank called his little community Ephraim (Land of Plenty). Harold S. Naess, writing in the Fall 1993 *Wisconsin Academy Review*, refers to Tank's community as a commune, a concept more fully developed by the communists almost seventy years later.

Reverend Andreas Michael Iversen, the leader of the Milwaukee (Wisconsin) Moravian congregation, came to Green Bay in late 1850 with his small flock to share in this new colony called Ephraim. Iversen's followers, however, wanted land ownership. Tank, according to Iversen, declared "in a thunderous voice that he would never give anyone a contract for land or lots." In the spring of 1853, Iversen and his break-away flock moved north to a harbor near Horseshoe Island and founded the present day Ephraim in Door County, which area will become part of this story one hundred years later.

So, how did the Andersons become a part of the Moravian diaspora? Charles J. Anderson, my great uncle, who was born in Ellsborg, Sweden, in 1863, one year prior to Otto Tank's death, became a member of the Moravian Church when he settled in Green Bay. Though Tank's idealistic concept of a commune failed, the Moravians who took up roots in the Green Bay area could have influenced Charles and convinced him to join the Moravian Church. Pure speculation on my part, but it's not too long a stretch that that happened, and it was Charles who got Grandpa Sam Anderson to join the Moravian Church when he arrived in Green Bay in 1906, thereby securing Joanie's, Terry's and my connection to a minor religious sect with a 500-year history. The Church's creed is: "In essentials, unity; in non-essentials, liberty; in all things, love." That philosophy was passed on to us by our mom and her parents.

Otto and Caroline's home, Tank Cottage, was built in 1776 by French fur trader Joseph Roi, one of the first settlers of La Baye (Green Bay). The house is the oldest frame structure still standing in Wisconsin. The home now serves as a museum at Heritage Hill State Park. I often visited it as a grade schooler when it was located in Tank Park.

"Hub, I've spoken to Patra and Ann (Sol Anderson's wife) and we're having a little family get together Sunday in Duck Creek. Don't you go off and make a golf game," Mom said in a somewhat threatening tone, as was often her manner.

It was probably the summer of 1941 as all five of us plus Gramma and Larry headed for the Barlaments' place in Duck Creek. Driving out Velp Avenue, we passed the

"Quarry."

"Mom! Can we stop and go swimming?" I asked, as we could see kids our age jumping off the cliffs into the small lake that was formed when a natural spring filled the rock quarry with water.

"Heavens no, Buster. I don't _ever_ want you kids to swim in there," Mom warned.

"Why? Why not?" Terry asked as he stood up on the front seat in Dad's new Oldsmobile, which was a pukey green color.

"It's too dangerous. The water is freezing cold and you could get cramps. And ... and there's machinery down on the bottom. If you jump off the cliff you could get tangled up in that equipment down there. No, it's just too dangerous. You kids can't swim there," Mom continued to warn us, which of course made the prospect of swimming at the Quarry even more alluring. Clandestine adventures to that forbidden place would be certain to follow.

The Barlaments, Walter and Patra, who were our great uncle and aunt, owned and operated a general store in Duck Creek at the intersection of Highway 41 and County Road J. Our second cousins, Merlin, Doris and Gerald, were a lot older than the three of us and cousin Larry. Merlin, in fact, had already graduated from St. Norbert's College in DePere and had signed up for the draft early in 1941. Congress, in 1940, had passed the Selective Service Act, and all twenty-one-year-old males had to register. Incredibly, Merlin's name, which was drawn randomly, was selected number 13 in the country. An auspicious number. At time of our family get-together Merlin was waiting for his marching orders, which were not only inevitable because of his low number, but the "Day of Infamy" was only six months away.

"You kids gotta be careful hitting those golf balls," Merlin yelled to Terry and me, who had discovered Dad's clubs in the trunk of our car. "You're gonna hit somebody," he cautioned us.

Terry, ignoring the plea of our older, wiser and concerned host continued to flail at the ball with the oversized golf club that my three-year-old brother had difficulty handling. Not noticing that Merlin was relaxing in a hammock nearby, Terry took a prodigious swing at the little white ball. He missed. While losing his balance and spinning out of control, Terry let go of the club, striking the unsuspecting Merlin in the back of his head!

Whack! The heavy head of the club careened off Merlin's "noggin." Shaking off the cobwebs and recovering from the blow, Merlin charged after Terry.

"What did I tell ya!" he shouted.

Terry ran to his dad for cover.

"Hub, ya better put your clubs up where the kids can't get their hands on 'em," Merlin suggested, obviously "put out" with Terry.

Dad grabbed the club in one hand and Terry in the other and headed for the back of the store, stopping briefly to smack Terry on his behind. As much time as Terry and I spent on the golf course caddying for Dad in the years to come, he never introduced us to the game. Obviously, he didn't want another club in our hands.

Fortunately, the incident didn't spoil the Sunday. Patra, Merlin's mother, and Hulda, my grandmother, enjoyed conversing in Danish and Swedish. The two languages sounded similar to me. They definitely understood each other. I learned that all Scandinavians understood each other even though there didn't seem to always be an "understanding" between the Norwegians and the Swedes.

None of us were ever in want of food to eat. It seemed that Patra, her sister Tillie and sister-in-law Ann (married to Soloman Anderson), and Gramma Anderson were engaged in a friendly "cook off" to determine who was the best chef. Hulda may have had an edge of sorts. In the 20's, after Mom and Elsie graduated from high school, she and Sam owned a restaurant on Walnut Street near the West Theater and Gramma, in addition to doing almost all the cooking, ran the small enterprise while Sam tended the bridge. In addition, Gramma and Sam owned a boarding house on the corner of Chestnut and Hubbard Streets during The Depression, and the boarders benefitted from Gramma's expertise in the kitchen. She did it all. She was an incredibly hard worker.

Almost all of the "fixings" for the family get-together were raised on everyone's small farms. Walter Barlament, Merlin's dad, grew just about everything at their place in Duck Creek, including strawberries that, along with ice cream from Dehn's or the home-made variety, were our favorite dessert. Walter's brothers were all fishermen. The Bayshore was only a hop and a skip away from the Barlament General Store and bass, perch, crappie and, on some occasions, pike and walleyes were the main course. Patra's brother, Soloman, raised chickens, and they would always bring their recipe of fried chicken that Colonel Sanders was, at that time, only dreaming about. (Actually the "secret blend of eleven herbs and spices" was developed by the Colonel in 1939 in Kentucky.)

Aside from the allure of the ever-dangerous "Quarry" and the swamps, Duck Creek had an aura of mystique about it. Because the town lay outside the city limits of Green Bay, it was the location of an over-abundance of taverns. Even during prohibition, alcoholic beverages were readily available. Merlin reports in his memoir that Frank Rodaer and his brother-in-law, with the appropriate name of Mooney, were the biggest bootleggers in the county. This enterprise, the taverns and other nefarious activities, attracted gangsters, particularly from Chicago, who probably fled to the area when the "heat" was on in Cook County. Merlin also reports that one such character was the infamous John Dillinger, "Public Enemy Number One." Evelyn Foechette, aka "The Lady in Red," was a native of Neopit, which was only a couple of miles from Duck Creek. She, of course, chiseled her name in the history books by fingering her boyfriend for the FBI who, in a fusillade of bullets, made Swiss cheese out of the mobster.

Quite often, all the Andersons, including the Barlaments, would get together at Gramma Anderson's house on Hubbard Street after church on Sunday. The Westside Moravian Church was located at the end of Chestnut Street, which was only six blocks from Gramma's. Their house had a large screened in porch where everyone would congregate on a hot summer day. I can recall many occasions when I would "stay over" at Gramma's and sleep on the porch on hot, humid nights, serenaded by the distinctive sounds of the crickets.

"Joanie? Joanie? Answer the phone in Dad's office!" Mom yelled from the basement, where she was doing the wash. Dad's insurance office was in the "card room," and he was out on calls.

"I'll get it. I'll get it," Joanie yelled back as she tore down the steps from her bedroom. She was now ten years old and was pretty good at taking messages. Dad's business was growing but he didn't want to have the expense of an office and a secretary. Mom seemed to be annoyed with the persistent calls. She shouldn't have. Each one had bread and butter on it.

Business was good enough for Dad to buy the 1940 Olds and there was optimism in certain areas, but the nation's economy was still struggling with high unemployment and a general malaise in the country. People had become accustomed to slow economic growth and were living conservatively. If there was a sense of apprehension as the conflicts in Southeast Asia and Europe grew more ominous every day, we, as children, had no sense of it, and our parents either avoided discussion of the prospect of war or they ignored it. Amazingly, there was a prevailing sense of complacency in our country amongst its citizenry. But, there was deep concern in the White House. I will defer to Doris Kearns Goodwin, who won the Pulitzer Prize for her book *No Ordinary Time, Franklin and Eleanor Roosevelt: The Home Front in World War II*, for an insight into the events leading up to "A Day That Will Live in Infamy" and to provide a backdrop to this critical moment in our time.[3]

Franklin Delano Roosevelt, affectionately or conveniently called FDR, had in November 1940 just been elected to a third term as president, something that neither Washington, Jefferson, nor any other president before him had accomplished. He had won 54.7 percent of the popular vote, defeating the Republican candidate, Wendell Willkie.

FDR wasn't devoid of his detractors, however. Goodwin says, "Critics lamented his deviousness, his lack of candor, his capricious experimentation, his tendency to ingratitude." She states that one of FDR's former aides "believed he had succumbed over the years to the 'intensifying and exhilarating effect of power.'" Some of the president's protagonists called him and the first lady the King and Queen of the U.S. Conservatives called him a Socialist for creating an alphabet soup of agencies and social programs to put the country to work. Some out and out called him a Communist. In a little more than a year the voices of derision and disagreement would disappear. Historians, novelists, journalists and pundits of all stripes have often raised the question, What did the president know and when did he know it? Did FDR know the Japanese would attack Pearl Harbor? Was the president deliberately looking for an excuse to enter the war that would override the isolationist attitudes of the majority of the American people? Was a war a means to end the decade-long Depression?

As Goodwin clearly outlines, Britain was on the verge of bankruptcy and couldn't afford to buy the arms, food and supplies it desperately needed to fend off the Germans. Winston Churchill and the president were related empathetically, philosophically, and by blood to each other. But only through FDR's deviously concocted "lend-lease" program was he able to assist the "Brits." Despite the fact that the German U Boats were sinking our merchant ships like shooting ducks on a pond, Congress and the American people refused to declare war on Hitler's Third Reich. Unless, of course, something dramatic happened. December 7, 1941, erased America's isolationism, but were the Japanese deliberately provoked so that we could enter the war against Germany?

In July 1941 the Japanese invaded Indochina and the U.S. supported the National Chinese leader Chiang Kai-shek. In order to force the Japanese to withdraw from Indochina, "Roosevelt had agreed to a policy of sanctions, including an embargo of high-octane oil. Implemented by subordinates ... the limited embargo he had sanctioned became full-scale. By the time Roosevelt realized that all types of oil had been closed to Japan, it was too late — without seeming weak — to turn back." Bottom line, Japan could not operate without oil. The issue of black gold was perhaps the final straw, or a green light to cast the first stone.

Did FDR's subordinates exceed their authority? Or, did they really carry out FDR's true wishes and leave the Commander-in-Chief a face-saving out? Goodwin doesn't open this door and she prefers not to go there, but that wasn't an issue with the American public at this moment in time. Most were oblivious to the gathering storm.

On November 27, 1941, the president knew that "a Japanese expedition was heading south from Japan," destination unknown. A few days later, Tojo, the Japanese premier, delivered a speech calling for immediate steps to remove the U.S. and British "exploitation in the Far East." Then there was the infamous Japanese telegraphed, fourteen-page reply on December 6 responding to U.S. demands that only transmitted thirteen pages, omitting the last page that terminated all diplomatic negotiations. The last page was delivered at exactly 1:00 p.m. Washington time — thirty minutes before the attack. Then, perhaps, the biggest blunder or deliberate device. Rather than phone all military installations in the Pacific, the critical alert was telegraphed and arrived after the holocaust began. Fifteen or twenty minutes could have saved hundreds of lives. The tragedy of Pearl Harbor is replete with blunders or devious designs.

The White House, the Pentagon and our intelligence community all knew the Japanese were going to attack, but was it the perception, at least at the top, that our leaders could not conceive or imagine that these near-sighted, diminutive, inferior forces could or would carry out a successful raid on Pearl Harbor? Was it unthinkable? Or, was it planned? Provoked, planned, or not, FDR and America faced their darkest hour since the Civil War. The defining moment that changed our nation and our lives was upon us.

1. *The Great Peshtigo Fire* (The State Historical Society of Wisconsin, 1999), pp. 54-55.
2. Robert G. Wells, *Embers of October* (Princeton, N.J.: Prentice-Hall, 1968).
3. Doris Kearns Goodwin, *No Ordinary Time, Franklin and Eleanor Roosevelt: The Home Front in World War II.* p. 283.

CHAPTER 3: A DATE WHICH WILL LIVE IN INFAMY...

Yesterday, December 7th, 1941 — a date which will live in infamy — the United States of America was suddenly and deliberately attacked by naval and air forces of the Empire of Japan....

SO SAID THE PRESIDENT as our family gathered together for this specific and historic purpose, to hear our president's speech to Congress.

Dad had hurriedly pushed his comfy reading chair to a position in front of the fireplace so that he wouldn't miss a word that the president was saying. I sat on the floor between Dad and the radio, which was a large floor-model Philco that served as our home entertainment center. It was big. I was five and one-half years old then, but I still couldn't see over it because it was so tall and occupied the bulk of the corner of our living room. The back was all hollowed out and Terry, my brother, and I used it as a favorite hiding place when Mom was trying to find us. I knew the news was bad and watched Dad's reaction as the president continued:

The U.S. was at peace with that nation and at the solicitation of Japan, was still in conversation with the government and its emperor looking toward the maintenance of peace in the Pacific.

I couldn't discern any visible reaction to the president's speech on Dad's face as I looked up at him. He had a somber look but there wasn't any anger or fear, which could be expected. Maybe it was an indication of his Swedish heritage, the Swedes being noted for their stoicism, you know. In fact, I can't even remember my dad ever exhibiting any real emotions except — except on one occasion. But, that was a long time after this day, December 8, 1941.

Indeed, one hour after Japanese air squadrons had commenced bombing in Oahu, the Japanese ambassador to the U.S. and his colleagues delivered to the Secretary of State a formal reply to a recent American message. While this reply stated that it seemed useless to continue the existing diplomatic negotiations, it contained no threat or hint of war or armed attack.

Mom was seated awkwardly on the edge of the piano bench directly behind Dad. In contrast to him, her entire body from head to toe was a picture of a wall of worry. She had kicked off her shoes and was scrunching up her toes on the carpet while at the same time chewing on her fingernails, which she always did when she was nervous. Her face was full of anguish, as if we were in immediate danger of dying. Dad had assured us that we were safe on Sunday after we heard that Pearl Harbor had been bombed. Maybe she was afraid that Dad, who was then 37, would have to go to war. Maybe she could feel things that only mothers can feel at the time of war, I don't know. Mom's lack of stoicism kind of debunked the Swedish image, but there are rules and exceptions to the rules. Mom was an exception.

It will be recorded that the distance of Hawaii from Japan makes it obvious that the attack was deliberately planned many days or weeks ago. During the intervening time, the Japanese government has deliberately sought to deceive the U.S. by false statements and expressions of hope for continued peace.

Joanie, my sister who was 10 and one-half years old at this point in time, was sitting on the on the arm of our living room couch, despite the fact that she had been told hundreds of times not to, and was nervously bouncing her feet off the floor. She was sitting on her hands, or else maybe she would have been biting her nails just like Mom. Joanie was old enough to understand the gravity of the situation, but I'm sure like most girls she would much rather have been somewhere else than deal with a man's war, as her constant fidgeting indicated. She fell off the arm of the couch as the president was saying:

The attack yesterday on the Hawaiian Islands has caused severe damage to American naval and military forces. Very many American lives have been lost. In addition, American ships have been reported torpedoed on the high seas between San Francisco and Honolulu.

My brother Terry, who was just three in August, was standing up facing the window looking out onto Dousman Street as snow flakes began to fall from an increasingly grey sky. Seemingly, Terry was oblivious to the president's speech and the significance of the moment. The typically frigid December day in Green Bay coupled with the warmth of our fireplace had built up frost on the inside of the corners of the windows, and Terry was scratching on the thin veil of ice with his fingernails. (This was the same window that less than a year prior I had broken. Dad had just arrived in the driveway, and in my rush to see him I hit the window too hard and my left hand shattered the glass. Here it is sixty years later and the scar between my fingers is still visible.) Looking more closely, I could see that Terry was drawing something. There was a series of jagged lines emanating from a core. "Ka-boom, ka-boom," Terry murmured softly in guttural tones, as he clearly understood that war meant bombs and bombs went ka-boom.

Yesterday, the Japanese government also launched an attack against Malaya. Last night, Japanese forces attacked Hong Kong. Last night, Japanese forces attacked Guam. Last night, Japanese forces attacked the Philippine Islands. Last night, Japanese forces attacked Wake Island. This morning, the Japanese attacked Midway Island.

Joanie, who was somewhat bashful and shy, took advantage of Dad and Mom's focus on the broadcast, slid off the couch, and made a beeline for the stairs and up to the safety of her bedroom. Mom didn't even say anything to her about sitting on the arm of the couch. I wanted to ask Dad if he would have to go to fight in the war, but he put his finger to his lips which was a signal for me to keep quiet. Reluctantly, I did.

Japan has therefore undertaken a surprise offensive extending throughout the Pacific area. The facts of yesterday speak for themselves. The people of the U.S. have already formed their opinions and well understand the implications to the very life and safety of our nation. As Commander in Chief of the Army and Navy, I have directed that all measures be taken for our defense.

All of us had been to church that historic and infamous Sunday. The three of us kids attended Sunday School at Grace Lutheran Church, which was located on the east side of the river, while Dad and Mom were at the main service, which ended at noon. Dad was an usher and helped to collect the parishioners' contributions at the end of the service.

Mom suggested that we stop at Gramma's house on the way home and check up on our cousin Larry, who was suffering from a bad asthma attack. Gramma's house on Hubbard Street was a half a block from St. Patrick's Church at Maple and Hubbard, and directly across the street from St. Paul Methodist Church. Despite their proximity to these churches, Gramma and Larry went to the Westside Moravian Church nearby. Dad also thought it was a good idea to stop at Gramma's, since he had just bought a brand new 1940 green Oldsmobile recently and, knowing how Larry was crazy about cars, he thought seeing the car might cheer him up.

Ironically, Terry and I were talking about playing "army" when we got home after we left Sunday School. We would set up our toy soldiers under the dining room table, using the legs of the table and the chairs as the "forest." The enemy, up to this point, was anonymous — not the Germans. We would spend hours fighting imaginary battles with an imaginary enemy. That was all about to change of course, but we had no inkling of what lay ahead.

As we got into the car to leave the church, Terry and I got into one of our usual "scuffles." Dad didn't want us to get mud and snow in the back seat of his new car so he separated us before we hit the ground. In order to keep us from going at it again Joanie had to sit in the middle of the back seat to keep us apart. She just hated to absorb those blows not intended for her, but what are big sisters for?

As we left Gramma's (Dad was right, Larry really was excited by the new car, especially since he and Gram didn't have one) and turned down Dousman Street, Dad remarked how odd it was that people were milling around outside their houses without any coats or hats. It was something that "Bayites" just didn't do in the winter — especially when it was below freezing. It was strange that the Quigleys, who lived only five doors down from us, didn't wave as we passed by. Something was wrong. It was eery. As we pulled into our driveway, Larry Fitchett, our next door neighbor to the east, who was standing on the sidewalk talking with our neighbors on the west side, the Rondous, ran up to our car and motioned to Dad to roll down his window. That's when we heard the news about Pearl Harbor. I had never heard about Pearl Harbor prior to this day, and most Americans didn't know where it was.

The phone lines were jammed. No one could get an operator. In 1941 you had to speak to an operator to get a call through, and there weren't many lines or operators available. Neighbors were braving the cold and spreading the word person-to-person. The shocking news penetrated just about everyone like a bullet, with an agonizing impact. The grownups were in shock and disbelief.

Every Sunday afternoon our family went for a "ride." It was Mom's afternoon out of the house. Often we went to Menominee to see Gramma Quist, or to Duck Creek to see the Barlaments, or to our favorite place, Door County. But, there wouldn't be a ride that Sunday. That day was different.

Always we will remember the character of the onslaught against us. No matter how long it may take us to overcome this premeditated invasion, the American people in their righteous might will win through to absolute victory.

A spark from the fire shot like an incendiary bomb over the fireplace screen onto the carpet and caught everyone's attention. Without fanfare I grabbed the little black shovel that we kept for such purposes and returned the small burning piece of charcoal to the fire. Somehow, without any visual reference as yet to the battle that had taken place the day before, I could picture thousands and thousands of large fiery objects like this one small one penetrating the sky at Pearl Harbor. Seeing newspaper photos and the Movie Tone News at the West Theater the next week confirmed what my mind's eye had seen.

I believe I interpret the will of the Congress and the people when I assert that we will not only defend ourselves to the utmost, but will make very certain that this form of treachery shall never endanger us again. Hostilities exist. There is no blinking at the fact that our people, our territory and our interests are in great danger. With confidence in our armed forces — with the unbounding determination of our people — we will gain the inevitable triumph — so help us God. I ask that the Congress declare that since the unprovoked and dastardly attack by Japan on Sunday, December 7, a State of War has existed between the U.S. and the Japanese Empire.

The president received an enthusiastic and supportive ovation from Congress. There was only one dissenting vote in the entire Congress on the declaration of war. I couldn't wait for Dad to turn off the radio. He had been listening almost non-stop since we got home from church. Joanie was sitting on the landing of the staircase immediately next to our Christmas tree that suddenly didn't seem important enough to decorate. Geez, I thought, "there might not be any Christmas."

"Dad, why did the Japanese attack us? Are you going to have to fight in the war? Will their planes drop bombs on us? And ...." Dad stopped me before I could blurt out another question.

"Ah geez, Buster, that's too many questions ... and, I don't have any answers. Everyone is in shock, you know.

I'm sure we're safe here in Green Bay. Let's wait until the paper comes this afternoon, okay?"

"Uh, okay," I said. "Will you read me the paper, huh?"

Terry added, "Me too ... me too."

"Yeah, sure. I'll read the whole paper to you if you want," Dad promised.

I can't remember if school was called off or not on that Monday. Dad was dressed in his blue suit and a funny looking red tie, but he didn't go out on any calls to see clients. Mom got us dressed for school as usual, but we didn't go. It was like we were all immobilized and on hold. Everything came to a stop.

After a couple hours of trying to find something to do, Mom said Terry and I were getting "antsy." (Which meant we had ants in our pants.) She bundled us up in our snowsuits and sent us out to play in the snow (that had now accumulated to a couple of inches) until the paper came. It was unquestionably the most important *Green Bay Press-Gazette* we would ever receive. Besides, Dad and Mom wanted to talk. I'm sure that they had things to discuss that they didn't want us to hear. They always did — like all parents.

———

"Congress Declares War" was the headline of the evening paper. Terry and I were throwing snowballs in the front yard at each other when our paperboy tossed us the paper from his bicycle.

"The paper is here. The paper is here," I yelled as Terry and I burst in the front door.

"Get your snowsuits and galoshes off before you come in," Dad demanded. We had an anteway inside the front door where we took off our snowsuits and hung them on a peg so they could dry. The suits were made of fuzzy-like material and the snow would stick to them. Dad brushed the snow off the paper into the fireplace and sat down in his reading chair. He put on his glasses and previewed the front page. Mom came in from the kitchen to listen. Joanie was upstairs in her room.

"The Senate voted 82 to 0 to declare war against

Japan. The House of Representatives voted 388 to 1. Can you imagine that? There was one vote against declaring war. Just one vote. I wonder why that lady from Montana voted against the resolution. Women just don't like war, I guess," Dad thought aloud as he read to all of us.

"The paper says that there were hisses and boos when she cast her vote. Here's an interesting comment," Dad said. "Senator Vandenberg of Michigan said, 'You (Japan) have unsheathed the sword and by it you shall die.' What is amazing is that Vandenberg was so opposed to the war. He was the leading isolationist." Dad, being from Michigan, knew who the senator was.

"How many people were kilt," Terry asked?

"The paper says there were about 1,500 fatalities, Terry. That's an awful lot of people to lose in one attack." (Actually the number was finally put at 2,433 Americans.)

"Geez, all the Japs sunk were one old battleship and a destroyer, but several other ships were damaged. We lost a large number of planes, though," Dad continued. (As we now know, the material losses of our Pacific fleet were much more extensive than the immediate reports indicated. We lost 18 warships and 188 planes. Fortunately, or by plan, all of our aircraft carriers were elsewhere.)

Were the reporters from the Associated Press and the United Press trying to ameliorate the situation? Were they trying to lessen the impact on an already devastated America, or were they given poor data from the military in Hawaii? The answer was probably all of the above. But, this is what we knew at that moment in time. Rumors, running rampant, indicated that bombs were being dropped on Los Angeles and San Francisco, which heightened the hysteria.

"Three Wisconsin men were killed," Dad said, bringing the war to our doorstep (although none of the men were from Green Bay). We learned later that a close friend of our neighbor Larry Fitchett, Pfc. Earl Wallen, was one of the casualties on the USS Arizona. Also, Lt. Colonel Austin Straubel was shot down over the Java Sea. (The Austin Straubel International Airport is now named after him.)

The editor of the *Green Bay Press-Gazette* wrote:

"Japan has murderously attacked our country without warning and as a skulking assassin she has launched fire and death with all the treachery known to thugs and outlaws. We are a united nation upon this score because we know our cause is entirely just...."

"You know what's amazing about all we're hearing and reading?" Dad asked Mom. "Just last week there were articles in the *Press-Gazette* saying that we should stay out of the war, and the country was divided. Now, the editor says, we're a united nation."

"Well, people didn't want war with Germany, Hub. That was different. You didn't either. Look, some of your closest friends are German. Like Otto. There are so many Germans here in Wisconsin," Mom interjected.

"Otto is a German?" Terry blurted out.

"Can't you tell from his accent? Sure he's German, but he's our friend," Dad reassured Terry, who probably thought the army or the police would arrest Otto. "The paper says that Germany will now declare war on us. That debate is over," Dad continued. He refocused his attention on the paper.

"Are you going to join the Army, Dad?" I asked.

"I don't know, Buster. It says here that General Hershey has been appointed National Selective Service Director, and he says that there are 1,000,000 Class A men ready for induction. I'll have to go if I'm called," Dad said.

As it turned out Dad was classified 4F, as unfit for service because of his rheumatic fever as a child. Terry and I were disappointed that our father was not going to fight the enemy, but we were also glad to have him home once we were assured that he wasn't afraid to fight. Every kid wants his dad to be courageous and without fear. Every kid wants his dad to be a hero.

Dad continued to read the *Press-Gazette*, and when he was through dinner was ready.

"Kids," Dad said addressing all of us at the dinner table. "We're going to be in for some real tough times. This war is going to be a long, long process. We're going to have to scrimp and save because everything is going to go to the war effort. I think we should all say a prayer for all our men in Pearl Harbor and around the world who are going to have to fight two enemies," Dad said as he accurately assessed the situation. We all prayed.

After dinner, Terry and I got out our toy soldiers. We couldn't play "army" under the dining room table because Mom and Dad wanted to talk, so we went into the card room, where we kept our toys. That's where Dad had his group over to play poker once a month. Dad's friends included Otto Rose, the German gentleman, who lived in our neighborhood. It was "icky" in the card room because of the old, stale smell of smoke, but we had no other choice but to play there that evening.

"I went back and re-read Saturday's paper, Thelma. There's a feature article on the front page regarding the negotiations between Washington and the Japanese in order to arrive at a peaceful solution to the problems in the Pacific. They had been in Washington with us for seven months while all the time planning to attack Pearl Harbor. What deceitful and traitorous bastards those Japs are. Roosevelt was waiting for a reply when the attack came. Geez n' plutz," Dad said. "The thing that really gets me is that we've been fighting this Depression for all these years and business was just starting to improve to the point where we can do some things and buy a new car, and now this. God Almighty, when will it all end? When can we enjoy life?"

Several years later, just before the war ended, Dad was playing golf at the Shorewood Country Club with Otto Rose and several friends. I caddied for Dad by pulling a cart with his bag on it. The conversation in the clubhouse after their game, which Dad recalled to me years later, was concerning the war.

"What I never could understand," Dad was saying, "is how the Japs could move that huge armada of ships all the way from Japan to 200 miles from Hawaii and not be detected. Not only by our ships or our planes but any merchant ships. Someone should have seen all those warships." And, he added, "How could we have been so unprepared?"

"It vas all orchestrated," Otto said, in his thick German accent. "Da Russians vas afraid dat da Japs vas going to attack dem from da east when dey had all der troops defending Moscow, yah, dey couldn't defend der eastern front. Da Germans and da Japs signed da Axis Agreement to assist each udder. FDR's right hand man, Harry Hopkins, vas in da Russians' pocket. He vas a commie. He gat FDR to lure da Japs into attacking us in order to get us into da war to save da Rooskies, yah. Da Germans haf surrendered. Da Japs vill soon and da American people vill neva know da real story."

"Geez Otto, you've never said that before. How come?" Dad asked.

"A'm German. Who vould listen to me? Ah haf to keep my mouth shut, yah."

Over fifty years later, facts revealed for the first time give some credence to Otto's theory.[1] As a 10-year-old I couldn't fathom it, but I sure was all ears.

"What's going to happen to us?" Mom asked nervously chewing her fingernails down to the quick, as the scene returned to December 8.

"Geez, I don't know. But, I'm sure glad I bought the Olds."

"Why?" Mom asked.

"I don't think there'll be any new cars for years and years."

"Why?" Mom asked again.

"Arms. GM is going to have to make tanks and planes. So will Ford. All production will go to produce weapons. And, another thing. We better get all kinds of food stuff that will keep. We better go to Farah's tomorrow morning and stock up. I think there'll be a rush to buy everything."

Dad's assessments were accurate as our nation, united as never before, prepared itself for its most defining moment.

As I was writing this memoir, the tragedy of September 11, 2001, conjured up comparisons as a second date which will live in infamy. Reflecting on this analogy a year after the terrorist attack on New York City, I concluded that these historic events did have two things in common. Both revealed, first, a massive failure of our intelligence community, which possessed vital information but improperly processed it, and secondly, the prevailing complacency in America that enabled these events to happen. What follows in this memoir provides an insight into the America of the war years and how its solidarity of purpose differs radically from the America at the beginning of the twenty-first century.

1. Herbert Romerstein and Eric Breindel, *The Venona Secrets: Exposing Soviet Espionage and America's Traitors*, (Regnery Publishing Co.), p. 608.

CHAPTER 4: THE WAR ON THE HOME FRONT

TURNING THE CLOCK BACK THREE MONTHS to September 1, 1941:

"Joanie, Joanie ... Wake up! Wake up!" I implored my older sister, who was sound asleep. "I don't want to be late for school."

It was my first day in kindergarten.

"What?" Joanie said as she reluctantly reached for the alarm clock on the table beside her bed. "Buster, it's only 6:00 a.m. Go back to bed! We don't have to be at school until 8:30."

My sister covered her head with her pink pillow and shut me off like a light switch.

At 7:00 a.m. we were at the breakfast table. Mom was fixing our usual hearty breakfast of scrambled eggs, bacon, cinnamon rolls, fresh orange juice and a large glass of milk. It put "meat on our bones," Mom would always say.

Joanie, who was already in the fourth grade, was nominated to take me to school, since Mom had to care for Terry and Dad was out of town seeing clients. Like everyone else in our neighborhood, there was only one car per family. You had to be really rich to have two cars.

"Joanie hurry. We've gotta long ways to go. I don't want to be late."

Joanie was a slow eater. She ignored her "baby brother," which she always called me — and still does. At last, we were out the door and on our way to Elmore School.

Going north from our house we had an unobstructed

pathway to our school. There were no homes behind our house. Only vacant lots, but we called them "fields." Don't know why, but everyone called them fields.

We crossed Division Street, then through the field to Kellogg Street, then over Elmore Street to Bond, and Elmore School was on the northwest corner of Bond Street and Ethel Avenue. I was awed by the imposing, brick structure that would be my home away from home for the next six years.

There were so many five-year-olds that attended Elmore School that year that Mrs. Hetherington, our principal, divided the students into two classes — one in the morning and one in the afternoon, each with a different teacher. The great number was due to the fact that the Catholic school at Annunciation Church, which was only a couple blocks away, did not have a kindergarten. About 12 students went to Annunciation School for the first grade.

We were on our own for the very first time, cautiously surveying the room and our classmates who would become our friends. We were beginning a journey that would take twelve to sixteen years to complete, without a compass or a road map and without a penny in our pockets. Sheer optimism and hope permeated the confines of our room despite an aura of trepidation.

"You'll all have name tags," Mrs. McCarthy said as she pinned a card on my new shirt that Mom had just bought at Pranges Department Store.

"Hi. My name is Dickie," the boy sitting on the floor next to me said, finally breaking the ice that seemed to freeze us in this yet cool and unfamiliar place.

"I'm Buster," I said as I pointed to the name tag which I couldn't read. We had all received our first lesson in school — identifying ourselves — as we started on a path to discover who we were.

By the end of the first day, the reserve and reticence changed to the clamor and chaos of thirty-eight kids talking all at one time.

Thanks to my classmate, Betty Meyers, I have a group picture of this historically significant Class of 1941, with most of the kids identified. In addition to Betty, some of the classmates that I remember that continued together for the next seven years are: Darlene DeGrand, Sharon Bookmeier, Tom Nack, George Grabb, Jerry Proctor, Harold Proctor, Calvin Whiting, Bob Caroline, Don Haupt, Margo Jesson, Patty Olson, and Connie Shaw.

Others, like Dick Maierle, Dan Caelwaerts, Tom Renard, and Paul Noak, went to Annunciation after kindergarten, but we remained close friends.

As I peer longingly at this remarkable photograph, I want to know what happened in the lives of all these innocent five-year-olds. Were they happy and successful and did they experience the joys of life, or did tragedy, misfortune and ugly circumstance darken their lives? If only they could all tell their stories. Mine is only one of thirty-eight.

The noise reached such a feverish pitch that the bell marking the end of our first day was muffled, like trying to hear someone talking close to a waterfall. I waited near the curb for my sister to walk me home. Dickie was pleading with his Mom waiting in her car.

"I want to walk home, Mom," Dickie said rather forcefully for a five-year-old. Looking around and seeing me he added, "I'm going to walk home with Buster. He's my new friend."

And, we did.

Dickie Maierle lived on Oneida Street, only a short one-half block from our house on Dousman if you cut through the Martins' and Rondous' backyards. We would become close "chums."

Recalling incidents or events as a five-year-old is difficult at best, but I have one archetypical experience that has remained with me for over sixty years.

When the winter arrived and we all made our way through the drifts and snowbanks playing along the way, most of us inevitably arrived at Elmore School with our snowsuits and knitted caps and earmuffs covered with snow. We hung them up in the corner of our one-room class near the large radiators to dry them out before we returned home. Our snowsuits were made of fuzzy woolen material, as waterproofed, water-resistant garments were non-existent.

What was so memorable? The smell! The entire kindergarten had the odor of a pack of wet, Saint Bernard dogs.

———

The War soon came close to our doorstep. Cousin Merlin Barlament, who had signed up for the draft early in 1941 and who was selected number thirteen in the entire country, was in basic training at Camp Wheeler, Georgia, when word of the raid on Pearl Harbor came. Unexpectedly, early in 1942, Merlin was reassigned from the 41 Infantry Division to a Medical Detachment and he soon found himself in Melbourne, Australia, where our troops were forced to retreat and regroup after the Japanese overran the Philippines. In his memoir, Merlin writes effectively and extensively of his wartime experience in the South Pacific.

Another member of our extended Anderson side of the family was George Leonard, who was a career seaman from the age of fourteen. George was the son of Anna Anderson Leonard, who was the sister of my grandfather Sam Anderson's half-sister Marie, who was born in Denmark. George's involvement in the war was transporting the precious cargo of the lifeblood of the war machine, oil, to our troops in the South Pacific. George, who lost all four fingers on both hands in a gas explosion at sea, often made Green Bay a port of call to visit the Barlaments and the Andersons. Cousin Larry remembers him well because of his unfortunate accident, but he should best be remembered for building his own ship and sailing it from the west coast of the U.S. through the Panama Canal to Denmark. George was a true seaman.

Our next-door neighbor, Larry Fitchett, who was thirty-three at the time, was at home recovering from a knee operation when the sneak attack came and he met us in our driveway. He soon recovered and joined the Flying Cadets, which was a part of the U.S. Army. While training in his AT6 trainer, it ground looped and crashed.

His injuries kept him out of combat. Most of the men in his unit, which flew P-39s, were killed during the War.

On the Quist side of the family, my oldest cousin Raynold at age 19 enlisted in the Coast Guard on July 7, 1942, and completed his basic training in Oakland, California. After radio training in Atlantic City he was transferred to San Diego, where he served as a radio operator in a lighthouse that was one of the mainstays of our coastline defense system. In addition, towards the end of the War, Raynold served on a cutter patrolling California coastal waters. After the surprise attack on Pearl Harbor, most everyone in America felt the U.S. was vulnerable to an invasion. The Coast Guard performed a vital vigil.

Cousin Norman, then age 18, enlisted in the U.S. Army in June 1943, and completed his basic training at Camp Wallace near Galveston, Texas, and advanced training at Fort Meade, Maryland. By February 1944, he was part of a large convoy crossing the Atlantic. He recalled that it was. "An exceptionally long trip due to a zigzag course evading German U-Boats. Everybody got sick due to the rough waters. One of our ships hit a mine and sunk." On June 9, 1944, Norm, still only 18, landed on Omaha Beach.

Recalling the incredible twenty-minute opening scene from "Saving Private Ryan," I asked my cousin, "Did you have to face that hellacious resistance?"

"No, I wasn't in the initial assault. Thank heavens. Good chance I wouldn't be here."

Very few survived.

Norm was discharged in November 1945, but re-enlisted in the Air Force in February 1947 and served an additional 18 years, attaining the rank of Sgt. Major. One of the most tense moments in his military career occurred during the Cuban Missile Crisis while he was stationed at the Strategic Air Command Headquarters in Omaha. He worked twelve hours a day, seven days a week underground until the Russians withdrew their missiles.

Cousin Keith fortunately had just turned 18 when the War ended in 1945. After the mass discharge of GIs following the War, Keith enlisted in the Navy in 1948, just prior to the Korean conflict. He served aboard the *USS Dixie*, which was the first ship to leave the US for Korea. His most memorable experience during the Korean War occurred when:

> *... Taking officers back from Subic Bay to the ship. We were using a 20' whale boat for the task when hit by heavy winds and huge waves. The boat was swamped and sunk. Everyone was in the water for about forty-five minutes before being rescued.*

Keith was discharged in 1952, as the Korean War ended and I started my junior year in high school.

William Anderson, born in 1920, and his brother Robert, born in 1923, were the sons of my great uncle Soloman Anderson and his wife Ann. They joined the Navy soon after the hostilities began. Both survived the conflict only to die of natural causes at the young ages of 34 and 27, respectively.

Most of the families in our neighborhood were young and their children were, like we were, in grade school. I can recall, however, the little royal blue star on a red and white flag in the windows, signifying that someone in that household was in the service. A gold star placed atop the blue star indicated that a member had served and died. Often, we went to the railroad station on Dousman Street as our parents would be saying goodbye to sons of friends. Green Bay, like most midwestern towns and communities all across America, was a tightly knit community. Everyone shared the angst of our friends and neighbors going to war. Many would never return.

Reading various accounts of this period, Christmas 1941 was one of the most memorable and heartwarming times in America. Not only did America unite and come together, the War understandably brought families closer together. The danger and the uncertainties were real. Our attendance at church was more than a weekly ritual, and our prayers were said with more passion and emotion. All the young boys our age wanted toy soldiers, tanks and battleships under the tree, but the stores sold out weeks before Santa Claus arrived. Food was abundant as Mom and Gramma fixed our traditional turkey with all the trimmings, but that was all about to change. All resources would go to the one supreme effort — the War. Rationing, wage and price controls, and shortages of just about everything brought a new reality into our everyday way of life.

In late April 1942, President Roosevelt, in his second fireside chat, said there is "one front and one battle where everyone in the U.S. — every man, woman and child — is in action ... that front is right here at home, in our daily tasks."

To bring all of us into the fray, FDR submitted to Congress in April, as I turned six, a seven-point program including heavier taxes, war bonds, wage and price controls and comprehensive rationing. By summer, all routine "rhythms of daily life"[1] were affected by the rationing of consumer goods. Men were asked to buy "victory suits" with cuffless trousers and narrower lapels to reduce the amount of cloth required. By the time the Beatles made their debut in the sixties this type of suit was "in." The two-piece bathing suit had its origin for the same purpose. The bikini soon followed in the fifties.

Since the Japanese now occupied and controlled the rubber plantations in Malaysia and Indonesia, and tires to keep our war machine rolling were critical, rationing of gas to limit driving was the War Production Board's solution to the problem. The majority of drivers received an "A" card, which entitled them to five gallons per week. "B" cards were given to war workers, doctors and others who required supplemental mileage. I vividly recall the "C" placard prominently placed on the front window of Dad's Olds and his telling me why it was there. An "X" card was for those who required unlimited milage. Gas stamps, however, were available on the "QT" for a price. I think Dad had some "connections" to get additional gasoline that enabled him to make appointments out of town.

Within a year or so, tire companies were able to produce "synthetic" tires, and the pressure to reduce driving was alleviated some what. (I think the 35 mph speed limit was increased to 50 mph.) I can recall my dad complaining about how hard the synthetic rubber was and what a rough ride it caused. In Green Bay the concrete highways had separators, or cracks, between the blocks of concrete to compensate for the freezing in the winter. Those cracks caused a rhythmic, thumping sound as we drove down the highway. With the new synthetic tires the sound and vibration were compounded. Sitting in the back seat I closed my eyes and anticipated each thump with a nod of my head and a click of my tongue against the roof of my mouth.

"Stop it! Stop it!" Joanie wailed.

"Stop what?" I asked mystified.

"That clicking noise you're making in your mouth. It's driving me crazy!" Joanie said, pleading with Dad to get me to stop.

As always, I was happy to comply with my big sister's wishes. That rhythmic thump continues today.

"Mom? What is that book of stamps for?" I asked as Terry and I walked down Dousman Street to Williquette's Store to get some groceries. We couldn't drive to Farah's. It was too far away.

"It's a ration book," Mom said. "We get forty-eight points each month for stuff we really need." Prior to the War, I would pull my American Flyer wagon to the store to get groceries, but Mom wouldn't trust anyone now with her stamp book.

"Does it have a stamp for a Twinkie?" Terry asked.

"No. Thank goodness we don't have to use them for candy." Mom replied.

When Mom gave me a list to take to Williquette's we could get penny candy in a paper bag for our effort.

"Any sugar today?" Mom asked Mr. Williquette.

"Nope, sorry Mrs. Quist," the grocer responded. "I don't expect any until next week." Sugar was hard to get. There were few ships available to import products except for military needs, and housewives were hoarding sugar. Even meat was scarce. We had a pretty steady diet of Spam (the kind you eat, not the kind that devours your computer), and relied very heavily on Dad's success fishing on the Bayshore. We couldn't go to Door County because of our limit on gasoline.

At Elmore School, Miss Hetherington, our principal, was mobilizing all of our classes to "pitch in" for the war effort.

In Miss Mahony's second grade class we collected rubber bands, rubber toys and scrap metal, and competed with the other grades to see who brought in the most. The kids who lived on farms on the other side of Velp Avenue easily won the scrap metal drive. I won the seed contest and got a certificate to recognize my efforts.

"The president wants all of us to grow Victory Gardens," Miss Mahony said, as the winter snow began to retreat and the prospect of spring was in the air. "We all need to grow our own vegetables," she said as she laid out a wide variety of seed packets on the desk in front of the class.

With Mom's help, Joanie, Terry and I turned our backyard and part of the field behind our house into a large Victory Garden. We probably grew more weeds than anything, but we had plenty of rhubarb, radishes, carrots, lettuce, pumpkins, squash and all kinds of veggies that Mom cooked. I got my first taste of selling as I combed the neighborhood for prospective buyers. I can distinctly remember that the rhubarb pie was pretty sour (*tart*, Mom called it) without sugar. We grew red raspberries and blackberries and ate them off the vine as well as in pies and jam. Gramma and Mom cooked and canned fruit and vegetables of all sorts that were preserved in mason jars. I don't think anyone went for lack of food like they did during The Depression, but certain items were "scarce as hen's teeth."

Many of the president's mandates irked a large number of Americans. The polls in advance of the mid-term elections were extremely unfavorable to FDR and the Democrat-controlled Congress. The Office of Price Administration (OPA) held a firm grip on prices and rationing, but when Leon Henderson, the OPA Administrator, announced that there would be a ration of one cup of coffee per day, per person, almost 85 million

Americans, who reportedly drank an average of three cups a day, were suffering withdrawal and the rancor reverberated across the land.[2]

In addition, the cost of living was rising despite the price controls and labor, with wages fixed, was demanding relief. FDR threatened to use his "war powers" if the farmers didn't stabilize their prices. Senator La Follete, whose constituents were Wisconsin farmers, accused the president of "placing a pistol at the head of Congress," but FDR won and inflation was cooled somewhat. Leon Henderson became the scapegoat and he figuratively fell on his sword to deflect the public anger away from the president.[3]

The following is one of a series of radio announcements broadcast every day on Green Bay radio stations and on virtually every station throughout the country:

The following announcement, in the Government Information Series, is an official release by the District Office of Price Stabilization, Green Bay, and is broadcast by this station in the public interest.

Mrs. Housewife! Price stabilization helps shield your budget from the weakening effect of inflation. Price stabilization helps preserve the value of your money ... by helping to keep the price level steady. The OPS January price freeze helped stop the rapid rise of prices. Now let's take a look into the future and try to see what the picture might be if these stable prices were not to continue. Probably you would worry about future needs, because you wouldn't be able to build up your savings. Now, although there will be strong inflationary pressures in the months ahead, we can hold the price line if all of us pull together. Homemakers, you have to help keep these stable prices. Support one of your strongest weapons against inflation: the price program. When you shop, buy wisely. ... Save all you can.[4]

———

"Thelma? They're real short handed at Northwest

(Engineering). They want me to work in the office," Dad said as we had dinner in our small kitchen. Northwest was the same company that laid off Dad in 1931.

"What will you do about your insurance business? You're just now making a go of it," Mom replied, concerned.

"Old Line Life objects to me working part time, but I've talked to another company. They'll go along with that arrangement. The job at Northwest is only until the War is over, you know."

"What company?" Mom asked as she was busy serving all of us dinner, featuring scalloped potatoes laced with little cubes of Spam.

"BMA ... Business Men's Assurance Co. Their home office is in Kansas City. I will be in a position to be their district manager when the War is over," Dad added, speaking optimistically about the future end of the conflict, as everybody did.

"Well, Hub, it's up to you, but you're one of the top men at Old Line Life. I hate to see you start over. You made almost $3,000 last year," Mom countered.

"BMA has got better plans to sell than Old Line Life and they pay a higher commission," Dad concluded as he got up and left for another appointment.

Dad made the right decision. His business flourished during the War, and with two jobs he began to save a considerable sum of money. There were few luxuries and no travel to spend it on, of course.

"You kids gotta eat your vegetables. We've grown all these carrots in our garden and you're going to eat them. They're good for what ails you," Mom, using one of her tried and true lines, said.

"But Mom, I like carrots raw out of the ground. I don't like cooked carrots," I responded, sort of gagging on the thought of eating those carrots in a creamy sauce which was now cold.

"Buster, you're going to stay here at the table until you finish those carrots. You hear me?" Mom said firmly as she stared me down. Mom was the disciplinarian in our family. She's the one who used Dad's leather shaving strap on Terry and me when we got out of line — which was pretty often. When Mom got real mad her head kind of "rattled." That was a sure sign that we had gone too far.

I was determined not to eat those darn carrots. An hour went by. It was now dark outside. Everyone, except me, had gone upstairs to bed. I put my head down on the kitchen table. I fell asleep.

When I woke up in the morning, I was in bed. I tiptoed downstairs and peeked into the kitchen. Next to my orange juice and a bowl of Rice Krispies were two raw carrots. Sheepishly and without a word I ate the carrots.

Women were experiencing discomfort from the government's strong-arm tactics — especially when it was announced that there would not be any more girdles manufactured due to the shortage of rubber. There wasn't any elastic in clothes either. Joanie recalls that the button holding up her panties came off while at Elmore School and she had a heck of a time keeping them from falling down to her knees. Nylon, which was used to make parachutes, was requisitioned and women had to bare their legs or wear wool stockings.

The War had a significant, beneficial impact on me personally. I wanted to know what was happening every day in the War, in detail. Dad wasn't usually home when the paper came and Mom was too busy to read to me, so I quickly accelerated my reading curve beyond Dick, Jane and Spot. By the second grade I could read, with the exception of the big words, the *Green Bay Press-Gazette*. While Terry was listening to Captain Midnight, Terry and the Pirates (his favorite of course), Jack Armstrong, the All-American Boy, Superman and other radio programs from four o'clock to dinner time, I was trying to read the paper.

"Joanie? What does *annihilation* mean?" I asked my sister.

"Buster, you've got the dictionary. Look it up," was her standard answer. So, I did.

By the time I was in Miss Donovan's third-grade class my reading was fairly proficient. I remember this incident, as if it were just a few years ago.

"Buster, you have such an interest in reading about the War, would you like to take this book home to read? It's about submarines," Miss Donovan asked.

"Sure, sure. I'd like to read it."

I took the book home. It was technical and difficult to understand, but I read it every day and late into the night. I brought the book back to class.

"Buster, why don't you read to the class. I'm sure they would like to hear about how submarines work," Miss Donovan asked. I'm sure she was trying to validate my claim that I had, indeed, read the book. I obliged. After school was out Miss Donovan asked me to go upstairs with her to the principal's office. There she asked me to read to Miss Hetherington. Apparently they were both favorably impressed. My report card, which I still have amongst all my cherished collectibles, has all "E"s (Excellent) for the four reading skills. The War shaped all of our lives in various and often positive ways.

"Dickie? Let's make war more realer," I told my best friend as we gathered in the field behind our house. After kindergarten Dickie went to Annunciation, a Catholic School that was on the northwest corner of Gray and Division Streets, only a long block from our house. Even though we never saw each other during school hours we always played together after school and on weekends.

"Whataya mean?" he asked, as we stood in the field with our crudely fashioned wooden rifles and old surplus World War I helmets.

"Let's dig some trenches and fox holes like the army does when they're fighting," I suggested with shovel in hand.

"That's a good idea," Dickie agreed.

Soon we enlisted Terry and our neighborhood buds, Lee Olson, David and Jeffrey Martin, Norbert and Jimmy Spitzer, Johnny and Mike Culligan and others to join our ranks and before we knew it, we had a whole series of trenches in our mock battlefield. There were over ten boys in our age group in the small area surrounding the field that was our battleground.

"Hey, I know what we should do," Dickie suggested.

"What?" we all asked.

"Let's cover the trenches with boards and dirt and make tunnels we can hide in," Dickie proposed, as he placed a piece of plywood over one of the tunnels and shoveled dirt over it.

"Geez! That's terrific," David said, as we all started scavenging around the field for material to cover the trenches. Before long we had a labyrinth of connecting tunnels and fox holes worthy of a platoon's effort. Playing army was now more real.

"Bang! I gotcha," I yelled as I took aim against the "enemy." Dickie, Lee, David, Jeffrey, Terry and I were matched against the Spitzer and Culligan brothers.

"No you didn't," Mike shouted, as he ducked into a fox hole.

"I got 'em, didn't I Dickie?" I asked for an impartial opinion.

"Mike? Buster got ya," Dickie claimed.

"He missed me. He missed me," Mike protested.

And the verbal confrontation usually went on indefinitely without resolution. Our scrapes and scratches were covered by the trusty, pink Mercurochrome. Often there were full frontal assaults that usually resulted in one of us getting our head or our ego bruised, but after school the next day everything was forgotten and another battle was on.

One day I ran home to change into my old clothes before engaging in dirty trench warfare. Terry, who wasn't in school yet, was standing on one of the mounds of dirt that all of us had excavated.

"Someone ruined it!" he cried out as I approached. "Someone filled in our tunnels."

"Jeepers creepers! Who did it?" I asked, shocked and dismayed by what I saw.

"I dunno. Maybe it was the enemy," Terry surmised.

The "enemy" of course were the adults in our neighborhood who were concerned about our safety.

Dickie thought it was our next door neighbor Mr. Rondou but it probably was a conspiracy hatched by a coalition of parents. Our war games were reduced to playing on a level field. That's what everyone wanted — a level playing field (like today), which wasn't as interesting.

My sister Joanie had no interest in war games. After Grandpa Sam's death she developed a much closer relationship with Gramma Anderson and spent hours with her after school and on weekends. I also suspect that she was retreating from her two "bothers."

Gramma taught her the art of homemaking. Gram's cooking and baking skills were virtually incomparable, but it was one particular talent that Gramma possessed that Joanie remembers fondly. Needlepoint. Gram had embarked on an ambitious project using this diagonal stitch technique to recover all of her dinning room and living room furniture. There must have been ten or more pieces that depicted remarkably consistent and intricate floral patterns on a black background.

While at a museum in Stockholm during my visit there, I viewed a furniture exhibit that portrayed everyday life in the mid -to late 19th Century in Sweden. The hand-covered, wooden chairs had a very similar pattern to those of my grandmother's. Did Hulda or one of her sisters or brothers bring these pieces with them from Sweden? An interesting conjecture. Amongst my sister's most prized possessions today are all of these chairs, still in pristine condition.

———————

Faced with declining morale due to military reversals in the Pacific, FDR endorsed a risky raid on Tokyo in April 1942. As Goodwin asserts, "The Japanese government had promised the people of Japan that their homeland would never be attacked."[5] Led by Lt. Colonel James H. Doolittle, sixteen heavily loaded B-25 bombers, which had never taken off from a carrier previously, carried out a raid that had a doomed exit strategy. After flying six hundred miles from the carrier and dropping their payload, there was insufficient fuel to return to the carrier. They flew on to mainland China, with no airstrip on which to land. The fact that any of our pilots, including Doolittle, survived in Japanese-held territory was an absolute miracle.

The physical damage done in Tokyo was minimal, but the psychological damage was monumental, both for the U.S. and Japan. Goodwin related that the raid forced Japan's hand, which led to their disastrous loss at Midway. That defeat, which cost the enemy 3500 lives, placed the Japanese on defense for the balance of the war. The bold raid on Tokyo bolstered an America desperate for good news.

Corregidor and the Bataan death march, however, negated the gains that had just been realized. In a strange twist of circumstance, I would have a connection to the horrible experience of the "death march." A soldier, Joe Smith, who was featured on the cover of LIFE magazine would have (incredibly) been my future brother-in-law. He was a prisoner in one of the more grievous episodes of WWII. He survived four horrific years as a prisoner of war, only to die in a civilian airline crash in 1949.

—————

Although it was a considerable distance (about two miles) from our house on Dousman Street to the Grace Lutheran Church on the east side, our family would never miss a Sunday, especially during the War. Our congregation was blessed with an outstanding pastor, Rev. Louis Frederick Gast, who came to Grace Lutheran in 1909 and served the church for 43 years. Since Rev. Gast was fluent in German as well as English, the congregation had a large German membership. Amazingly, there was never any consideration of the Germans as potential risk to American security while over 100,000 Japanese-Americans were interned in prison camps.

"I'm going to teach Sunday School for the high school kids today," Dad said, as we headed for the Walnut Street bridge. It was a grey overcast day, punctuated with snowflakes darting at the front window like white sparks from a firestorm.

"Dad? Why don't you teach our class?" I asked.

"Mrs. Forsythe teaches your grades. She'll be your teacher until you get to junior high," Dad informed me.

Terry and I went to Sunday School in the basement. Dad's class was upstairs in the church. Joanie was in the choir and practiced before the main service. After the service Dad was out in front of the church talking to Rev. Gast and another person.

"Buster, this is Robert Suess. He is one of my students. He goes to West High and plays basketball on the "Y" team that I sponsor. Visit with him awhile, I need to speak privately with Rev. Gast."

"Okay."

"Your dad is a wonderful guy, Buster. He really made our class interesting, and it was so nice of him to sponsor our team. We just got our new uniforms," Robert relayed to me. It was the last year that Dad was associated with Old Line Life.

"Yeah. Everybody likes Dad. He was a good basketball player too," I added, although I really didn't know that was true for certain. "Have you been a member of Grace Lutheran very long?" I asked. I felt awkard trying to make conversation with a high schooler; I was only six.

"As long as I can remember. My aunt, Elsie Bruechner, is the organist and my mom, Lillian, is the secretary for the church. I took my confirmation class from Rev. Gast," Robert informed me.

"What's he like ... I mean Rev. Gast? I'm kinda scared of him," I said a little apprehensively, as he stood nearby. Rev. Gast was an imposing figure and the whole religious ritual was mystical and mysterious to me.

"He's terrific. He's not the old stuffy guy you think he is. Don't get me wrong, he doesn't allow any 'monkeyshines' in his class, but you should see him when he teaches us how to memorize the Books of the Bible. He's like a cheerleader leading a cheer for our basketball team. You'll never forget it, by golly," Robert elaborated, excited by the mere mention of his experience.

Robert, who was of German descent, joined the reserves immediately out of high school and by 1945 he found himself fighting in France after the Normandy invasion. He was badly wounded when the Nazis unleashed the massive counter-attack known as the "Battle of the Bulge" in August

1945. Fortunately, Robert recovered from his wounds and was able to relate his relationship with my father and his war experience to me fifty-seven years later.

One of the great traditions at Grace Lutheran was to make a gift of a Bible to every young member of the church when they reached the third grade. Amongst my memorabilia is a small photograph attached to a pamphlet entitled, "The Books of the Bible," commemorating the event. I and ten of my Sunday School classmates are standing with open Bibles, dressed in heavy coats with ear muffs. It is late April, yet the trees in the background are void of leaves. Spring time in Green Bay! We were probably praying for the winter to end.

Elmore School was named for the first mayor of Green Bay after the city had been merged with Fort Howard. Built in the late 30's, it was a relatively new school with its own gym. Teachers' salaries were $1,260 per year in 1942, and almost all of our teachers were single. Our teachers were women, particularly during the War, and if they married and got pregnant, they were immediately fired. Many, wanting to remain employed, stayed single all their lives. They were truly married to their jobs. We were their "kids."

The neighborhood that was serviced by the school was populated by what was described as "up and coming families," according to Helen Fersleu who, at age 84 when we renewed our acquaintance, was still "sharp as a tack." Parents took a very keen interest in their children's activities. The parents, who had just lived through The Great Depression, wanted their children to have what they didn't have. They eagerly supported all the programs at the school and backed the teachers 100%. We had a perfect learning and disciplined environment. But, we had a lot of fun too.

"Snowball fight! Snowball fight!" Jerry Proctor yelled, as we almost knocked the doors down getting outside for recess. It was like a dogcatcher had just released a bunch of cooped up, mad dogs from the city pound.

Before we could pelt each other with snowballs the teachers stepped in and called a cease-fire. They did allow us to throw at the "wall" however, in order to burn off our excess energy. The wall was the northeast corner of the school. It had no windows. After recess the entire face of the sandy-beige brick building was peppered with white, inverted pot marks. Mine was one of the highest, suggesting that, at an early age, I was blessed with a pretty strong right arm. Late in the day when we went home streams of water descended down the wall like tears flowing down the cheeks of a wounded giant.

This same northeast corner of our playground was also home plate for our softball and kickball games at recess when spring finally would make its always delayed appearance. A well hit ball down the left field line would slam against the same gigantic wall that withstood our snowball attacks. Jerry Proctor, Tom Nack and I would do our best to impress the girls by hitting the monster target. But some of the girls were very athletic too. Patty Olson and Connie Shaw could swing the bat as hard as most of the boys, and Sharon Bookmeier, who I thought was the prettiest girl in our class and who I had a "crush" on, was one of the fastest runners. Our favorite class then, as it probably is today, was recess. Unfortunately, in the forties and fifties, there wasn't any competitive athletic endeavor for the girls through all the grades and into high school.

One of the unusual rituals at school during this period was our requirement to take iodine tablets to prevent an enlargement of our goiter. The foul-smelling and icky-tasting tablets that had to be chewed were darn near inedible until they were chocolate flavored. Once they tasted like candy we no longer had to demonstrate to our teacher that we, indeed, had digested the loathsome medicine.

While citizens were dealing with everyday life under an ever present cloud of uncertainty, the president and our allies were dealing with clear, unfettered realities. The Russians were retreating from a massive onslaught from the Germans that brought the enemy literally to the doorstep of Leningrad and Stalingrad. Stalin was demanding a second front in France to relieve the pressure and force Hitler to focus on the west. And, there was the treaty between Germany and the Japanese. An invasion by the Japanese from the east could sound a death knell for our Russian allies, so the public was told.

There was a new danger rising ominously, totally unknown to not only the civilian population, but to most of Congress and our military. As early as 1939, FDR knew, by virtue of a letter from Albert Einstein, "that scientists in Berlin had achieved the fission of uranium atoms and the release of incredible amounts of energy."[6] The Allies were faced with the prospect that the Germans could be the first to develop an atomic bomb, with a madman dictator that wouldn't hesitate to use it. That horrific possibility was the instigator for the "Manhattan Project," the Los Alamos Laboratory and an all-out effort by the U.S. to develop a nuclear bomb.

Vyacheslaw Molotov was the Russian Foreign Commissar. He was sent to Washington with Stalin's orders to get a commitment from FDR to initiate a second front in France. Goodwin says, "So unswerving did Molotov prove, content to sit in his chair for hours on end sticking to his argument, that Roosevelt later nicknamed him 'Stone Ass.'"[7] Molotov, making certain that he had the support of Eleanor Roosevelt, charmed the First Lady and returned victorious to Russia with FDR's commitment.

Winston Churchill, upon hearing of FDR's meeting with Molotov, flew immediately to Washington to meet with the president. He was adamantly opposed to a full frontal attack on the continent, reminded of the loss of 60,000 British soldiers in one day at Somme. Despite the "little bulldog's" furious rhetoric and tenacity, FDR approved the formation of plans for the invasion of Europe.

Most Americans have long forgotten or may have never known the name Harry Hopkins. Much has been written about Franklin and Eleanor, their relationship and the tremendous influence that Eleanor had on the president and the policies of his administration. Few, however, remember the extraordinary influence that Hopkins had on the president. Goodwin acknowledges that Hopkins was a "confidant," an "alter ego," and a "number one war adviser" in describing Hopkins' relationship with the president. One of Hopkins' detractors called him "Rasputin," the Russian mystic who literally controlled Czarina Alexandra of Russia less than one-half century earlier. The inference was scurrilous, but make no mistake about it: Hopkins, who lived in the White House for three and one-half years, even after he married, had an enormous influence on the president. A recent book, *The Venona Secrets: Exposing Soviet Espionage and America's Traitors*, by Herbert Romerstein, *et al.*, raises the significance of this relationship to a new level. The authors, after obtaining records from previously secret Soviet archives, maintain that Hopkins was, in fact, a Soviet spy.

By the fall of 1942 there was an acute shortage of workers to build the tanks, planes and armaments of all sorts. The War Manpower Commission had run out of men. "Rosie the Riveter"[8] was born, and her image on billboards and in newspapers dressed in overalls and bandanna appealed to women's patriotism to meet the call of "Uncle Sam Needs You." The money was substantially greater than most women had ever earned, but it also was the recognition by the public, and men in particular, that they were of value to others that coaxed them out of the kitchen and into the work place. Our mom never ventured out. She had her hands full with us kids, and since Dad was working two jobs, he wasn't home to lend a hand.

When the war ended, problems quickly developed. When the boys came home women were competitors for their jobs. Men in general wanted their women at home where they were "in the good old days." The rise in juvenile delinquency was attributed to the absence of Mom at home. The picture of juveniles smoking was an image that reinforced the need for Mom to return to her rightful responsibilities. To many historians and sociologists the working woman of WWII was the onset of woman's independence. Feminism, to some, was born when Rosie became a riveter. And, if you carry the point to its ultimate conclusion, this was the beginning of the breakdown of the family unit (an interesting and thought-provoking thesis on which I have no view). But, one thing is for certain, the War had an enormous impact on our society and those who lived it.

My cousins and their comrades in arms were fighting a grisly war not of their making. Merlin writes extensively of his experiences in the Pacific.[9] Some excerpts:

I had been out of water for several hours. Despite warnings of untreated water I flopped on my belly and scooped up a couple of handfuls. Out of the corner of my eye, I spotted a slight movement upstream. There — much to my horror — was a dead, very bloated Jap floating in the stream. I practically turned inside out, heaving the water up.

I had just sat back in my slit trench with my cup of instant coffee when something told me to <u>DUCK</u>. It was as if my 'guardian angel' had tapped me on the shoulder. I rolled face down in the bottom of my hole almost at the same instant as a shell crashed on the edge of my hole. When I shook the dirt off that had partially buried me and looked up — I saw the fellow seated in the hole next to mine had been decapitated.

Just as Merlin heard that the atomic bomb had been dropped on Hiroshima, he was headed back to (appropriately) Duck Creek. Aside from several encounters with malaria and a bad episode of dengue fever my cousin survived the entire four years unhurt, but only eight of his original unit of 120 medical detachment members made it home.

At home we sought refuge from the war at the movies. Incredibly, out of a population of about 135 million in the U.S., 90 million went to a movie once a week.[10] Walt Disney exploited all of our archetypal fears of separation, rejection and abandonment with *Dumbo*, the outcast baby elephant with big ears, and *Bambi*, the baby deer whose mother was shot and killed leaving her offspring without protection and homeless. It wasn't a message that children needed during the War, but somehow it worked positively for me and my generation and made Disney famous and wealthy. Escapism from the harsh realities of the War was undoubtedly responsible for the meteoric rise in attendance, but I can recall how anxious I was to see the Movie Tone News. It was the only visual representation (other than newspaper photos) that we had of the War. The news was always deliberately positive, which reinforced our feeling of optimism that everything would turn out right. Mom would usually take us to the Strand or the Orpheum on Saturday afternoons. I believe that Mom's ticket was 25¢, mine was 10¢ and Terry's was free for a double feature.

I loved the Disney cartoons but never dreamed that "Minnie Mouse" would appear in my future picture.

Bill Maudlin, the Pulitzer Prize-winning cartoonist, provided us another view of the War through his two principal characters, Willie and Joe. Any romantic image that we had of our fighting men in the trenches was shattered by this laconic pair of unshaven, slump-shouldered and weary, dogfaced G.I.s. Maudlin, himself an infantryman, passed away in 2003, but his unique presentation of the War will never be forgotten by those from our era. General Patton despised Maudlin's portrayal of our G.I.s.

Sometime probably in the late 1930's Dad took up the game of golf. Despite the fact that during the War all the younger and healthier men were in the service, the Green Bay Industrial League was a competitive and stress-reducing release for those men at home. Dad played on the Northwest Engineering Team with Matt Wells, Martin Deere and Urban (Slim) Jensen. According to Larry Fitchett, our next-door neighbor, they were the best team in the league:

I was into hero worship. I really looked up to the athletes. Your dad was good at every sport — softball, basketball, golf. He was an incredible athlete and he was probably in his late 30's then, I guess.

Dad was a stockholder in the Shorewood Country Club, which was located on the east shore of Green Bay just north of Bay Beach. It was a beautiful sight looking down from the bluff on the blue waters of the bay. I vividly remember the rickety, wooden footbridge suspended high over a ravine. Dad's foursome usually included Lee McFazzen, Dan Raymond, Slim Jensen and occasionally his neighbor and good friend, Otto Rose. One incident is still as fresh in my mind as my last hole-in-one, despite the fact that it occurred almost sixty years ago.

Number 18 at Shorewood was a very difficult hole. It was a little over 400 yards long, but it played much longer because a steep hill in the ball's landing area prevented any significant roll. There was a small pond on the right in the driving area, and trees on the left that would block a golfer's line of flight to the green. To make it even tougher, there was a tree directly in the middle of the fairway that could render a perfect drive virtually worthless.

Standing in the fairway, most golfers could not see the green — the approach shot was blind. There was a bell to the left of the green and when the players left the putting surface they rang the bell to signal that the green was clear. Someone didn't wait for the bell to ring. Dad, waiting for his foursome to putt out, was hit directly on the back of his head by the blind approach shot. He collapsed like a puppet whose life-giving strings had been severed.

"Telma! Telma!" Otto said in his heavy German accent, unable to pronounce the "H" in her name. "Hup has been injured. Vee haf to take him to da hospital, yah."

I was standing next to Mom when the call came in from Otto.

"Buster, get your brother. We have to go to Bellin. Your dad is in the hospital," Mom said somewhat panicky. She panicked pretty easy, which was a portent of things to come.

I grabbed Terry and we jumped into the Olds. We were off to see Dad, not knowing or fully understanding the nature or the extent of his injury.

"Is Daddy kilt?" Terry asked. "Is he going to die?" he added, standing behind the front seat as Mom was driving with one hand on the wheel and biting her fingernails on the other.

"Dad's going to be all right. Dad's going to be all right," Mom reassured us as she was trying to reassure herself.

Anxiously we opened the door to Dad's room at Bellin Memorial Hospital (where all three of us were born years earlier). Dad was conscious and sitting up with a large bandage that looked like a turban on his head.

"Daddy? You're not gonna die, are you?" Terry asked wishfully.

"No. No, Terry. I'm going to be okay. Otto made sure I got to the hospital quickly. He drove like a bat out of heck to get me here," Dad said, looking at his tall, thin, wiry friend.

"Das goot," Otto remarked. We always had a hard time understanding what he said.

During the War there was a constant subliminal fear amongst children that, like "Bambi," we would lose a parent. Never, however, could we conceive that it would occur on a golf course. A non-contact sport if there ever was one. Dad was in the hospital three days.

Forty years later I would suffer a similar fate with a blow to my head from a golf ball. After regaining consciousness and spending two hours at the hospital getting an MRI and twenty-one stitches, I returned to the golf course and finished my tournament round. Dad would have been proud of me. He rarely said anything to me face-to-face, but he told anyone who would listen what I had accomplished.

On a recent visit to Green Bay, I joined Richard (Soup) Campbell and Whitey Stuiber for a round of golf at Shorewood. The course had changed. The University of Wisconsin had claimed nine of the holes to expand its campus, but the aura of the place revered by my father was still intact. "Soup" and Whitey will recall that we were a threesome that gorgeous June day, but to me Dad was with us also. In my mind's eye I could see him in his Ben Hogan-

style golf hat, full, pleated slacks and winged-tip golf shoes strolling the fairways with us. He smiled and tipped his hat as I parred the difficult 18th that nearly became his "signature" hole.

During the War Mom also took up the game of golf. As a child, I never pictured Mom as athletic, but at 5'8" and probably 160 pounds she was a strong and well-built woman.

Viewing movie film of her playing in the late forties, I was impressed with her ability to strike the ball. Gramma or Joanie would babysit Terry and me while she played at Shorewood with Edna Rose (Otto's wife) and Christie Mann, who were her best friends. It was during one of her outings with Edna after the War that Mom learned of Dad's dark "secret."

Despite the occasional loud, sharp whistle from the Fairmont Dairy signaling a blackout for an air-raid drill (monitored by wardens volunteering for the Civil Defense), Christmas went on undeterred. Prange's was Mom's favorite department store downtown, just over the Dousman Street bridge at Washington and Pine Streets. One of Green Bay's greatest traditions was a life-sized animated display in the windows at Prange's. It drew huge crowds, and we waited in line to get a glimpse of the eye-popping spectacle. What followed was a tour of the toy store and a visit with Santa on his knee (divulging later to Mom what was on our wish list). Our mom was super practical. She focused on clothes, like underwear and shoes, and stuff like that.

"Ah geez, Mom. I don't want to wear knickers any more. They're for sissies. Jerry and Harry and Dickie don't wear knickers. I want pants like the other guys wear," I implored to my mom. Lo and behold I won. No more knickers with long socks!

Jerry and Harold Proctor, along with Dickie Maierle, had become my best friends. Jerry and Harold were twins, but I had a difficult time believing that since they weren't identical and Jerry was taller than Harry. The Proctors were a huge family. Jerry and Harry had three brothers and three sisters, and one brother, Dick, was in Joanie's class. They, understandably, had a large house on Velp Avenue and they invited me to play there often. I guess Jerry and Harry's mom would hardly notice one more kid around, and their house was out in the "country" so there were a lot of neat things to do. Our favorite treat was to load up all of us in the car and go to Barney Farah's A&W Root Beer Stand on Broadway. There were no root beer floats like A&W in the frosted mug.

Joanie was now a teenager. There wasn't much music in our house until she started to play the piano. Then she got a portable phonograph player, which was a big deal. It was in a light blue box with a crank on the right side, and the popular war songs from the "Big Bands" emanated from her room. Some were, "In the Mood," played by Glen Miller's band; "I'll Be Seeing You," by Harry James; " 'Til We Meet Again," sung by Margaret Whiting; and crazy hip songs like "Mairzy Doats" and "I'm Looking over a Four Leaf Clover." I must have been listening. I can still remember the words of a good number of the War songs.

While researching for Rediscovering America! *I made an incredible discovery. My cousin Larry mailed me an article in the* Green Bay Press-Gazette *that reviewed events in Green Bay during the 1940's. Under a heading "Swimming at Bay Beach, 1943" is a picture of bathers swimming at the beach just north of Green Bay. Who are two of the kids featured in the photo making sand castles? Larry, my brother Terry and I didn't realize what he had discovered! Under the photo is this caption: "The beach has been shut down intermittently through the years, triggered by concerns of industrial pollution and botulism."*

The pollution was primarily from the waste dumped into the Fox River by the paper mills. The smell of rotten eggs still arouses foul senses in my memory. I suspect that Bay Beach was one of our few options in 1943 and the pollution drove us north to Door County to clear, clean water. In this same series of articles, one dated November 5, 1943, reinforces my earlier point: "Nineteen Green Bay residents who work in the shipyards at Sturgeon Bay had their 'A' and 'C' gas rations suspended for a period ranging from 10 days to a year and two months for driving their automobiles above 50 mph on Wisconsin 57 between here and Sturgeon Bay."

The OPA police were lurking everywhere to catch violators. We lived in a tightly controlled and managed society. In that same article, we are reminded that county highway workers (laborers) who then made 50¢ an hour were filing for a 10¢ pay increase (20%), and bowling at the Columbus Club at the cost of 18¢ per lane on weekends. The pressure to increase wages was enormous. Inflation was a real problem despite the OPA controls.

By the spring of 1945 the Allies were winning the War on all fronts. As I had done since I was six years old, I viewed the map of Europe in the *Green Bay Press-Gazette* each day tracing the progress of the Allies as they pushed towards Berlin from the east, west and south. A black solid line like the screws of a massive vise was clamping down on the once mighty Wehrmacht. As the inevitability of the War in Europe ending brightened each day, the nation was unprepared for the unexpected darkness that would shroud the Capitol and the country.

Grace Tully, the White House secretary, remarked after the president returned from a four-day weekend at Hyde Park that the weekend "had failed to erase the fatigue from his face."[11] That was March 29, 1945. A station agent at Warm Springs, Georgia, FDR's favorite place of respite, said, "The president was the worst looking man I ever saw who was still alive."[12] Those in the president's inner circle may have suspected that the end was near, but the nation did not.

"I have terrific pain in the back of my head,"[13] the president said as he sat for a portrait in his cabin at Warm Springs. Those were his last words. He died of a cerebral hemorrhage on April 12, 1945. Harry Truman was our new president.

Dead was the man whom America perceived with almost single-minded resolve, and who had guided this nation through two of its most defining moments in the twentieth century. Gone was the man so crippled by polio that he could neither stand nor walk on his own, but who was the pillar of strength when the very foundation of the nation was threatened. Regretfully, Franklin Delano Roosevelt did not live to see the end of the War.

I can vividly recall sitting next to the fireplace (as I had done four years earlier, in December 1941), listening to radio accounts of the president's casket making its last journey by train to Washington. The nation was in shock and in tears. We went to the theater to get a visual remembrance of this defining moment. It was the only way, really, that we could pay our respects. In addition to an expected outpouring of grief there were some reactions that were unexpected.

When Joseph Stalin was informed of FDR's death, he "sent a message to the State Department asking that an autopsy be performed to determine if Roosevelt had been poisoned."[14] A reflection, perhaps, of the paranoia of the inquisitor or a recognition that the president did, indeed, have his detractors. Those who insisted that the president was sympathetic to the cause of the Russian Revolution may have been suspect in Stalin's mind.

To Eleanor Roosevelt, her husband's death was exacerbated by the revelation that the president's long-time mistress, Lucy Mercer Rutherford, was at his side at the moment of his death. In addition, Eleanor discovered that Anna, their daughter, was the liaison between Lucy and the president. Eleanor felt she was betrayed by both her husband and her daughter. Anna, a child caught between two parents, found herself in a no-win situation. I understood Anna's plight. Fifteen years later I would be faced with a similar dilemma.

Miss Donovan entered our third-grade class at Elmore School with a big grin on her face.

"Children, I have good news. Germany has surrendered. The War in Europe is over."

A raucous cheer went up from our class. Quickly the entire school erupted in yelling and noise-making that only gradeschoolers can elicit. After the celebration subsided, I asked:

"Is school out?"

Another cheer, equally boisterous, broke out.

"No, No. School is not out," Miss Donovan asserted.

Even as children, we felt that we were an integral part of this massive effort to win the War. In the archives of the Brown County Central Library, with the assistance of Mary Jane Herber I discovered a written report, by Joseph D. Donovan, the County Superintendent, on the history of the War efforts of the Brown County Schools.

The schools served early in the War as centers for draft registration, the distribution of ration books, the sale of defense bonds and stamps, the sale of seeds for Victory Gardens, and the collection of paper and milk weed floss (which was used for life preservers and jackets for pilots), and as depositories for scrap iron, rubber and rags.

In 1943-1944 the students and teachers sold $77,826 in bonds and stamps. In 1942, the schools brought in 809,309 pounds of scrap metal and 17,748 pounds of rubber. Most of us enrolled in the Junior Red Cross and prepared gifts for refugees and soldiers. Yes, we felt that we were a part of a team. A team that had to be victorious in order to preserve our way of life. That's why we held up the two fingers in each hand in a V sign for days after the announcement that the War in Europe was over.

The headline in the Monday, May 7, 1945, evening edition of the *Green Bay Press-Gazette* read:

"GERMANY SURRENDERS"

After five years, eight months and six days of bloodshed, the War in Europe was over. Elation turned to glumness, however, at the realization that the invasion of Japan was ahead, and of the brutal reality that hundreds of thousands more Americans could lose their lives in order to bring World War II to an end.

Residents of central New Mexico knew that something was afoot in July 1945 when the dark early morning sky was prematurely ignited by a radiant light of unknown origin. Speculation was rampant about a new weapon with horrific power, but until "Little Boy," the atomic bomb that literally vaporized Hiroshima, Japan, on August 6, 1945, the nation and the world could not possibly fathom what devastation mankind had unleashed.

The bomb exploded 1900' above Hiroshima. Temperatures near the center of the explosion surged from 5400° to 7200°, and an estimated 100,000 Japanese citizens died the first day. As we subsequently learned about the effects of radiation, we realized that many more died years later. On August 9, 1945, "Fat Man," with twice the power of "Little Boy," was dropped on Nagasaki, killing 74,000 Japanese. On August 15, 1945, the Empire of Japan surrendered.

Overwhelmed by euphoria with the cessation of World War II, and the relief that hundreds of thousands of American lives would be spared now that an invasion of Japan was not necessary, little focus publicly was devoted to the obvious. Why didn't the U.S. warn the Japanese, perhaps with an offshore demonstration of the "A" bomb, of the terrific annihilation they faced if they didn't surrender? Why was a second bomb dropped just three days after Hiroshima, not allowing the Japanese sufficient time to reflect upon their fate? More importantly, in this writer's opinion, the debate that followed didn't delve into the overriding issue surrounding the war that was supposed to end all wars.

After their successful attack on Pearl Harbor, the Japanese Fleet Admiral Isoroku Yamamoto was reported to have said, "I fear we have awakened a sleeping giant." Yamamoto's famous line could have been translated, "I fear we have awakened a sleeping military-industrial giant." Goodwin acknowledges that "It was during the war years that the links were forged that would lead to the rise of the 'military-industrial complex' in postwar America,"[15] but it wasn't within the purview of her book to develop this issue further.

President Dwight D. Eisenhower, in his farewell address in 1960, warned America of the enormous threat of the new "military-industrial complex." Who better than "Ike" would comprehend the awesome power that WWII had spawned, which dominates America's geo-political role today.

Prior to "a date which will live in infamy," American industry was struggling barely above the levels during the depths of The Great Depression. Unemployment was still in excess of 20%. Bank lending was flat as consumer sentiment remained negative and demand for goods was modest at best. People were saving money, not spending it. Roosevelt fought The Depression with an aggressive array of programs to stimulate the economy, which had only limited success and were of short duration. The War changed everything. Goodwin says in her book:

> Between 1940 and 1945, the U.S. contributed over three hundred thousand war planes to the Allied cause. American factories produced more than two million trucks, 107,351 tanks, 87,620 warships, 5,475 cargo ships, over twenty million rifles, machine guns and pistols and forty-four billion rounds of ammunition.[16]

The War did awaken the sleeping giant and its economy. At the beginning of the War Japan had eleven aircraft carriers, which had taken twenty years to build. Within four years the U.S. built one hundred aircraft carriers. The War made American industry profitable and robust, and its owners rich. Due to tens of thousands of government contracts with a guaranteed (cost plus) margin of profit, the banks were anxious to supply all the money necessary for industry to buy the material necessary for the manufacture of arms and supplies. Those banks which had survived the "bank holidays" of the 1930's also became enormously profitable. As a result, wittingly or unwittingly, WWII created an alliance between American industry, the military and the U.S. money center banks. Eisenhower's term was confined to the "military-industrial complex" but a tripartite partnership including a funding mechanism was necessary to make it function. The most persuasive and longest lasting legacy of WWII has evolved into an unspoken and unwritten mantra of "perpetual war for perpetual profit." Without question a cynical view but readily demonstrable.

Beginning with the European Recovery Program (aka the "Marshall Plan") after WWII, lending to rebuild countries devastated by war has become one of the most lucrative sectors in global banking. Why? The loans are principally guaranteed by governments, i.e., taxpayers — U.S. taxpayers — you and me. Sixty years ago the banks financed the reconstruction of Japan and Europe. Today it's the Balkans, Afghanistan and soon it will be Iraq. Though at the time of this writing the war with Iraq had not yet begun, the U.S. government had already taken steps towards awarding $900 million in construction contracts to repair and rebuild the country.[17] And that amount is "just a beginning" according to *Time*. The United States Agency for International Development (USAID) sent out confidential requests for construction proposals to companies such as Fluor Daniel, Kellogg, Brown & Root, Perini, Parsons, the Louis Berger Group, and Bechtel, prior to a single shot being fired. The same cast of players that helped rebuild the Balkans and Afghanistan. As Perry Mason would say, "I rest my case," but I find no solace in the discovery that Dwight D. Eisenhower's admonition was amazingly accurate. Few Americans understood Eisenhower's admonition of forty years ago. Given contemporary events at the turn of this century, Ike's message screams to be heard. Americans have traded the absolutism of kings in the past for the collection of power in the hands of a select few who determine why we fight.

As the war in the Pacific approached its inevitable but shocking end, gas rationing eased and our family looked eagerly to a summer vacation in Door County. Prior to the War, we had camped out in Peninsula State Park near Ephraim. I can vividly remember how Mom and Dad would lay blankets over ropes attached to trees to cordon off an area for privacy while we "camped out." Gramma and Larry were almost always with us. I'm almost certain that the photographs taken with Grandpa Anderson in the late thirties, when I was about two, were taken there.

The summer of 1945 would be different. After V-E Day everyone wanted to "get away." I suspect that finding a place to rent in Door County was difficult but Dad secured a large cabin on the bay in Egg Harbor, which was a new area to all of us. A cabin for the whole month of August. Jeepers Creepers! The only negative was that the beach was rocky — no sand. But, with golf nearby at the Alpine Inn and Cottages and fishing unlimited, Dad was in "hog-heaven."

"Let's see who can skip stones the best," I suggested to Terry as we stood on the rocky beach. The rocks were perfect — round and flat, polished by centuries of waves lapping against the shoreline.

"These rocks are smooth," Terry, who would be seven in a week, said.

"You need to side-arm your throw, Terry, so they skip better," I informed my younger brother, who already showed indications that he also had a strong right arm.

"Look at that one!" Terry exclaimed. "It skipped six times."

I questioned his count.

I moved forward and dipped lower to deliver my next throw on to the placid, rippleless water.

"Eight skips!" I shouted as I raised up, admiring my success. Suddenly, I felt a sharp, stunning blow to the back of my head! My eyes blinked. Fragments of light like shooting stars darted across my pupils. I had caught one of Terry's throws to the back of my head!

"Mommie! Mommie!" Terry shouted as he ran up to the cabin, which was on a ledge above the bay.

Mom ran out on the porch. "What happened?" she asked my little brother.

"Buster is hurt. He's bleeding. He's bleeeeddding! Come quick."

"What happened? How did he get hurt?" Mom inquired as she scrambled down the rocky slope to the Bayshore.

"I dunno. I dunno." Terry said (not revealing the cause of my agony).

After a quick trip to the doctor's office and some stitches and ice packs I recovered. What was humorous (years later, of course) was that Terry didn't want to admit that he threw the stone that hit me, when there was no other logical conclusion. Accepting blame was tough for any of us as kids, but it's something we learned effectively. Our generation assumed responsibility for our mistakes. And, still do.

This incident was only the first of many hits on my "noggin." Any one of them could have caused a brain tumor, but that comes later.

Up the hill from our cabin and across Highway 57 was Gilson's Variety Store. Terry and I went up there often for treats. One day I had just left the store and looked both ways so that I could dart across the highway. Suddenly all the cars were honking their horns! Everyone was shouting. People came running out of their houses and cabins along the highway. I was dumbfounded. Then I heard someone shout:

"The War is over! The War is over!"

It was August 15, 1945. I was nine years old and I've returned to that exact spot numerous times. Some of my friends and family think that is strange and shrug their shoulders when I recall the moment. History has always been meaningful to me. We are products and beneficiaries of history. Some, unfortunately, are victims of it.

Our cabin was one of three owned by Paul Bertschinger and managed by the Alpine Inn and Cottages. The Inn itself, south and west of our site, was built in 1921 by Paul and his brother John. Now known as the Alpine Resort, three generations of the Bertschinger family have operated this magnificent place for 83 continuous years.

Paul managed the golf course. It's safe to assume that he and Dad made connection through the game, and this is how we came to be renting the cabin during this memorable moment in time. Paul's son Bill, at the time 18 years of age, remembers that day as if it were recorded on film, complete with sound. Following is a conversation Bill and I recently had:

"I was about to get drafted so the War's end was very meaningful to me," Bill said. "I immediately enrolled in the University of Wisconsin and received a deferment. I remember three major things that happened that day.

"One, all the cars formed a convoy and paraded between Egg Harbor and the Inn honking their horns. (So, my memory was correct.) Second, soon all the guests and employees formed a 'conga line' and danced in and out of the resort. Lastly, I was a drummer in the band and we played until the wee hours in the morning. I had a date with Millie that night and we didn't get together until 2:00 a.m."

"I recall the wild party that evening at the Inn," I added. "Terry and I, armed with confetti, showered those on the dance floor with curly ribbons of crepe paper that would unroll when you threw them in the air."

"You're right again," Bill said. "The party was totally unplanned though. It just happened. We served 42 cases of beer that evening. On an average night we normally served two or three."

"Terry and I stayed up real late and my sister Joanie, then 14, danced more that night then ever before. Bill? How were the War years? With limited gas how did people get to Alpine?"

"First we thought that the Navy was going to take over the resort for a training base, but fortunately that didn't happen. A guy from Manitowoc came to my dad and uncle John, saying he needed some financial help to buy some buses so he could bring guests from Chicago and Milwaukee, from the port in Manitowoc (on Lake Michigan) to Egg Harbor. Our family helped him, and he would bring in five bus loads of 190 people and return the same number back to the port. As it turned out, we had some of our best years during the War."

Yes, VJ Day was a happy day for us and all Americans. It's one of those days that you remember exactly where you were when the announcement came, even if you were only nine years old.

Just as at the end of WWI, Johnny would come marching home again, hurrah, hurrah, along with cousins Merlin and Gerry Barlament, William and Robert Anderson, Raynold and Keith Quist, and George Leonard. We were indeed blessed, and thanked God for all of our family's safe return. 185 Brown County residents,

119

unfortunately, did not make it home.

As Paul Harvey is wont to say, "Now, you'll hear the rest of the story." Or at least another side of the story, courtesy of Richard J. Mayberry. Richard is a historian, economist, and writer who is the editor of Richard Mayberry's Early Warning Report for Investors, and whom I have met and exchanged ideas with. The following is taken from his notes to be used in his soon-to-be published book, The Rest of the Story About World War II.

After the Freedom of Information Act was passed in 1966, the other side of the WWII story began to emerge. And I Was There, written by Edwin L. Layton and published in 1985, as well as Day of Deceit, written by Robert B. Stinnett and published in 2000, give a different view from our family's and the American public's long held perception of the events leading up to the surprise attack on Pearl Harbor and U.S. entry into WWII.

According to Mayberry, Layton, who was the chief intelligence officer at Pearl Harbor, says in his book that FDR entered into a secret agreement to enter the war on the side of Britain should the Japanese strike British territories, months prior to December 7, 1941. That covered what was then Siam (Thailand), the Dutch East Indies and the Malay Peninsula. None of these areas were U.S. territories. The problems with this secret agreement were multifaceted. It violated the Neutrality Act, which the president signed in 1935, and the U.S. Constitution, which required Congressional approval; and the president failed to notify his military commanders in the area of their commitment to protect British interests. Mayberry believes FDR's act was treasonous.

Another perception supporting the above, from Goodwin's book, is that the U.S. agreed to a "second front" in western Europe to save the Russians from Hitler's invasion of Russia, and that the U.S. had to enter the war to prevent the invasion of Great Britain.[18] Not so, says Mayberry.

The battle for Britain ended on October 31, 1940, more

than one year before the U.S. entered the war, according to Mayberry. Hitler realized that there was no way that the German Army could invade the British Isles. They had no landing craft to effectively conduct an invasion. Bombing continued, for certain, but the threat of a direct assault on Britain ended when Hitler turned his attention eastward towards the "Big Bear," Russia. On June 22, 1941, the Germans invaded the Soviet Union. It was the beginning of the end for Hitler's troops when on September 12, 1941, snow began falling early on the barren plains of Russia. Like Napoleon before him, Hitler made the same error. Germany could defeat the Russian troops (which they did) but they couldn't defeat the Russian winter, where temperatures soon dropped to 50° below zero according to Mayberry.

The writer and historian says, "In June 1941, the Germans had gone into Russia with a half-million vehicles. By November, only 75,000 were still working. By December German transport was almost by horse and sled." Deep into Russia, on the outskirts of Stalingrad, the "Russkies" cut off the German supply lines; the Germans were weakened and vulnerable to attack by the weather-hardened and aggressive Russians. In truth, the war in Russia was over within a year as the Russians drove the Germans back into the "fatherland." According to the Guinness Book of Records, *the battle for Stalingrad, which lasted five months, resulted in a total of 1,110,000 deaths on both sides. Incredible as that number is, Stalin, in his reign of terror, caused the deaths of 43 million people[19] — mostly citizens of the Soviet Union.*

Mayberry's point is that FDR didn't have to enter the war to save the Russian Bear. The widely held American perception, then and now, is that the U.S. entered the war to stop Hitler, the most evil and dangerous man in history, when in reality Stalin was far more brutal and was then, and would remain, a greater threat to the security of the U.S. during the cold war.

Why, then, did the U.S. enter the war in Europe? To liberate France and other nations under control of the Nazi's? Or, as I alluded to earlier, did Harry Hopkins, as an agent for the Communist Party, prevail upon FDR to strengthen Russia's cause while depleting our own human and material resources? We'll probably never know, but given the power vested in Hopkins and the "military-industrial complex" fixed behind the throne, the president, like so many before and after him, is but a facilitator of their will.

The overwhelming view of the War as effectively illustrated by the movie Why We Fight, produced by Frank Capra, was as a battle of good vs. evil. Our parents never questioned our government's motives or complicity in provoking the War, and these beliefs were passed on to us. Mom and Dad went to their graves firmly believing that good triumphed over evil. The good guys did win, but now more than ever, as the "powers behind the throne" engage and involve our country in Afghanistan, Iraq and entanglements all around the globe, we must ask, Why?

Goodwin's book alludes to the fact that President Roosevelt goaded the Japanese into attacking Pearl Harbor, but she fails to pursue that line. Mayberry, quoting from Stinnett's book Day of Deceit, leaves little doubt that an eight-point plan hatched by Lieutenant Commander Arthur H. McCollum, which concludes that "Japan could be led to commit an overt act of war," was used in part to provoke the start of WWII.[20] It's unconscionable to think that 2,433 men lost their lives on December 7, 1941, as part of a scheme to inflame us and change America's desire for neutrality, but to those in power who pull the strings our soldiers are but puppets on a grand stage. That was not only true in 1941, as it is true today, but perhaps it has always been that way. The absolutism of kings in the past has been replaced by an unholy alliance that determines why we fight. Adding to the travesty of Pearl Harbor was the blame affixed on Admiral Husband Kimmel, who was the naval commander, and General Walter Short, who was the army commander, at Pearl Harbor. They were the designated scapegoats who had to fall on their swords for the president.

In 1953, the highly respected Fleet Admiral William F. Halsey wrote: "I have always considered Admiral Kimmel *and General Short to be splendid officers who were thrown to the wolves as scapegoats for something over which they had no control.[21] ... They are our outstanding military martyrs."*

But it wasn't until 1999 that the U.S. Congress declared that Kimmel wasn't responsible for what had happened at Pearl Harbor. This is some vindication for the Kimmel family but the widely held perception in America, postulated by Goodwin in her book, remains the same, and Roosevelt is the president who won "the big one."

1. Doris Kearns Goodwin, *No Ordinary Time: Franklin and Eleanor Roosevelt: The Home Front in World War II.* (New York: Touchtone, 1994), p. 339.
2. Ibid., p. 384.
3. Ibid., p. 394.
4. Brown County Central Library, Office of Price Stabilization.
5. Goodwin, op. cit., p. 340.
6. Ibid., p. 346.
7. Ibid., p. 344.
8. Ibid., p. 364.
9. M.A. Barlament, *Footprints in the Sands of Time*, p. 26.
10. Louis Gianetti, Flashback: A Brief History of Film, (Princeton, N.J.: Prentice Hall, 1986), p. 199.
11. Goodwin, op. cit., p. 598.
12. Ibid., p. 598.
13. Ibid., p. 602.
14. Ibid., p. 605.
15. Ibid., p. 610.
16. Ibid., p. 608.
17. Adam Zagorin, "Notebook," *Time*, March 3, 2003, p.
18. Goodwin, op. cit., p. 342.
19. R. J. Rummel, *Death by Government* (New Brunswick, N.J.: Transaction Publishers, 1994), p. 8.
20. Robert B. Stinnett, *Day of Deceit* (New York: Touchstone, 2000), p. 8.
21. Admiral Robert A. Theobald, *The Final Secret of Pearl Harbor* (New York: Devin-Adair, 1954), p. ix.

Hulda Andersson and Sam Anderson Wedding Picture

Is this the Kungsskogstorp (Andersson) farm or the
Kungsskogen schoolhouse in Varmland, Sweden? It could have

The Andersson Sisters
L/R: Elin, Marie, Hulda

Green Bay Industrial League Football 1901
Sam Anderson, top right

Menominee High School Basketball Team, 1921

Herbert A. (Hubby) Quist
Menominee High School, 1922

Thelma E. Anderson

The Quist Family, Menominee, Michigan, ca 1925
L/R: Raymond (Reinhold), Valberg (Ray's Wife), Robert, Knut, Clara, Fre and Herbert

The Quist Cousins at Grandfather Knut's Funeral March, 1938

Nicolet Bay, ca 1939

The "Quiz" Kids
L/R: Joan, Buster and Terry
Green Bay, Wisconsin, ca 1941

Buster and Billy, August 16, 1946
Probably Lake Michigan

1948

Above is the Elmore school team, champion
~~st~~ Side Sixth Grade Basketball league conduct
~~tor~~ Pintz. Front row, left to right, are **Calvin W**
~~y~~ Andersen and John Farr. Back row—**Harold P**
~~ry~~ Proctor, Buster Quist and Bob Boguski.

Elmore Elementary School, Sixth Grade, 1948
Jennie Hetherington - Principal (middle row left)
Buster Quist (top row right, next to Richard Williams)

Green Bay YMCA Junior Leaders, 1949-1950
Lee Prodehl (top left) and John Scovell (top right)

CHAPTER 5: A PERFECT TIME, A PERFECT PLACE

"HUB? I DIDN'T EXPECT YOU HOME until dinner time," Mom said. Dad, appearing glum, set his briefcase down in the multi-use office in our house.

"I didn't feel like making any calls. I had lunch with Bill from the bank at Kaap's (restaurant) and he put me in such a bad mood, I didn't feel like making any calls," Dad said with a decidedly dejected look on his face.

"What happened? You look like something the cat dragged in," said Mom, suspecting something bad was up.

"I wanted to discuss my plans for setting up my new office and my prospects for expanding my business, and Bill threw cold water all over it," Dad continued.

"Geez, I don't understand. Why would Bill be so negative?" Mom asked.

"Bill thinks that we're going to have another Depression. He says that all the G.I.s are coming home and there aren't enough jobs for them. And, since the plants are not making armaments any more, they'll be laying off those who are working. Just like my job at Northwest. They don't need me any more. It doesn't make any difference to me. I want to concentrate on insurance, anyways. But, the other guys need jobs," Dad explained further.

"Goodness gracious. If it's not one thing it's another," Mom said, using one of the well-worn clichés of the day.

"Here Gil (Gilbert Diehl, the Wisconsin Branch Manager for Business Men's Assurance Co. and Dad's immediate supervisor) wants me to set up an office and hire agents and Bill says it's a mistake. Geez n' plutz. I don't know who to believe. I've already committed to office space at the Columbus Building and looked at furniture and stuff. I just don't know what to do," Dad detailed, obviously perplexed and somewhat despondent. Dad was always optimistic so this revelation coming at this point in time was a real downer.

"Well Hub, you need to do what you think is right. You know best what you can do," Mom said, encouraging Dad to push forward with his plans. Privately, she wanted Dad to have an office — out of the house.

Bill and many other bankers all over the country were biased based upon their devastating experience from The Great Depression that continued to haunt them like a bad horror movie. One of the best anecdotal experiences that illustrate this perception was a banker in not-too-far-removed Duluth, Minnesota. So convinced was Maurice Florance that another depression was at hand that he sold his bank and other interests and moved to, of all places, Albuquerque, New Mexico, where, in a career change of gigantic proportions, Maurice formed an oil and gas exploration company. His prognostication of the future for the economy proved to be wrong, of course, but his nose for the smell of oil and gas proved to be fortuitous. Maurice, along with others, developed what was to become one of the largest untapped oil and gas reservoirs in the U.S. — the San Juan Basin. Maurice, or "M.J." as friends called him, was one of the pioneer icons and truly interesting characters in this new frontier. Ironically, the call and promise of opportunity from the desert plateaus of New Mexico would also come to 1140 Dousman Street a few years later. I had the good fortune to interface later with some of these rich and famous entrepreneurial "cowboys" like M.J., which will enrich and reward the reader in Books Two and Three.

What Bill, other bankers, economists, journalists and pundits of all stripes failed to assess was the pent-up demand for goods and services that had fermented during the four and one-half years during the war, and the amount of liquid cash savings that had been accumulated by the servicemen and a populace that had few opportunities and little desire to spend it.

There was a drastic shortage of housing in Green Bay

(and the entire country) as the Vets returned home and were anxious to start or re-start their families. A housing authority came into existence in Green Bay. The "baby boomer" generation was born but few recognized a phenomenon had been created which would impact the economy and our lives for decades to come.

Cousin Merlin Barlament, unable to find a place to live for himself and his new wife, Dorothy Wenell, soon gravitated from architecture to the building business, which would become his career after first building a home for himself.

If you wanted a new Chevy or Ford you put your name on a list at the garage, and with luck you might get a new car within six months. Top asking price. No "Deals." The less desirable lines like Nash, Studebaker, Hudson and Packard were available on a shorter waiting list. Dad opted for a blue 1946 Nash Ambassador 4-door Sedan. I think he actually made money on his pre-war "Olds." The G.I.s had to have a car and would pay a premium for a used car. Dad wouldn't buy a Studebaker because, he said, "You can't tell whether it's going forward or backwards." A well-worn joke of the day.

"Thelma, I'm sure glad I opened my office. I've got so many people and companies to see I have to have a full-time secretary to keep up," Dad, beaming, told Mom as he came home for a bite to eat before his next appointment. He hired a perky, young brunette by the name of Mabel Wall who became his "number one gal."

Another post-war phenomenon was occurring. People wanted health insurance but employers were reluctant to incur the cost of providing group health insurance coverage for employees and their families. BMA, Dad's new employer, was one of the originators of "wholesale" health insurance. These plans were a cross between what was then known as "true group insurance" for large companies, paid in part by the employer, and individual health insurance. BMA's "wholesale" health insurance plans were designed for employers who would not participate in the cost of the coverage, but would permit payroll deduction for the payment of the premiums. For that, BMA would discount the premiums. Dad was, if not the first, amongst the pioneers offering this type of coverage, and accumulated clients as fast as a snowball rolling down a steep slope.

Dad wrote coverage on the teachers who were members of the Brown County Teachers Association, the Green Bay City employees, the hospitals (including the nuns at St. Mary's and St. Vincent's) and a wide range of smaller, privately held companies. Dad was gregarious, outgoing and popular with his clients. Most importantly, they trusted him. His business flourished and soon within a few years it seemed that almost everyone in the town of 45,000 knew or had heard of "Hub" Quist, the insurance man.

About this time period a picture appeared in the *Green Bay Press-Gazette*, on the society page, featuring the three "Quist kids." We were three "soft, rosy-checked Swedes" favoring the fair complexions of our heritage. Mom had a beautiful complexion all her life, as did Aunt Fre and Grandmother Quist. I also benefitted from this genetic trait until the devastating and dangerous southwestern sun took its toll. Genetically, our ancestors from the cloudy and cold climes of Northern Europe weren't equipped with a natural sun screen.

"Dad? I'd sure like to have a bike for Christmas," I not so subtly suggested to my father, as Christmas 1945 approached.

"That might be tough. Just like getting a car. They're as scarce as hen's teeth. But, I'll tell you what ... if you'll help me sell Christmas trees at the Y (YMCA) this year, I'll see if I can find a bike for you," Dad proposed.

"Geez Dad, that's a deal," I responded, as I pictured myself riding down the sidewalk.

Terry, overhearing our conversation piped up.

"Dad, I want a train set. A Lionel train set with lots of track and lots of cars. Huh? Okay, Dad?"

"Well, same for you Terry. You can help me at the Y also and I'll see if Prange's has any train sets," Dad offered. At ages nine and seven, we no longer made a wish to Santa at Prange's. We went directly to the source, and he wasn't at the North Pole.

Dad was on the board of directors (or was soon to be) and he contributed considerable time to the Y, including the annual Christmas tree sale held in the parking lot. I can still feel the chill of the Green Bay winter as we helped the trees up, using holes in mounds of snow for the stands. Most of the spruce trees were one dollar. The large double balsams were $3.00. High cost, I'm sure but the sales were a fund raiser. On the day or two before Christmas Eve we practically gave the remaining trees away.

How can I possibly remember this seemingly insignificant event so long ago? My sister thinks my head is cluttered with irrelevant facts, but the recollections are there in the cortex of my brain and they keep popping out as I fondly recall those marvelous days when life was simpler.

"Shhh," I whispered to Terry as we eased our way down the stairs on Christmas Eve. Dressed in our PJs, we were anxious, as all kids are, to see what Santa would bring us as gifts. We knew Dad was Santa but we continued to carry on the tradition in spirit, anyways.

"Dad is settin' up my train set!" Terry whispered in my ear barely able to contain his excitement. (The complete set with real smoke and a whistle then cost about $30.)

"There's my bike! It's red. Geez, just like I wanted," I said softly as I could hear Dad and Mom talking in the kitchen. We scrambled up the stairs and jumped back into bed. It was difficult to sleep.

"The Schwinn is re-conditioned, Buster," Dad said. I didn't know what that word meant but my very own bike was perfect as far as I was concerned. (At $20, it was a terrific bargain.)

I also got a chemistry set, which was a big surprise. And, a model airplane kit. A P-38, as I remember. I spread it out on a table in the card room and worked on it most of Christmas Day. Mom was amazed that I could sit still that long in one place. Working meticulously with a special sharp hobby knife, balsa wood, glue and special paper I finished the P-38 and hung it by a string in my bedroom. Dad and Terry focused on his Lionel Train, and they had track laid out all over the living room floor. I can't remember what Joanie got for Christmas (and neither can she), but it probably was a coat or something practical.

In 1943, when I was seven, Dad introduced me to what was to become one of my most life-defining experiences. I became a member of the Young Men's Christian Association (YMCA) at the outrageous cost of six dollars per year. More importantly, I would meet a man, John M. Scovell, who would become my mentor and, next to Dad, the most important and influential man in my young life.

John M. Scovell, or "Johnny" as he allowed us to call him, came to the Y about the same time that I was born, in the midst of The Depression. A graduate of St. Norbert's College, Johnny, unable to find a full-time job, worked part-time at the Y as a locker boy. Over forty years would pass and John, a legend in his own time, would still be at his post at the Y. Counting the years back to his membership in 1925, John was a fixture in this great place of youth development for over fifty years.

There are YMCAs all over the country. What made this Y so different, so influential in building the bodies and character of young men? It was John Scovell and the dedicated YMCA Program Staff at the Green Bay Y. Thanks to my mom, who started a scrapbook for me at age ten, I can give the reader a precise insight into the thoroughness and the challenge of John's extensive athletic programs.

All boys, ages eight to fifteen, were broken down into three classes and competed with others in their same age group. Each boy was awarded points based upon his performance and attendance, and the ultimate goal was to eclipse 1000 points (the 1000 Point Contest) during the year from September to June. Not only were points awarded for performance in specific events, the competitor would also earn points for health habits, sportsmanship and leadership. We were instructed on how to take a shower properly. Mom believed cleanliness was as close to Godliness as you could get, so I scored highly in personal grooming. Once per month we had a Physical Achievement

Test and a report card to take home. A large, mimeographed report was mailed to my parents listing all of my marks.

"Buster! You're next," Johnny shouted, as it was my turn to climb the rope to the ceiling of the gym.

The report card says it was 18' to the band of white tape at the end of the rope, but to a kid nine years old I thought it was the height of the Empire State Building. It was scary. I was always afraid I'd lose my grip and fall to the mat below.

"You're almost there," Johnny shouted encouraging me to finish the climb. "Hurry! You can beat your record."

According to my report card, my best time in 1945-46 was 12.5 seconds, for which I earned 77 points. Several cards simply show a "P" for the climb, which I assume meant "pass" but over the time limit. My best score was 100 points in the Spring Board High Jump (5'1") and my poorest was free throws — only two out of ten. I also scored well in the other three jumping events, but finished just average in the sprints.

At the end of the Y year in June I had accumulated 782 points and finished second to Jack Stacker, who had 870. I remember Jack well. He had an amazing athletic build at age 13 when, at three years younger, I was still working off "baby fat." I edged my friend Tom Ruffing, who finished third, by 43 points. I suspect that it was my persistence and attendance that enabled me to finish second. I can't remember ever missing a Saturday at the Y until I got hurt.

According to my report card in December 1945 I was 5'0" tall and weighed 96 pounds. I was competing with ten year olds but I was only nine. How come? I have to admit, for the first time to anyone, that I lied about my age! Something a young Christian certainly shouldn't do. Why then, did I?

Johnny had formed a special group which he called the "Junior Leaders" and this elite corps all wore white uniforms with the red triangular Y emblem intertwined with a very distinctive L for Leader in the middle of their chests. To be a member, however, a boy had to be at least ten years old. In the fall of 1945, I was nine. My buddies Tom Docter, Tom Ruffing and Dick Jansen were all older and all Leaders. I wanted desperately to be like them. So, I lied and prayed that no one would find out. Something I've always regretted and swore to myself that I would never, ever do again.

The number one point-getter for 1946 was my friend Tom Docter (1016 points), who was a year older than I was. Tom went to Annunciation, the Catholic school in our neighborhood. Father Kiernan, the headmaster at Annunciation, wasn't in favor of his kids joining the Y. I never understood why, since we were all Christians, but Dickie, my closest friend, didn't join and I sure wanted to share the experience with him. Phil Thompson, who was 14, was second with 1002 points, and he and Tom both got gold ribbons. Phil was an outstanding athlete, especially at swimming as was validated later in his college days. (He also assisted me with his input on this book.)

After each gym class, and on each Tuesday afternoon, we hit the shower and the pool. I learned to swim, according to my dad, when I was four, so I didn't fear the water. That wasn't the case for some of my friends. One, in particular.

Otis Foster, whom we called "Otie" (everyone had a nickname except me because my name was already a nickname), had a phobia. Aquaphobia.

"Otie, you're shaking! What's wrong?" I asked my diminutive and skinny buddy as we stood on the edge of the pool, waiting our turn to determine how many lengths of the pool we could complete.

"I... I... I'm cold," Otie said, sliding his hands up and down his legs covered with "goose-bumps."

We were nude and it was the middle of winter so yes, it was cold, but there was more to it than that. Otie looked up at me sheepishly with sorrowful eyes and said softly:

"Buster, I, I...can't swim! I'm going to drown!"

"Geez, Otie. Tell Johnny," astonished, I replied.

"I can kinda swim in the shallow end but I'm afraid of

the deep end. Johnny thinks I can swim but I can't," Otie added, as my name was called to begin my laps. Worried about my friend, I jumped into the pool to swim my laps.

Somehow Otie made it. One lap at least. Adrenalin from fear can often propel a person to accomplish the unreachable. Otie overcame his fear and went on to become an excellent swimmer, as well as one heck of a basketball player. And, basketball was THE sport at the Y.

While waiting for our gym class my age group would shoot hoops in the small gym adjacent to the main gym. We closely observed the bigger boys like Eddie Mathews, Lyle Tobin, Dick Purath, my cousin Larry and others to glean what we could from their advanced skills, while at the same time trying to avoid getting run over and knocked to the floor. At 6'2" and only age 12, Terry Rand was the biggest kid and the best basketball player at the Y — despite the fact that he was an "eastsider." By the time Terry was 18 he would grow to 6'9." In a couple of years, I would be old enough to play on the Leaders team.

Our Saturday classes began at 8:30 a.m. and lasted until noon. Often, if I had a quarter, I would have lunch at the Y cafeteria. The chicken and dumplings were absolutely out of this world. I could get the dumplings, veggies, pie and a large glass of milk for 25¢.

Early in the fall or in late spring I would walk to my dad's office at the Columbus Building a couple blocks away, and he would take me with him to Shorewood Golf Club and I would caddie for him. Dad, like most everyone else, worked on Saturday mornings. Quite often I would walk to Gramma's house, which was about a mile away, and have lunch with her. She would always have fresh baked cinnamon rolls or "kaffekucken" waiting for me. The most fun, however, was "riding" the bus home in the winter on Tuesday nights.

"Otie, the streets are packed (with snow and ice), let's ride the bus home," I said to my short, wiry, little buddie.

"You mean holding on to the bumper?" Otie asked. "Uh, uh — that's too darn dangerous for me."

"Oh, geez, Otie. It's not dangerous. Dick (Jansen) and I are going to do it. Geez, you can save a nickel in fares," I suggested.

"Nope! I'm goin' <u>in</u> the bus, not behind it. Besides, you could let go and some car would run over you," Otie added.

"Oh geez Otie. You're a 'scaredy cat,'" I admonished my friend.

Otie got aboard the bus. Dick and I waited for the bus to leave the curb and then we ran and latched on to the bumper. Aside from the exhaust fumes it was a thrilling ride.

Until —

The bus stopped before passing over the Walnut Street bridge. More people got on. The bus couldn't move. The rear wheels were spinning on the ice in the gutter. Suddenly, the bus driver appeared around the corner of the bus.

"Hey you kids! Get outta there!" the driver shouted belligerently.

The burly driver grabbed me by the large collar on my coat and knocked me around pretty good. Dick took off running. The driver stormed off and got in the bus. Otie waved to me from the back window as the bus pulled away. I never rode "free" again.

New Year's Day 1946 was considerably different than the first day of the year anywhere in America today. There were a few football bowl games, but there was no such thing as T.V. and the perennial couch potato hadn't yet bloomed. Where and how did the Quists celebrate New Year's Day? At the Y.

January 1 was an "Open House" for Dad, Mom and the family. All the boys in the Y program performed for their parents. Gymnastics were called tumbling and the flying rings and parallel bars were performed on an "apparatus." My Junior Class held an Indian Club Soccer game, but I couldn't tell you how it differed from the game as we now know it. We demonstrated each of our achievement tests and concluded with a basketball game. I'm certain that my parents were favorably impressed with the formidable and extensive program that Johnny had designed for the members. I'm absolutely certain that they felt that, for $6, they certainly got their money's worth. The return on my parents' investment was, and still is, incalculable.

In 1941, the summer before the War, when I was five, I went to Y camp which was located at Chute Lake at Mountain, Wisconsin. I was several years underage but Dad was a counselor so I got to go, as did my cousin Larry. I remember one incident as if it occurred as recently as a few years ago — give or take sixty.

"Okay boys, we're going to test your swimming ability," Dad said to all the boys in our cabin as we stood on the dock. "I want you to jump in off the dock here and swim out to the raft and return back here. One at a time, okay?"

Almost everyone said, "okay."

Some of the boys jumped in. Some dove off the dock. Some exhibited great form as they made it out to the raft and back smoothly. Some "dog paddled" and were exhausted by the time they got to the raft, and couldn't make it back. They failed and would have to confine their swimming to an area cordoned off close to the beach. I thought I would be "different."

I dove in. The water was dark and murky. I stayed underwater using a crab stroke. My goal was to reach the raft out of the sight of everyone.

A few seconds elapsed. I didn't surface.

Fifteen seconds or more passed. Still no sight of Buster.

Dad panicked and he jumped into the lake!

Another counselor serving as a lifeguard in a dinghy paddled vigorously to my presumed spot. My cabinmates peered anxiously at the murky but unsullied surface of the lake looking for a sign, some movement. There was none. Everyone on the dock was anxious.

Out of air and my lungs bursting I finally surfaced! Incredibly, almost adjacent to the floating raft.

"There he is!" Someone shouted. I heard a few cheers. Then, I heard my father's wrath.

"Buster! Get back here right now!" he shouted.

As I made it back to the dock I sheepishly climbed the ladder.

Dad, dripping wet but hot with embarrassment and anger, grabbed me by my arm forcibly.

"Showing off, huh? Don't you ever do a stunt like that again or I'll ..."

Dad never finished the sentence but I got the message. My friends thought it was swell, though. My propensity to "show off" surfaced early in life. Couldn't help it. It must have been in my genes.

The real summer activities, however, centered around the city parks. Terry and I participated at Fisk Park, which was only a couple of (long) blocks from our house. Larry Fitchett, our next door neighbor, worked for some time for the park department, and his close friend Lee Dalforge headed up the various youth programs at Fisk. Like the Y programs, the Green Bay City Park system was well organized and everyone involved dedicated themselves to providing the best possible guidance and motivation for all the city's youth.

Softball was number one on my list. I played third base on the Fisk Park Junior Midgets Softball Team from 1946 to 1948. At ten years of age I was probably one of the few kids who could get a throw on the fly from third to first. A brief episode caught on color film shows me taking practice swings in our flashy, satin-like maroon uniforms.

Tom Ruffing played first base. I admired his loosey-goosey approach to the game and his ability to scoop up every ground ball and bad throw that came his way. Maybe it was because Tom had a famous baseball name that I thought he was good, and he certainly was one of our team leaders.

Jerry DeGroot was our pitcher. All teams rely on their pitchers and Jerry, a tall, lanky, blonde, curly-haired kid stood out as an exceptional performer. Tragedy would soon strike my friend.

My best friend Dickie played outfield. He would stop by my house each day and we would ride our bikes to the park together. Tom Docter, as exhibited at the Y, was one of our outstanding players, as was Paul Noak, our catcher (who was also an April Fool). Tom Renard, our alternate pitcher, and Calvin Whiting, my friend from Elmore School, were also on our team. Dave Evjue, who lived adjacent to the park, backed up Tom at first base. There were a lot of moms that didn't have to worry about their kids — where they were and what they were doing. We were safe and preoccupied at the park.

We played teams from all the parks on the west side. Jerry and Harold Proctor played at Tower Park, as did many of my friends from Elmore School. There were teams at Tank (we incorrectly pronounced it like an army tank), Seymour, Fort Howard (where my buddy Otie played), Marquette and probably other parks, and the west side champ would play our adversaries from across the river for the city championship at the end of July.

Our coaches were appropriately named "Parkies" — senior high school and college students who worked and managed all of us kids during the summer. I never missed a day at the park — except when it rained.

The erosion of time does not wash away certain events in one's life — particularly those that conjure up the fear of dying. Without the benefit of research I can recount this event stamped with indelible ink on the cortex of my mind.

In January of 1946 a young girl (six years of age) in Chicago was kidnaped and murdered. Her name was Suzanne Degnan. Her abductor, as I recall, maneuvered a ladder to a second story porch where he was able to enter her bedroom and kidnap her. As I read the account of this heinous crime I had visions of a sinister-looking character placing a ladder to our second floor porch and carrying out a similar deed. I must have been traumatized by the event. I was afraid of that porch and I recoiled with fear in the summer when my parents kept the windows and the porch door open for ventilation.

I have often regretted the fact that I could read at an early age. That aptitude plus a hyperactive imagination elucidated a number of goblins and ghosts.

At times divine intervention seems to guide my hand as I write this memoir. On January 13, 2002, a TV news special carried the story of the commutation of the life sentences of *all the convicted murderers at the state prison in Illinois. One of the felons was "The Lipstick Killer." The killer of six-year-old Suzanne Degnan in 1946 wrote in lipstick on the bathroom wall, "Stop me before I kill again." He did kill again. Two more times. This traumatic event <u>was</u> chiseled in my mind. Was this discovery 57 years later a strange circumstance? Or, is something else at work here?*

Then, on December 31, 2003, on a TV program, "American Justice," the convicted killer of Suzanne Degnan, William George Heirens, appeared on the show proclaiming his innocence 57 years later. Heirens, only age 17 in 1946, claimed that he was the victim of mass hysteria created by the press who sensationalized the murder. There were, in fact, three murders. In addition to Suzanne there were two adult women who were similarly and gruesomely dismembered. It was a quiet period after the War where six newspapers in Chicago were competing for business and each was trying to out scoop the others. The grisly stories mandated that the police solve this heinous crime, and in Heirens' opinion he was the only one they could circumstantially connect to the crimes.

As the summer softball season of 1946 came to a close there were great expectations ahead for next year's team, but storm clouds, like premonitions of doom, were building on the horizon, casting a dark shadow on all of our future lives. A devastating and frightening epidemic had begun to incubate, but wouldn't reach our hamlet for almost two years.

"Thelma?" Dad said as he burst into the kitchen after parking his new Nash in the garage. "I got us a big cabin at Fish Creek for two weeks in August. Isn't that terrific?"

"How big is it?" Mom asked.

"It's a 3-bedroom. The Edgewater Cottages are right on the main street close to the beach. Grandma, Larry and all of us will fit in comfortably," Dad elaborated.

"Geez Dad, what's Fish Creek like?" Joanie asked.

"It's fantastic … just fantastic," Dad replied.

"Sounds great Hub. How much does it cost?" Mom asked. Always concerned about Dad's spending habits, it seemed.

"Forty bucks a week. Isn't that terrific?" Dad responded enthusiastically, because cabins were hard to find now that people could, and wanted to, travel.

Thinking about last year's experience on the rocky shores of Egg Harbor I naturally asked, "Is there a sandy beach, Dad."

"Yup — and it's only half-a-block away. I saw it myself. I was in Sturgeon Bay to call on the shipyards and I went up there. We're going to enjoy Fish Creek," Dad said.

Dad, I learned much later, had established a "beach head" of sorts in Door County. His clients owned several of the shipbuilding companies in Sturgeon Bay, the gateway to the upper peninsula of Door County.

———

Of all of Dad's interests and avocations, golf and fishing had to be foremost, in both time spent and satisfaction gained. He was quite proficient at both. Fish Creek, appropriately, was the perfect spot for the latter.

My first recorded fishing experience with Dad was memorialized by a photograph taken, as best I can determine, in the summer of 1938 in Peninsula State Park, when I was approximately 18 months of age. Dad is holding me in his left arm in the back seat of a small fishing boat with a fly rod gripped firmly in his right hand. A pith helmet is protecting Dad's bald head from the bright summer sun, as his attention is divided by his love for the sport and his son.

Another and even more precious photograph depicts my grandfather, Sam Anderson, with Joanie, my cousin Larry and myself on a dock, with Grandpa holding a fishing rod with his line in the water. The picture was undoubtedly taken the same summer of 1938 as the picture with my dad, as I appear to be about eighteen months old. It is one of only a few surviving pictures of Grandpa Sam, and the only one with his grandchildren. Grandpa died shortly thereafter in 1940, as I indicated earlier.

Vivid memories of actual fishing experiences,

reinforced by numerous home movies, date back to this year, 1946, at Fish Creek. By then, at age 10, I was not only schooled in the art of fishing but I was allowed to operate our 12-foot Petersen fishing boat, with its 5 horse power Johnson motor, within the confines of the harbor at Fish Creek. Sans life jackets Terry and I would cruise the harbor at Fish Creek with the stipulation that when the swells in the bay were high enough to sport "white caps," we had to dock the boat. Amazingly, with that proven track record of mischief and mishaps that Terry and I earned with dubious distinction over our formative years, there were no boating or water-related incidents. It was the only unblemished record that we earned, that I can recall.

Terry and I learned early how to "pack the boat" for fishing trips. We developed a mental checklist for all the necessary tools of the trade needed to spend several hours on the water. Mom almost always fixed sandwiches, and the ice cooler had A&W Root Beer, Coca Cola, and Orange Crush soft drinks. All along the Door County peninsula, a successful catch for the day would include smallmouth bass, perch, bluegills, crappie, walleye and, if we were lucky, a sturgeon or a Northern Pike. Dad's primary target was the smallmouth bass. Pound for pound he thought they were the best fighters in the bay. The ultimate goal was a 5-pounder, but they were as rare as ending a day on the water without a mosquito bite. To Dad, however, the highest fisherman's echelon was stream fishing. Armed with his fly rod, he would forge the streams in his "waders" catching rainbow and German brown trout. The beautiful multi-colored rainbow was a special prize, as exhibited in several films and photographs.

For two young, energetic boys however, several hours on the bay could be pretty darn boring. Aside from the periodic, "Have you had a bite yet?" from Dad, not much dialog was usually exchanged. (The incident below being an exception.) Often I would lie down on the seat cushions with my casting rod braced against the side of the boat with an eye on the bobber. Recorded in my mind is the rhythmic sound of the small waves lapping against the side of the boat. The sound was and still is hypnotic.

Along with the occasional thrill of the catch and the immeasurable pleasure of soaking in the omnipresent panorama of the bay's clear blue water, the evergreen forests and the contrasting sky, was the grimy and messy "stuff" — cleaning the fish and hunting for bait.

Using a 6 or 8 inch knife to remove the scales on the fish was easy. Puncturing and splitting the belly of the still living, breathing creature and then unceremoniously, like a medieval executioner, cutting off the fish's head was the tough part. Removing the blood and guts completed the necessary process. I can't say that Terry and I enjoyed this aspect of the sport but we accepted it with few complaints, and by the time we spent the entire summer in Door County in 1949, we were responsible for almost all the fish cleaning. Occasionally, Mom was pressed into service on the cleaning end as well as the cooking, but Joanie wasn't a party to the "man's sport."

Although we often used artificial lures to catch the fish, most of our bait was natural. Angleworms or nightcrawlers (earthworms) were the primary candidates. At night, after a heavy rain, Dad, Terry and I (and occasionally Cousin Larry), armed with a flashlight, would go to Fisk Park and search for the long, slimey, brown worms that would abandon their wet, saturated, subterranean world for a drier environment. Stretched out in the short grass, they were an easy target if we moved fast enough. It always amazed me that these eyeless earth worms could react to a light they ostensibly couldn't see, and quickly retreat down an invisible hole. We gathered them by the dozens into glass jars and transferred them to a dirt filled box at home until needed for the next fishing trip. Some anglers maintain that it's the odor of the earthworms that attracts the fish. If that's true they must like some pretty smelly stuff.

Another type of bait that was irresistible to bass, in particular, was the mayfly, or what we referred to then as the "Green Bay Fly." These are flying insects about the size of a man's thumbnail, that develop from aquatic nymphs and transform butterfly-like into a flying insect. They have fragile, translucent wings and enjoy a very limited life span in the month of May. Given the right weather conditions they could populate the early evening sky like a swarm of locusts. In the evening, Dad would skewer a couple of them on a hook and, casting delicately with his fly rod so as not to rip them off the hook, he would attempt to catch bass feeding in the shallow water. I can recall numerous times seeing the mayfly floating on the placid surface in amongst the lily pads near sunset, while Dad, like a puppeteer, mimicked the fly's moves with a barely perceptible flip of his wrist. Suddenly and usually with great fanfare and splash, the fly would be swallowed by the hungry fish. Unfortunately, it usually was "may day" for Mr. Bass.

Dad, like any other experienced fisherman, had his "spots." He also had certain spots for certain times of the day. Like afternoons near Camp Meenahga — the girls' camp near Fish Creek. One day about 1:00 p.m. Dad, Cousin Larry, and I headed for the camp. I was in the front of our boat manning the anchor. Larry was the pilot and Dad was in the middle seat. Our modest 12-foot fishing boat was all hard wood and was well maintained, since we had just sanded and varnished her that spring.

Camp Meenahga, named for a verse in Longfellow's epic poem *Song of Hiawatha*, was a private summer camp for "city girls" that was founded in Peninsula State Park in 1916. Unfortunately, or fortunately depending on your perspective, the raft that was the center of the girl's swimming activity was close to Dad's "spot." The conversation on this day after arriving in Fish Creek in 1946 went something like this:

"Slow her down, Larry. We're near our spot," Dad shouted to the back of the boat over the engine's noise. "Get the anchor ready, Buster. Drop her when I tell you, okay?"

"Okay, Dad. I'm ready," I replied.

"Cut it Larry," Dad instructed, as our boat slowly drifted to a stop. "Drop the anchor on this side, Buster; get it on top of the ledge. It's too deep on the other side," Dad advised as he dropped a second anchor at the rear of

142

our boat.

"That's good ... that's good. We should be able to hold her here guys, even though the waves are getting up," Dad said, addressing both of us.

"Whataya think we should use here, Hub?" Larry asked.

"Why don't you guys start with worms and a bobber, okay?"

"Okay," we both responded in unison.

"And ... let's see ... set the slip bobber about 20' up from the hook, okay? It's deep off the ledge. I think about 20' is about right. I'm going to use my casting rod and see if they'll go for the ole daredevil today," Dad said as he laid out our game plan.

Larry and I got our lines ready. I added a little more lead sinker to my leader but had to take one pellet off because it was too heavy for my bobber. Larry had his line in for only a few minutes.

"Got a bite, Hub!" Larry said excitedly as his bobber danced on the water like a duck bobbing for snacks on a pond.

"Let him take her, Larry. Let him get a taste of that nightcrawler," Dad said as he watched the action of the bobber. "He's got it Larry ... gentle now ... set the hook."

"I got 'em. It's a bass, I think."

"Yeah, it's a bass. I can tell by looking at your rod. Let him run but keep your line tight ... don't give him a chance to spit it out, Larry."

"Geez ... he's a fighter," Larry said as his outmanned opponent fought for his life. The battle continued for four or five minutes.

"He's pooped out Larry. Bring him close to the boat. I've got the net ready," Dad said.

"Whoopsie Daisy," Dad said as he missed with the net. On the next pass with the net Dad deftly brought the bass into our boat.

"He's a dandy ... about two pounds, I'd guess," Dad said. "You handled him well, Larry. Good start, huh?" Dad added.

No sooner had Dad said that and was helping Larry get the hook out of the bass' mouth when I felt a nibble on my line.

"Dad, I've got a bite," I said, suppressing both my enthusiasm and sound fearing I would warn other fish below.

"He's probably just nippin' on the worm, Buster. Wait until the bobber goes under."

"Okay."

More nibbles and then my prospect took the bait. I gave a quick pull on my rod.

"Ah nuts," I said. "He got away."

"That's okay," Dad said. "You're going to miss a few. Probably a small one anyway. Most nibblers are. Check your line. He may have taken your bait."

"Okay," I said as I reeled in the line. "Geez, Dad, he ate the whole worm."

"Fish are pretty smart, Buster. Put another on and go back down and get him," Dad offered. "He's still there."

All was quiet for a few minutes as Dad cast his line about sixty or seventy feet out over the deep water. He wanted to draw the bigger bass out from under the ledge using a red and white striped daredevil lure. You could see the bright spoon-like lure dance in the clear water as he reeled it in. Suddenly, a dark shadow darted out from under the ledge and grabbed the lure.

"He's got it," Dad said, pleased that his strategy worked. "Got a dandy."

Dad played his catch masterfully, like a musician would play a violin. Larry handled the net as the exhausted bass couldn't even do the usual flopping around on the bottom of the boat.

"Hmmm. Good size, huh?" What do you guys think ... three or four pounds?"

Larry thought the smallmouth bass weighed about three. I thought it was bigger than that. No matter. It was a "dandy."

Within an hour or so we had six "keepers." We threw three back hoping they would go down and tell their grandparents about the menu du jour we offered.

All was going well until the screaming and yelling started. The girls from the camp had arrived for their afternoon swim and within minutes half of the squadron of screeching and giggling teenagers were on the raft within 50 yards of our boat.

"Gosh darn ... they're going to ruin the fishing Dad. All that noise and splashing will scare all the fish away," I protested.

"Naw, it won't. The fish are used to it. The girls swim every day," Dad assured me.

While I was focused on my bobber, Dad and Larry were paying more attention to the girls! In fact, Dad had put away his casting rod and taken out his movie camera and began taking pictures of the noisy "intruders." Larry's attention was obviously directed to the raft also.

"Hey, are we goin' to fish or what?" I asked. Dead silence. Dad and Larry were so goggleyed that they didn't even hear me. But, I was right. Over the next thirty minutes or so, there wasn't a single bite. Finally Dad said:

"We've done all the good we can do here guys. Let's move on over to Weborg Point and do some casting."

It was a good day, I guess. We caught an assortment of bass, perch and a couple of crappies. When we returned to the dock at Edgewater Dad told Larry and me to clean the ten fish and he would unload the boat. That was okay because I wanted to talk to my cousin since he was fifteen and I was only ten. There was something I needed to know and I sure didn't want to ask my Dad. We started cleaning the fish next to the dock below our cabin.

"Larry, what does 'stacked' mean? You and Dad said a couple of those girls at the camp were really 'stacked.'"

"Yeah ... that red-head was built like a brick .... house," Larry said.

"Huh? Whataya mean?"

"She had a terrific figure ... you know, a great body."

"Yeah, but what does 'stacked' mean? I don't get it."

"She has great boobs ...," Larry informed me.

"Oh, that's what they're called?"

"Yeah. Geez, you don't know s—- from shine-ola do you?"

"Geez Larry, I'm only ten. I don't know anything about girls. I can't ask Dad. You can tell me, can't you?"

"Sure. Sure I can but don't tell your parents, okay?"

"Okay."

With that introduction thus began my first lesson on the birds and bees and all that stuff. What began as just another fishing trip turned out to be one of life's memorable experiences.

"One thing I don't understand Larry."

"Yeah, what?"

"Why did Dad take movies of those girls at the camp? We don't know any of them."

"Geez I don't know. Maybe he just likes to look at girls, huh?"

"Yeah, I guess," I said, unconvinced that Larry's answer was the real answer.

But, that really was the real answer, as I would soon learn.

———

"Dad! Dad! There's a Viking ship at the dock. A Viking ship!" I yelled as Terry and I burst into the front door of our cabin.

"Really?" Dad, questioning our seemingly outlandish claim, said.

"Come on. Come on. We'll show you," Terry suggested as he attempted to pull Dad out of his comfy chair.

Reluctantly, Dad agreed to journey down to the main dock, which was only a block or so away. But sure 'nuf. We weren't kidding. There was the Viking ship just as we had said.

"Well, I'll be darned," Dad said, as he surveyed the 36' replica of a Viking ship that had particular significance to us as Swedes.

The Viking ship, named "Serpent of the Sea," was the creation of Charles A. Kinney, a shop teacher from Skokie, Illinois, who built the ship in 1925. Kinney established the Adventure Island Camp for boys, which was located on the largest of the Strawberry Islands, approximately two and one-half miles from Fish Creek. Kinney, known as "Skipper," operated the camp (incredibly) for 35 years.

The "Vikings" who sailed and rowed the boat were boys our age. Terry and I desperately wanted to join their ranks and return with them back in time to their "Adventure Island," but Dad wouldn't concede to our request. We did meet some of the boys at the "Summertime Gift Shop" and they shared with us their imaginary experiences as Vikings and pirates while enjoying a chocolate malt or shake. The "Summertime" was also our favorite place to get a penny box of "SunMaid Raisins."

Terry made another remarkable discovery.

"Daddy! There's a goat <u>eating</u> a license plate on a car next door."

Dad amused, laughed, not believing what Terry reported but curious enough to venture outside.

"Well I'll be darned!" Dad exclaimed. "That billy goat has eaten half of the plate!"

As it turned out, the Illinois plates were made of a composite material that wasn't metal, and the goats loved it. Since a large percentage of the vacationers to Fish Creek were from the Chicago area, the goats found the black and orange plates quite a treat.

Joanie soon met and became fast friends with Barbara Bondie, an attractive, tall and slender blonde who was from Milwaukee and, along with her parents, resided in the cottages adjacent to the Edgewater. I remember Mr. Axel Bondie well, especially after one particular incident.

"Axel? Geez, that's a funny name," I pondered as we sat on the porch of his cottage, which was directly on the Bayshore.

Well, you don't think the axle on a car is funny do you, Buster?" Mr. Bondie, who was a very tall and large man with silver-blond hair, replied.

"Oh, yeah ... an axle on a car," I said as I reflected for a moment. "I think I'll call you axle grease," I said for some unknown reason.

Mr. Bondie jumped to his feet and, towering over me like a Goliath, his white, powdery complexion now reddened with anger, said:

"Young man! You are to call me MR. Bondie! Do you understand? I hate smartalecks — especially kids who are smartalecks!"

I was devastated. Joanie was embarrassed. Cowered, I said, "I'm sorry Mr. Bondie. I didn't mean to be fresh."

"You should address all adults by Mr. or Mrs. Don't you ever do that again," he admonished me.

I never did.

Despite my impudence, Joanie and Barbara remained best friends, as did our families. Not all our new acquaintances, however, were long-lasting with pleasant memories.

Residing in the same cottages as the Bondies was a boy exactly my age. His name was Billy. I don't remember his last name or what his parents looked like, but the memory of him has haunted me since this summer of 1946. One photograph of us together on the beach must have been taken just days before tragedy struck suddenly and without warning. In my mother's handwriting the inscription on the reverse side of the photograph says, "Buster and Billy Aug. 16/46."

"Buster? Billy's mother is here," Mom said as she answered the door of our cabin. "She's looking for Billy."

"I haven't seen Billy since this morning, Mom. We were fishing for crabs down near the main dock but I got a couple of blood suckers on my legs and I quit and came home," I informed Mom while Billy's mother peered into our cabin.

"Did he stay there near the dock?" Billy's mom asked looking concerned. "I thought he was still with you."

"Geez, I don't know. I just kinda left 'cause I was having trouble pulling the suckers off and I wanted to get some salt to pour on them," I informed Billy's mom.

"Oh, goodness," Billy's mom sighed. "Will you help me look for him, Buster?"

"Sure. Oh geez, sure," I offered as Terry and Mom

joined me. Gramma stayed at the cabin.

Terry and Mom went west on Main Street. I went with Billy's mom down to the Bay shore and showed her where we were fishing for crabs. We used a string with a little cheese on the end of it to coax the little rascals out from under the rocks. They would pinch the cheese and we'd pull them up. They were like miniature lobsters.

We were calling for Billy when we noticed a crowd of people on the main dock. Billy's mom, seemingly sensing that somehow the gathering crowd related to her son, began running to the spot. Tentatively, I followed.

"What happened?" I asked one of the men standing in the crowd. I couldn't see what everyone was looking at.

"A young boy has drowned. They just pulled him up," the man said.

I had a sickening feeling in my stomach. I didn't want to look but I inched my way past the legs of the grownups that formed a barrier between me and the center of attention on the dock. I broke through the crowd. I could see Billy's mom on her knees, crying with her arms around her son. I was stunned. Billy was a faint bluish color. He was dead. I turned and ran. I didn't stop until I got home.

"If I hadn't left and gone home Billy wouldn't have died," I said to Mom, tears streaking down my cheeks, as she held me close and stroked my head. "It's not your fault Buz. It's not your fault," Mom reassured me.

Apparently when the bay gets a little rough and the swells crash against the dock, currents can develop that can pull a person under the dock. In my mind's eye I can still picture places in the concrete structure that were open under the dock and the water would swirl and rise and fall, often violently, in and out of those openings. Billy must have ventured too close. It was my first experience with death. (The openings under the dock are no longer there.)

In retrospect, another amazing aspect of our experiences at Fish Creek was our lack of fear of the dangers of the water. Terry and I, at the ages of ten and seven, often went to the beach alone, without our parents, and we never wore life jackets when we tooled around the harbor alone in our boat. The three of us learned to swim early and we swam well, but then again I imagine so did Billy. We were lucky.

When you're a youngster two weeks seems like an eternity, but the remaining days at Fish Creek vanished all too quickly. Maybe because of Billy's death, I wanted it to end. All the summer fun seemed to dissipate like the air from a birthday balloon. I don't know but suddenly the Labor Day weekend was over, which always marked the end of summer. I started fifth grade at Elmore School. I was anxious to be back and see old friends. They helped me to try to forget about Billy.

Now at about five feet three inches tall I was, for the first time, as tall as my teacher. Helen Ferslev was a diminutive, attractive, well-groomed young lady, about thirty years old, dedicated to the education of her kids. She was also Scandinavian (Danish) and seemed to take a particular interest in an 11-year-old Swede with an inquisitive mind.

"Your son is interested in everything, Mrs. Quist," Miss Ferslev said to Mom during her first parents' conference in the fall of 1946. "He has a keen interest in history. Wisconsin history is of particular interest to me so I have much to share with him."

"Does he behave himself in class, Miss Ferslev?" Mom asked.

"He's a very energetic young man, but he's respectful and takes instructions seriously," Miss Ferslev replied. "We've had field trips to Fort Howard Hospital, Tank Cottage and the Hazelwood Historical House so far this year. Buster is full of questions when we're on the field trips."

"I hope he doesn't make a pest of himself," Mom interjected. (Mom had a favorite saying — you're a P-I-S-T, pest. I don't know what she was alluding to but she used it often.)

"Heavens no," Miss Ferslev responded. "Children who are curious are almost always the best students. My guess is that Buster will be a good student and will probably have a genuine interest and sense of history."

Miss Ferslev was right. I had the good fortune to interview her at age 84 to record her impressions. Helen, as she permitted me to call her, achieved considerable success in her life-long profession. She co-authored It Happened Here *in 1949, which was a history of Wisconsin. She also did extensive research on the Moravian movement, which I've explored because of my relationship to this relatively obscure religious sect. Helen was recognized by her peers by being elected President of the Wisconsin State Principals Association and became President of the National Association in the 1960's.*

In 1976 she wrote, for the benefit of gradeschoolers, in A Young Look at Old Green Bay: *"My mother remembered farther back than I could. My grandmother remembered farther back than she could. My grandmother knew people who remembered even farther back. Each family could tell the younger ones some of the things that had happened in the past."*

Miss Ferslev told every class, "If you know your family history, your memory will stretch back for decades." Little did either of us know at the time that the seed for this memoir could have germinated in 1946-1947 at Elmore School. My greatest hope is that in the creation of Rediscovering America! *I've delivered a valuable gift to future generations of family and those that share my sense of history and the wonderful era we grew up in.*

"I've got a surprise for you boys," Dad said as he held a large box in each hand. Terry and I were mystified. Eagerly we tore open the boxes like lions ravaging their prey. (Packers as you may not know, were named for meat packers, so I had to use another analogy.)

"A helmet!" Terry exclaimed. "A football helmet." It had a black leather top with a beige front.

"Look carefully," Dad enjoined. "It's a special helmet."

"It's got names on it," Terry observed.

"Holy cow! Here's Tony Canadeo's signature. And Ted

Fritsch ... and Irv Comp ... and Don Hudson and Jack Jacobs. Gosh!" I effused, finding it difficult to contain my enthusiasm.

Dad had secured the autographs of many of the Green Bay Packers. We were the envy of our friends as we played make-up games at Fisk Park and in our backyard field, memorialized on yards of film. I played quarterback and Terry, now quite stocky and powerfully built, was a running back. Our dilemma, however, was that as we continued to use our coveted helmets, the autographs began to fade.

Given the number of boys in our neighborhood, we had some pretty good games in the field behind our house. Dickie, of course, along with Norbert and Jimmy Spitzer, Johnny and Mike Culligan, Lee Olson, Jeffrey Denison and others enabled us to have at least five players on each side.

The Packers, of course, brought enormous recognition and pride to Green Bay which, at this point in time, had a population of approximately 45,000 totally dedicated fans. The team, owned and coached by their founder, Curly Lambeau, was one of the original professional football teams in the US dating back to the 1920's, prior to the formation of the National Football League.

Through Dad's connections with the team we also enjoyed an unusual privilege. Coach Lambeau owned (or had access to) a magnificent vacation home on a large tract of land in Door County, which he utilized as a pre-season training site for the team. I can vividly recall on one of our trips to Fish Creek being permitted to watch a practice session at Curly's home. Both the autographed helmets and our ability to be permitted into a "closed" practice session were testimonies to Dad's stature in the community. But, all that was subservient to the real McCoy — a Packer game. One game in particular, for several reasons, sticks out in my mind.

It's October 11, 1947. It was a "nippy" but sunny day at the East High Stadium, which was a modest, old wooden facility even in that day. Dad memorialized the game on film. I suspect that Terry and I were both in attendance, taking Mom's place in the stands. Many of the record crowd of 25,502 fans had come to see the Chicago Cardinals star running back Charley Trippi. We weren't disappointed. He was the star of the game and the "Cards" won the hotly-contested battle 14-10 to take the lead in the NFL's Western Conference. Several aspects of the game were memorable.

In an unnamed sportswriter's account of the game in the *Green Bay Press-Gazette* the next day, the writer wrote: "Trippi, running hard, returned Indian Jack Jacobs' punt twenty-two yards to start a drive."

Every time Jack Jacobs' name was mentioned in this and every written account while he played at Green Bay was preceded by the designation "Indian." An accepted and possibly expected practice of the day but I wondered what the writer's purpose was. I had a classmate at Elmore School, Connie Webster, who also was an Indian (now Native American), but she wasn't singled out as such. I recall that she was a neat, well-dressed, attractive girl who was quiet and unassuming. I didn't think she was "different," but the adults must have.

Although he didn't start on this day, Irv Comp was a quarterback. What made Comp stand out in my mind is that he had only one eye.

As a youngster, I thought it was remarkable that a quarterback could play with one eye. Every quarterback with <u>two</u> eyes was vulnerable to a "blind side" sack. Imagine the prospect with only one. Later, as a QB myself trying to "see the whole field," I always remembered Irv Comp, the one-eyed quarterback, with admiration.

This game was memorable also for one significant event that took place off the field. As Dad panned the field just prior to the kickoff while all the fans were standing, he focused the lens on an attractive young lady one row below and four seats to our right. She was Mabel Wall, my dad's secretary, who, unbeknownst to me or, more importantly, to Mom, played an important role in my Dad's life. Mabel's husband, to her right, smiled graciously as he waved at the cameraman.

In one of life's little ironies, the Chicago Cardinals would

153

migrate, like their namesakes, south to a warmer climate. First to St. Louis and then to nest in the "Valley of the Sun," Phoenix. A move that would much later be followed by this writer.

I'm certain that the Bidwell family, the owners of the Cardinals who were the NFL champions in this year, 1947, never envisioned or anticipated that 50 years would elapse before their beloved team would make the NFL playoffs again.

At a visit to the Green Bay YMCA in 1999, in the lobby amidst a collection of historical photographs, I found one that portrays and represents this era that I have dubbed, "A Perfect Time, A Perfect Place."

Jack Stacker, in the center of the photo, hangs suspended on the flying rings, with twenty-one members of the Junior Leaders attentively focused on Jack's pose. On the left is our inexhaustible and motivating instructor John M. Scovell. If the viewer looks closely, directly behind Johnny's left thigh and hand, one half of a face is peering out behind the human obstruction. That unrecognizable kid is me. My place in YMCA history was, by chance and photographer's error, obscured. No matter. Maybe the incident provided some motivation to be more recognizable in the future.

The Y year 1946-1947 got off to a bad start, both physically and emotionally. Lee Prodehl came on board to assist Johnny with his ambitious and demanding program. Lee was a young, athletic man, probably about thirty years of age, who shared Johnny's enthusiasm and dedication to building young men. He, too, was a super guy.

"We're going to work on the parallel bars this morning, guys," Lee said as we lined up along the mat awaiting further instructions.

Lee demonstrated several basic moves on the bars for us Leaders. Since Johnny was now in his mid-forties I suspect that he probably preferred that Lee handle the more vigorous and demanding exercises.

Positioned with his body between the parallel bars and arms fully extended, Lee rocked back and forth and then allowing his momentum to carry his legs up and pointing directly towards the ceiling, he came to a full stop in a handstand. Dismounting, Lee said:

"Now I want each of you to perform this routine. I'll be here to 'spot' you so you won't fall."

Jack Stacker, who was an excellent tumbler (the word gymnast wasn't in our vocabulary then), performed the routine easily, as did a number of the older guys. Then it came down to the eleven and twelve year olds.

Eager to prove that I could do the handstand also, I jumped up on the bars. Under Lee's watchful eye and assistance I managed to get my body extended in a vertical position. Lee had one hand on my hip and the other on one leg as I tried to hold the handstand. I was fighting to maintain the correct position but my arms were weakening. They were shaking, unable to support my weight. Before Lee could bring me down one arm collapsed and, missing Lee's attempt to catch me, I fell to the mat with a resounding thud.

"Buster! Are you okay?" Lee, concerned, asked.

"My chest hurts real bad, Lee," I replied, gasping for breath and obviously scared by the fall.

As I recall I pulled some intercostal muscles and injured my sternum. This kept me out of the program for quite some time. I couldn't swim or climb the rope or do anything the required the use of my arms. In short, this long, protracted story is a faint attempt to explain my poor performance for the year. A total of 1,031 points on a new point system (which was far below Jerry Gibble with 2,134, and Tommy Rand (Terry's brother) who had 2,122). Tommy was only ten but was already establishing himself as a terrific athlete. As disappointing as this year was, it paled in comparison to another event that took place about this time.

"Buster? Do you wanna walk home together?" a friend, who shall remain anonymous, asked. My friend, who was a couple years older, lived about a block west on Dousman and we often walked home together from the Y.

"Sure," I replied. "I was thinking of going to the Orpheum this afternoon but yeah, I'll walk instead if you want to."

"Geez, that's great. I wanna stop at one of the stores on the way home and look at a BB Gun," he said.

"A BB Gun? Geez. Are you going to get a BB Gun?" I asked, excited at the prospect of having a close friend that had one. Every kid wanted a BB Gun.

"Yeah, I've got some money saved up," my friend assured me.

I don't recall the name of the store and I can't remember if the clerk wouldn't sell him the gun because of his age, or without his parents' presence, or whatever, but anyways my friend didn't buy a BB Gun.

"Boy, I sure liked that Red Ryder gun," I remarked as we made our way from the store towards the Dousman bridge.

"Yeah. That's the one I got," he said.

"Geez, whattaya mean?" I asked, perplexed. My friend pulled me aside off the street into an alley, where he proceeded to pull out the gun from his pants! Somehow, without being observed, he had stuffed the BB Gun down his pants leg and walked out of the store with it. I was stunned.

"Geez n' plutz! That's stealing. You're going to get into big trouble stealing that gun," I admonished my friend.

"Who's going to know?" he said with a sly look on his face. "My parents knew I was going to buy one anyways and you're not going to tell, are you?" I didn't reply.

We continued on home. I realized that I had a dilemma. I _was_ the only one who knew the gun was stolen. If I told anyone my friend would know I was the tattle-tale. At school anyone who "told" on someone else was derided by our classmates saying, "tattle-tale tit who can't get over it." I didn't want to suffer that indignation.

"Buster? Something is bothering you? You've been 'moping' around the house all day," Mom said as she observed me wrestling with my conscience.

"I can't tell you Mom, I don't want to be a snitch," I

said as I tried to absorb myself in starting another model plane, as I was developing a real proficiency in building them.

"Snitch on whom?" Mom, now really intent on discovery, persisted.

"Mom? If you know someone who did something bad and that someone was your friend, would you tell on them? Even if it will make them mad?"

"Buster ... you always must tell the truth no matter what the consequences. You know that. Dad and I have preached and preached that to you since you were a little boy. Now, tell me what happened."

I gave in and told Mom the whole story. My parents chose to call my friend's parents and advised them. Next thing I knew, Mom, Dad and I were walking down the street to my friend's house. I cringed at the thought of facing my friend. Why did I have to go through this ordeal? There was a very good reason why.

"It was Buster's idea," my friend said as we sat in their living room, with the Quists on one side and the other family on the other. I was shocked at his claim. I simmered silently with anger. Suddenly, I exploded.

"Liar! Liar! You're a damn liar!" I blurted out as I rose up out of my chair and made a move to physically assault my accuser.

My dad, detesting nasty confrontations, demanded that I stop my tirade and we quickly left the house. It was probably the first time my parents had ever seen an outburst of anger from their easygoing son, but it was the first time that my integrity and my honor had been challenged and called into question.

"Dad, he's a schmuck! A liar and a schmuck!" still fuming I said as we walked home.

"Where in the world did you learn that word, 'schmuck,' Buster?" Dad asked.

"Oh, I just heard it around. All the kids use it," I replied.

"Do you know what it means?" Dad asked, obviously very curious and anxious.

"Geez, no."

"Buster, don't you ever use that word again," Dad said emphatically.

Dad was right. It was a very bad expression. How a Yiddish word found its way into our vocabulary in Green Bay has always remained a mystery to me, but my friend's act and duplicity by deflecting the blame to me justly fit the word. Mom and Dad finally believed my side of the story. That was the most important aspect of the whole ordeal. If my friend learned as much as I did from this unfortunate experience, one of life's critical lessons would prove to be invaluable. There's a theory that "who we are is where we are at the age of ten." There's no doubt in my mind that this wonderful place where I lived and the values learned began to define who I was and what I would become.

Profanity, swearing or taking the name of God in vain was strictly verboten. *"Geez," presumably, was an acceptable derivation of Jesus. "Gosh" or "gad" was probably a substitute for God. Any transgression of the unwritten code of language, whether at school or at home, was met with instant rebuke. I can vividly remember on at least one occasion my slip of the tongue resulting in my mouth being "washed out" with soap. A memorable archetypical experience if there ever was one. Language speaks loudly of the time in which we live. Our loss of civility, evidenced by the manner in which we speak to each other today, is reflected in our language. I suspect that there isn't sufficient soap on all the store shelves to stem the "tide" of the use of four-letter words today.*

Fisk Park also was a center for winter activities. The area that served as our baseball diamonds was flooded during our long winter and served as a skating rink. East of the rink was an area we used for hockey. At ten and eleven I worked hard to learn the game of hockey, as well as speed skating. I didn't particularly distinguish myself at either, but amongst my collection of mementos is a white ribbon signifying third place in the Boys Midgets 220 Yard Race. I learned a valuable lesson in that seemingly unimportant event.

In the city's finals, which were held on the east side, I was matched against an older and much more proficient racer. I can't remember his name but I was clearly intimidated. Rounding the last turn of the 220 yard race I was surprisingly close to my opponent, but with his superior technique and strength he began to pull away. Cognizant that I was probably going to lose, my skates went out from under me and I slid unceremoniously into the snow bank surrounding the race track.

After the race Dad said:

"Too bad that you slipped, Buster. You might have won."

What Dad nor anyone else ever knew is that I didn't slip. Facing certain defeat I <u>intentionally</u> fell. I couldn't accept defeat. I wanted an excuse. Hardly the mindset for someone who wanted to be a competitor.

I was also guilty of this same behavior that past summer. Often I would meet my buddies at the park to hang out in the evening. We decided to foot race to see who was the fastest runner. There were two pathways that led into the park off of Dousman Street, one from the west and one from the east. Together with the sidewalk down Dousman, they formed a triangle ending at the point by the park headquarters near the main baseball diamond. My opponent to race around the triangle was my one-year-older and good friend, Tom Docter.

We were shoulder to shoulder as we tried to make the last sharp turn of the triangular track to the finish. Tom, huffing and puffing but appearing stronger to me, was edging ahead towards the finish line. I fell!

"Gee whiz Buster. Bad break. I think you would have beaten me. I was tired," Tom said as he put his arm around me.

An undesirable and unfathomable trait was becoming a habit. Why was I retreating from competition at <u>the</u> critical moment? Why was the fear of defeat preventing a chance at victory? Somehow, someway, my own self-humiliation motivated me to overcome this propensity to wilt under pressure, and I learned to blossom when the sun shined the brightest. From this self-deprecating level of esteem I would become a fierce competitor. (Book Two)

It was December but it rained all day. Then, as the weather often does in northern Wisconsin, the temperature plummeted like a skydiver in a freefall from a plane.

"Mom! Dad!" I yelled as I broke into their bedroom at daylight on what must have been a Saturday or Sunday morning. "Everything is covered with ice. The trees, the lawn, the sidewalk — everything! Everything is silver-like."

Sure enough. An ice storm had blanketed the city and froze everything in place. Memorialized on film, the eerie scene looked like a surreal winter wonderland. All three of us broke out our skates, along with the Rocheleau girls (Peggy, Helen and Barbara), who also lived on Dousman. We skated around the corner and on Oneida we ran into Dickie and his sister Mary, the Christman girls (Shirley, Susan, Sandy and Mary Jo), and Jeffrey and David Martin. The Culligans (John, Mike and Pat) and our playmates Norbert and Jimmy Spitzer, who lived behind us on Kellogg Street, also joined us. It was like skating at Fisk Park, only we had our own neighborhood rink.

Cars, if they ventured out at all, ended up against the gutter hopelessly, like whirling dervishes, spinning their wheels. Green Bay was frozen in time. A heavenly day for kids but a devilish one for city workers.

This snapshot made me recall a similar event that occurred while I must have been in the second grade (because Joanie had graduated to Franklin Junior High and Terry was not yet enrolled at Elmore School).

A considerable amount of snow had already fallen. The winds circulating behind our house and between the garage left a six foot snow drift directly under the clothesline. Whenever that occurred Terry and I would dig tunnels with our friends into the massive drift and make an "ice house."

On this particular day it appeared that the worst of the storm was over. Mom dressed me up in my snow suit, galoshes, mittens, hat with ear-muffs and a woolen scarf wrapped around my neck. Only my eyes were visible.

Typical attire for a winter day in Green Bay. But, this day turned out not to be typical.

"The snow is pretty deep Buster. Go through the field to Division Street and then stay on the sidewalk down to Annunciation and Gray Street. Don't go through the other fields. Do you hear me?" Mom instructed me.

I could hardly hear her because I was so bundled up but I wasn't listening anyways. It was so much longer to walk to Gray Street when I could take my normal shortcut to school. Trudging through the deep snow I finally reached Division Street. I then headed, against Mom's instructions, towards Kellogg Street through the vacant field.

The wind started whipping up the snow, hindering my ability to see. Then, it started snowing harder. Stuck in the middle of the field between Kellogg and Elmore Streets I couldn't see anything. No houses, no trees. Nothing but white on white. I was in a dreaded whiteout! My short legs in the deepening snow, encumbered by bundles of clothing, imperiled my progress and now were threatening my survival.

"Why didn't I listen to Mom? Why did she send me to school, anyways?" I thought to myself.

Plodding and often crawling through the snow, not knowing which direction for sure that I was heading, I moved on. As I became disoriented, fear gripped me. I was lost. Tears froze on my cheeks and the snot from my nose caked as icicles above my upper lip. I was scared. I was only seven years old.

Suddenly and miraculously I could see a backyard fence of a house that fronted Wilson Street. This was where the path, now covered in snow, that I followed every single day to school was located. I was in a familiar place. Eager and now reinvigorated by hope, I plodded north along the fence to Bond Street. The snowplows were clearing the street! I was safe! I ran to the door. I was greeted by Mr. Duchateau, our janitor.

"Buster! What in the world are you doin' out in this weather?" he asked, seemingly flabbergasted.

"Mom sent me. I almost got lost," I confided to Mr.

Duchateau.

"Holy cow! That's amazing. You're the only kid here. The school has been closed."

Miss Hetherington, the principal, was there, though. She took me to her office and called Mom. Dad must have been out of town because after the streets were cleared later in the day, she drove me home.

As I recall several other kids and some teachers showed up also, but what has intrigued me all my life is why Mom sent me and Joanie off to school that day. She was so protective of us kids. Often, overprotective. Fortunately, in later years, we could both laugh about the "whiteout." It was my first brush with death, but there were more to come that sure as heck weren't Mom's fault.

Christmas 1946 brought a new joy into our home and into our lives. Maybe Mom's resolve was broken down by the "whiteout" incident or whatever, but she finally relented: A little, black, curly-haired cocker spaniel with a white mark on his chest that we named "Laddie" became our first pet. I didn't need Dad's movie film to refresh my memory of this rambunctious creature that immediately took control of our house. He demanded and received constant attention and refused to live in the cold and clammy basement where Mom wanted him to reside. He was instant and constant energy and would only stop when we went to bed at night. Unfortunately, Laddie was a chewer and he exercised his teeth on anything and everything that he could fit in his mouth or get his chops around. His days at 1140 Dousman Street were numbered right from the start.

Spring 1947 brought two huge surprises to the Quist family.

A feature article with Dad's photograph appeared in the business section of the March 8, 1947 *Green Bay Press-Gazette*. The headline read:

QUIST RANKS HIGH AMONG
COMPANY'S INSURANCE AGENTS

Herbert A. Quist, supervisor for Business Men's Assurance Company in this territory, ranked eighth

*in the entire United States in personal production for
his company in 1946....*

The article went on to say that Dad was the top
producer in the state and that in January 1946 he had
written a record 62 individual insurance applications. Also
noted was the fact that BMA's hospital and surgical plan
was endorsed by the Wisconsin Medical Association. Proof
positive that Dad's business was booming, which created a
number of perks for him and his family.

"Where are we going for our Sunday ride?" Mom asked
as we headed home from church.

"Got a big surprise for you," Dad informed all of us
with that generous, inviting smile that was his trademark.
"Change into your play clothes and we're going to take a
ride to Door County."

"Geez, Door County!" Terry enthused. "Can we bring
Laddie?"

"Sure, sure," Dad said, while Mom rolled her eyes.

After lunch, we all jumped into the Nash and headed
north on Highway 57 near Namur and Brussels (the
Belgian communities where so many people had died
seventy-six years prior during the great Peshtigo fire), and
we seemingly headed towards Sturgeon Bay.

"Are we going to Fish Creek again?" Terry asked.

"Nope," Dad replied, intent on keeping our destination
a secret.

Unexpectedly, Dad turned left off of Highway 57 and
north on County Road MM and then west on County Road
C.

"Gosh, Daddy, this is way out in the country. Where
are we going?" Joanie, getting as impatient as Terry and I
were, asked.

"Big surprise. Big surprise. You'll know when we get
there," Dad, knowing he was teasing our curiosity to the
limit, said.

Terry asked the inevitable, "Are we there yet?"

"I'm looking for May Road, Thelma. Did you see a
sign?"

"No, there aren't any signs, Hub. Don't you know

where you're going?" Mom asked, indicating that she hadn't been where we were going either.

Suddenly ahead of us was a magnificent sandy beach. An old, faded sign said we were at, appropriately, Sand Bay. Before we could jump out of the car, Dad backed up and proceeded west until, he got to a small, poorly defined road and turned in. We stopped aside a cluster of cedar trees covered in vines, with a view of the bay directly ahead.

"This is it, kids," Dad said as we piled out of the car.

"This is what?" Mom asked, perplexed as we were.

"This is our land. This is where we're going to build our cottage," Dad informed us.

"You bought this property, Hub? My gosh, how much did it cost?" Mom wanted to know as always.

"'Bout six hundred bucks," Dad said, obviously proud of not only his ability to buy the land but finding such an exquisite place.

Joanie, Terry and I tore down to the beach like we had been shot out of a cannon, with little Laddie right at our heels. Mom, perhaps still in a daze over the "surprise," stayed back to talk with Dad. I never knew if she knew what the surprise was.

There were three large lots that had just recently been subdivided. To the east of our lot was an old house, no longer occupied, that was the home of Oscar Haines, who at one time farmed the area. That parcel was purchased by Mr. and Mrs. Gilbert Brandes from Milwaukee, who would soon become our close friends. The lot to the west was purchased by Dad's good friends from Green Bay, Mr. and Mrs. Gordon Ware who, with their two sons, would become our summertime playmates. There was an old log cabin on the Ware property that served as a perfect playground for four boys until the Wares tore it down.

After we toured our lot (which extended from the beach all the way to Snake Island Road) on foot, we drove back to the beach area, which seemed to be the place where boats were loaded. There was a small store just up from the beach. According to the sign above the door it was "Johnson's Store."

"Are you Mr. Johnson?" Dad asked. "Your name sounds Swedish," he added.

"Yep, parts anyways," Mr. Johnson replied. "What brings ya up heres before tha season?" Mr. Johnson asked as the three of us looked for candy and snacks.

"We just bought the property next to the old house," Dad said proudly.

"Oh, ya did eh," Mr. Johnson replied.

"Yes, we're going to build a cottage as soon as we can. We plan to spend our summers up here," Dad continued. "How's the fishing?"

"'Bout as good as yul find in all of Door County," Mr. Johnson proclaimed, which, of course, is exactly what Dad wanted to hear. It turned out to be true.

Mr. Johnson, I learned from my research, bought the land from Mr. Haines back in the 1930's and built the small general store. Johnson was kind of a "crotchety" old guy and wasn't as personable as most Swedes, but maybe, as he said, he was only part Swede. How did Dad find this magnificent place? I've pieced together a logical scenario.

During the War, Dad wrote health insurance on the employees of a number of the shipbuilding companies in Sturgeon Bay. The shipyards built PT boats, LSTs (Landing Ship Transports), rescue boats and corvettes (small support ships). Alex Meunier, a life-insurance agent in Sturgeon Bay, undoubtedly knew Dad and they possibly could have worked on the health insurance business together, given Alex's relationship to the company owners.

Alex, who at one time also served as the County Sheriff, presided over a sheriff's sale (foreclosure) of some of the Haines' property at Sand Bay, and from this event, according to his son Miles, Alex learned of the enormous potential for the development of Sand Bay. He and a couple of friends formed a partnership and subdivided lots in Sand Bay. I suppose that it was probably Alex who led Dad and the Quist family to this promised land. Fond memories of this enchanting place will always be prominent in my heart and in my mind. You'll soon discover why.

The second surprise was that Dad had qualified for BMA's national convention, to be held in September in Banff, Canada. He told us we were going with him and Mom. For someone that had only traveled as far as Menominee, that <u>was</u> a big deal. But, that was still five months away.

"Mom? Can I have a birthday party?" I asked as April Fool's Day approached.

"Sure, Buz. Who do you want to invite?" Mom was now calling me Buz. Don't know why. Dad called me Buster, Joanie spelled my name Buzz, Terry called me Buzzie, Gramma called me Bus, and I was soon to get a new name. It's difficult to discover who you are when you have to answer to a slew of names, but I knew my birthday was on a special day even if I was the brunt of many jokes.

"Dickie of course, and Jerry and Harry Proctor, Tom Docter and Tom Ruffing, Lee Olsen, David Martin, Calvin Whiting, Bob Caroline and Jeffrey Dennison. And, the most important one, Sharon Bookmeier," I listed.

"Buster, you're inviting only one girl," Mom said. "Sharon will feel out of place with all the rest of your guests being boys."

"Oh, that's okay. Sharon won't mind. She plays baseball just like us guys, anyways."

I didn't think Sharon felt ill at ease. She was the focus of all of our attention and, after all, she got to meet her future husband (that was a few years off in the future). She remembers the party well, naturally.

While at Elmore School Sharon was (secretly) my "girlfriend." She lived on Elmore Street near our school, and we often played together at her house or at the home of her best friend Margo Jesson who lived close by on Ray Avenue. On one occasion Mom and Dad drove us downtown and we went to a movie. Under the cover of darkness inside the theater we held hands. That was truly a big deal. Our parents didn't know that we were at risk sucking in a sea of smoke. The haze was so thick it diffused the picture on the screen.

Sharon's mother, Edna, knew Mom very well, as they

worked on a fund raising campaign for the Y together. Mrs. Bookmeier was also a good friend of my Aunt Elsie so both of our mothers approved of our relationship, which was mandatory at this point in time. Mom's circumspection would become more pronounced in the future.

One of my birthday presents was a crystal radio set. Using earphones I would search for various stations with a pin that looked somewhat like a phonograph needle. The crystal, which was a small, clear, hard rock magically produced sounds from its little cracks and crevices. Sitting under one of the large elm trees in our front yard I could "tune into" the Chicago Cub games, and I sat there for hours following the exploits of Phil Caveretta, Andy Pafko and my heroes.

Little did I know then that only seven years in the future the "Cubbies" would be interested in me.

"Hi, Mr. Bookmeier," I said as I opened the door to Sharon's father's store on Chestnut, just one-half of a block from my grandmother's house on Hubbard Street.

"Well, Buster, what brings you here?" Mr. Bookmeier asked.

"I'm stayin' at my Gramma's house and I had nothing to do. Can I look at your machines?" I asked Mr. Bookmeier, who sold and serviced juke boxes, pool tables, pinball machines and other games.

"Sure Buster. Would you like to see how they work?"

"That would be swell Mr. Bookmeier."

I got a full tour and marveled at the inner workings of all the devices that were our predecessors to video games.

"Hub? Can I use the Nash this week? Whitey (Stuiber) and Bob (Markham) and I are going out to the Friday night dance at Bay Beach," Larry asked my father while he was at our house.

"Sure. That's okay. I'm playing at Shorewood in the afternoon. You can pick me up around noon and caddy for me," Dad offered.

"That would be great Hub. Thanks a lot. I'll wash the

car too," Larry proposed.

About nine o'clock in the morning the phone rang. Mom answered it.

"Thelma? It's Laurie" (Aunt Elsie used that name but Mom refused to call her Laurie.)

"Yes," Mom said with a cool sound in her voice.

"Do you know where Larry is?"

"Well, he took the car to go to Bay Beach last night. Why?"

"He's sitting right here in my apartment on Lincoln Park West (Chicago)."

"Oh my Lord, what ..."

"Joy ride. Larry and his friends went on a joy ride. I'm sending them home right now," Laurie said obviously miffed.

Aunt Elsie was obviously concerned that her son would take Dad's car unauthorized on such a long and dangerous trip. But, she also didn't want her son "interfering" in her lifestyle. Elsie was Luke Barkhausen's girlfriend. Barkhausen was a multi-millionaire entrepreneur who was one of the original founders of Ducks Unlimited, and had a penthouse on Lakeshore Drive. Elsie operated a women's dress shop in the Loop called "Suzy Q," presumably financed by Barkhausen.

When cousin Larry visited his mother on prearranged visits in Chicago Mr. Barkhausen's chauffeur would meet him at the train and take him to the Barkhausen penthouse where, on several occasions, he would have dinner served by a full-time staff. Larry's mother's life was difficult for the teenager to comprehend, but he "behaved as a good boy should." Ironically, just after Larry made his unauthorized trip to Chicago, an event occurred that would dramatically change the course of his mother's life.

On July 27, 1947, Larry's mother was visiting in Green Bay with a friend from Chicago, Mrs. Ada Owen. They were in the company of Clarence A. Cross, a Green Bay clothier and avid sportsman. Ironically, the three were driving out to visit the Barkhausen game sanctuary when Cross' car ran off County Trunk J and Elsie suffered severe lacerations to her arm. My aunt ultimately received a settlement of $28,872, a significant sum in 1947, due to her injuries but, unfortunately, she acquired a penchant for pain-killing drugs and alcohol, and gradually she lost her grip on the comfortable life she had become accustomed to.

Just twelve years later, in 1959, in Chicago, while I was at the top of my athletic career at the age of 23, I called on my aunt in the company of two of my teammates. I expected to find Elsie in comfortable surroundings, but in one of the most revealing reality checks in my young life, I was astounded at what I discovered.

My aunt was living off the Loop in a modest apartment house. Her living quarters were a one-room studio apartment. She had to retreat behind a folding partition to finish dressing. All of her outdated fashions were hanging everywhere for lack of closet space. I was embarrassed in front of my friends. I felt sorry for my aunt that I had always shied away from when she hugged and kissed me. She was no longer the attractive, well-groomed, fashionable and desirable object of a rich man's affection and money. Her only real friends that she could rely upon now were booze and drugs.

I was standing on the front porch of our home with Mom when Larry returned Dad's Nash to the driveway. Looking east on Dousman I could see Larry's friends hiding behind the shrubs at the Quigleys, five houses down the street. Larry quickly parked the car and made a beeline towards his friends. Dad was at the golf course.

"Larry! Larry! Come back here. I want to talk to you," Mom said emphatically.

Larry never turned around.

Strangely, Dad never confronted Larry over the car caper. In fact, a couple of months later, after a parade, Dad approached Larry.

"Wouldn't you like to take Phyllis (Kessler) home after the parade?"

"Geez, Hub. Sure. Thanks. Thanks a lot," Larry, finding it hard to contain his enthusiasm, said. Phyllis was the West High School and the Packers' head majorette and Larry's heartthrob. Even I, at the curious age of eleven, knew she was a "babe." "Hubba, hubba," the guys would say as she, baton in hand, marched by. We have significant footage of Phyllis in her attractive, attention-getting uniform.

Dad, typical of his desire to avoid anything unpleasant, never scolded Larry about the unauthorized use of his car.

June 1947 arrived. School was out. My classmates were delirious but I strangely possessed a feeling of sadness. It was such a good year and I enjoyed my time in Miss Ferslev's room enormously. She was such a good teacher and now it was over. As I walked towards Gramma's house (for some reason that I can't remember) down Elmore Street, Gail Plutchak, an attractive, blonde classmate, was walking on the north side of the street, carrying all her books in both arms pressed against her chest. We didn't have backpacks then and our books were heavy and cumbersome.

I said to myself, "you should help Gail with her books." I stopped several times to yell to her but the words couldn't come out. At eleven, despite my relationship with Sharon, I was still shy approaching girls. Particularly one as pretty as Gail. I was "bothered" by my lack of confidence and initiative to approach her. I'm sure she would have welcomed my assistance and company. Funny how such a small event can remain so prominent in your mind for over fifty years.

Our Fisk Park Junior Midgets Boys Softball Team was, as anticipated, a very good team. Anxious to practice, I rode my bike with Dickie to the park every day, rain or shine. I can remember during the cold days in March and April pitching to my friend Dickie in his basement. For some reason I envisioned myself as a pitcher but Jerry (DeGroot) was still our number one guy. Most memorable, however, was a practice session behind our house where I nearly lost my best friend.

"I'll hit you some 'fungos,'" I said to Dickie, as we often

170

had pick up games in our backyard. Since there were only the two of us we wanted to create a fun practice. Standing about fifteen to twenty feet away from me, Dickie lobbed me a pitch underhand and I would bunt or take an easy swing and hit the ball back to him. Dickie would field the ball and then repeat the same action. We called it "fungo practice."

I got the bright idea to take a full swing at Dickie's slow pitch. As the ball approached me waist high I drew back my bat and with a Ruthian swing from my heels I swung with all my might.

Whack! I made a perfect contact. A line drive.

Dickie, only twenty feet away, had absolutely no time to react. He never saw the rocket-like projectile. It hit him right between the eyes on his forehead! My best friend crumpled to the ground like he was felled by a .357 magnum. I was horrified!

"Mom! Mom!" I yelled as I headed towards the back door of our house. "I killed Dickie!"

Mom, slamming the screen door behind her, dashed to my buddy's aid. He was out cold as a cucumber!

"Oh my Lord," Mom cried out as she assessed Dickie's dire situation. I stood over my fallen comrade praying that he wasn't dead. Mom ran back into the house. She returned with a large wide-bladed carving knife that we used to cut the Christmas turkey.

"Mom? What are ya going to do?" I asked frantically.

"His forehead is swelling," Mom related, as I could see a lump the size of an egg growing quickly to the size of a baseball on Dickie's forehead.

"Are you going to cut it?" I asked, thinking Mom was going to lance this rapidly rising and ugly knot.

Mom, kneeling down, took the knife and pressed the flat blade hard against the rising spot. Dickie, groaning, opened his eyes.

"Is he okay Mom? Is he okay?" I asked anxiously.

"Dickie? How do you feel?" Mom asked my woozy friend.

"I ... I saw a bunch of stars, Mrs. Quist," Dickie, trying

to find his senses, replied.

Fortunately, my buddy and teammate survived and we went on to win the 1947 City Championship. I have a large "Award of Merit" placard signed by B. Christenson (the playground leader) as evidence that we were, despite "fungoitis," winners.

This incident wasn't the only brush with disaster that Dickie and I experienced while practicing baseball. About this same time Dickie and I were playing catch in his backyard, throwing the softball high into the air to replicate a fly ball. Misdirected, the ball flew over the backyard fence into the neighbor's yard. Two problems prevented us from easily retrieving the ball.

One, the Maierle's neighbor had a Doberman pinscher, inappropriately named "Bing," that was mean and ferocious and whose sole purpose in life seemed to be to prevent anyone from entering the yard. Secondly, there was an ornamental wrought iron fence with sharp spikes at the top about our chest height, either to prevent anyone from getting into the yard or the dog from devouring the neighbors. Don't know which, but it wasn't a piece of cake to get the ball.

"I think Bing is in the house, Dickie. Do you think we dare try to get the ball?" I asked, scanning the yard.

"I'll get it. I'll get it," Dickie volunteered. I was skeptical.

Carefully, Dickie climbed over the fence avoiding the spikes at the top of the fence. Just as my buddy retrieved the ball, the Doberman came tearing around the corner of the neighbor's house.

"Dickie! Look out!" I cried as my friend pitched me the ball.

Dickie scrambled to get over the fence. Bing, his large white fangs bared, grabbed Dickie's pants leg. He lost his grip and slipped. He fell towards his own yard but the back of his right knee caught on the iron spike as he fell towards the ground.

"Ouch!" he cried in pain as the arrow-like spike punctured and penetrated the area behind his kneecap.

Dickie's leg was impaled on the fence!

The Doberman, smelling blood, was in a shark-like frenzy. I tried to lift Dickie's body up to release his leg from the spike. Dickie grabbed the fence at the same time, exposing his hand to the awesome teeth of the sleek black and brown aggressor. Finally, he lifted his leg off the spike and he was down safely in his yard.

"It hurts like all get out," Dickie cried. He was bleeding profusely. I half carried him to his house.

It was a nasty gash that required hospitalization, but fortunately he would recover and go on to become an outstanding All-State football player at West High and a first-team starter at Marquette University. At the rate that we were going, though, it's a marvel that either of us made it to junior high.

August arrived and all the family, including Gramma and Larry, were back at Fish Creek at the same cottage at Edgewater. Bad memories of Billy still lingered, but the lure of the beach and our freedom to cruise the harbor in our fishing boat helped erase the demons of yesteryear.

"Bus? Would you like to take a hike in the park?" Gramma asked (Peninsula State Park, which was directly north of town).

"Sure Gram," I responded, shortening Gramma to Gram.

"Can I go too?" Terry asked.

"Sure, sure. The walk will do us all some good," Gramma elaborated.

We proceeded down to the Bayshore, past the municipal beach where we spent hours every day, and waded across the mouth of Fish Creek (from which the town derived its name), into the park where paths were clearly marked for hikers.

"This is so beautiful, Bus. It's just like home. Just like Sweden," Gram said as she examined the flora which she identified for us. We continued our hike.

"Bus. I've run out of gas. I just can't make it any further," Gram said as she sat down on a log next to the path.

"Are you okay?" Terry asked while I also expressed my concern.

"Yes boys, I'm okay. Your Gramma just isn't up to hiking anymore," reluctantly Gram admitted. Future walks were limited to visit Sunset Beach at the west end of Main Street. Gram would gaze into the sunset, perhaps fondly recalling her days in Sweden as a young girl. It was a magnificent sight.

Gram was then sixty-two years of age. In recalling this experience I was reminded of my hiking adventure in the Grand Canyon when I was the same age as Gram was in 1947. I've hiked both into the canyon and out. There's approximately a 6,000' vertical rise from the Colorado River at the bottom to the top of the rim, and temperatures were 100° at the bottom during my last hike out. The last 1,000' up Jacob's Ladder is a switchback virtually straight up. It was an exhausting hike but one of the best physical and emotional experiences in my lifetime. An experience that could never have been enjoyed by Gram or my parents at a similar age. We've made great strides in the improvement of our health, and our lifestyle has changed dramatically in the past fifty years. Gram and my parents would be absolutely amazed that in my sixties I still work out, lift weights and ski, as well as hike. And, I still play competitive golf.

"Buster? How would you like to caddy for me today? I'm playing golf at the park," Dad asked, as I was looking for something to do.

"Gosh ol' fish hooks. That would be great," I responded.

The Peninsula State Park golf course was built in 1916 and was situated on the bluff overlooking Ephraim, just five miles or so from Fish Creek. It was a hilly course and a challenge for an eleven-year-old pulling the golf cart up those hills. My primary job, however, was looking for balls.

"If I happen to hit one into the woods be sure you watch where it went in Buster," Dad instructed me. "Be on the lookout for any Acushnets," he added.

Acushnet (which later became Titlest) was a premier

ball of the day. Probably one of the few golf-ball manufacturing companies during or at the end of the War to use real rather than synthetic rubber in their balls. Anyways, Dad thought they went farther than any other ball. I traipsed through the woods in search of the prized white spheres. My reward was a quarter for each one I found. It was tough, especially when you had to look out for poison ivy. Nobody wanted to get poison ivy on their hands or legs. The itching would drive you crazy. I had been there and done that before.

"Give me the niblick," Dad said, as we stood on the tee box of a short 100-yard hole that was perhaps 100 feet up on the bluff above the green. It was probably the "signature" hole at Peninsula State Park, with a panoramic view of the harbor at Ephraim to distract the golfer as he or she teed off. Movie film taken during this same time period captures my mom teeing off from this scenic hole. Not a good swing, however.

Dad was a pretty good player. Now age 42, he probably shot in the mid-eighties on this difficult course. Fifty-two years later, in a wonderful return to our past, I broke 80 from the "tips."

"Good job, Buster. You deserve a malt at Wilson's before we go back to the cottage," Dad offered as he finished his round with three other men he met at the course.

Wilson's was the number one fun place in Ephraim. This town was founded by the Moravians, which allowed me to have some connection to this magnificent place that rivaled Fish Creek in its beauty and uniqueness. I had my usual — a chocolate malt, extra thick, with crackers. What a treat. Just about as good as Dehn's in Green Bay.

"Can we stop at Eagle Tower on the way back Dad?" I asked.

"Sure. We've got time," Dad said as we got in the Nash. Eagle Tower was a 75' tower located on the bluff, 200' above and overlooking the bay to the west. The present tower, built by the Civilian Conservation Corps (CCC) during The Great Depression, replaced a previous "lookout" tower that had to be closed. I climbed the tower quickly to get a spectacular look at Horseshoe Island and the Green Bay. What an unforgettable view. One that would take on more significance in a few years.

Dad's favorite golf course in Door County was Maxwelton Braes Golf Club, located on the east coast of the Peninsula just south of Bailey's Harbor. Cousin Larry caddied often for Dad at this course but I don't think I ever did. Often, when the weather was hot and humid in Fish Creek, we would make the short trek across the Peninsula where it could be twenty degrees cooler on Lake Michigan. Mom and Gram fixed sandwiches and we would have a picnic on the beach while Dad played golf. Most often, the water was cold and we didn't swim much in the lake, but the beach with all its sand dunes offered a perfect place to play "hide and seek."

Our two weeks were soon over, but the sadness of leaving Fish Creek was offset with the excitement of going to Banff, Canada. There was one big, sad surprise left, however.

"Kids," Mom announced to us, "we're going to leave Laddie here with Mr. and Mrs. Wesa. Their son Jerry will take real good care of him and we'll see him each summer." We never considered the fact that we weren't coming back to Fish Creek.

Terry came unglued. Laddie was his constant companion. He cried crocodile tears as he wouldn't let go of this scrappy, affectionate creature that we all loved. It was a pathetic sight to see Terry getting his last look at his little buddy out the rear window as Jerry Wesa held on in fear that our faithful companion would break free and follow us.

Dad stopped in Sturgeon Bay on the way home, presumably to meet with the architect and contractor who were working on our cottage in Sand Bay. Mom and Dad, both in the front seat, tried to keep the conversation to themselves.

"How are they doing, Hub? Will we have a cottage by next summer?"

"Geez it's tough. There's such a shortage of housing here in town you can't get anyone to work in Sand Bay.

The workers don't like it out there. No electricity, you know. They have to cut all the wood out there by hand and there's a waiting list for all the plumbing and light fixtures and everything. I sure didn't count on those types of problems."

Despite the logistical problems, however, construction, which was as slow as ants trying to build a colony in concrete, did start that fall.

It was late August 1947 when Mom and Dad loaded up the Nash and we began our long trek to Canada. Gramma Anderson went with us. Joanie, for some reason, preferred to stay at home. Dad, by now a film fanatic, recorded the entire trip for posterity, which I've transferred to video.

Driving through South Dakota I asked:

"Why do they call these the 'bad lands,' Dad?"

"They look pretty bad, don't they?" Dad replied as we all laughed. Mount Rushmore, however, was a marvel to see, and uplifted our impression of South Dakota.

Yellowstone Park piqued our interest as nothing had ever done in our lives. Terry and I cringed with trepidation as two massive bears pressed their paws and noses up against our car window. Old Faithful did its thing right on cue as we "oohed and ahhed" at nature's fountain as it gurgled and then spewed forth its payload of water and steam into a clear blue sky. In Canada Terry and I are pictured with a real, honest-to-goodness Royal Canadian Mounted Policeman, and enjoyed probably our first ever ride on horseback.

At our final destination we awoke in Banff to discover almost a foot of snow had fallen overnight, and it was only the first of September. Terry and I stayed with Gram at a cabin in town while Mom and Dad were at the luxurious Banff Springs Hotel.

"Wow! Look at the snow," Terry yelled to me as we woke up in a winter wonderland. "Let's make a snowman," Terry suggested.

As we ventured out of the cabin to a bright sun-filled sky, Terry made an incredible discovery. A small fawn was standing in our front yard.

"Don't scare her," I warned Terry.

"It's Bambi, it's Bambi," my nine-year-old brother proclaimed as he sidled up to the innocent-looking creature. Surprisingly, the fawn held its ground and Terry began petting the small deer.

Suddenly, Bambi's mother appeared out of nowhere. Neither Terry nor I saw her coming. She charged my brother like Bronco Nagurski (the famous pro football player), head down, taking dead aim at the enemy who would harm her offspring.

Thud! The doe's hornless head hit Terry right in the behind, sending him flying through the air and landing face-first in the snow. I didn't know whether to laugh or cry. Fortunately, Bambi and its mother took off running, leaving Terry wondering what had happened. Bears and other wild animals continued to make their way into town foraging for food, but we stayed out of their way.

It was a great trip for the two of us but, more importantly, it was a wonderful change of scene for Mom. Dad received numerous accolades for his superb sales performance and Mom basked in his recognition. Other than Mackinac Island, Mom hadn't seen much of the country either. Her fondest memories were of this and other BMA trips.

The long, arduous and boring trip home was punctuated with playing the nickel slot machines in Montana, and finally discovering why all the billboards had been boasting about Wall Drug. Our best game to break the monotony was identifying the cars as they approached us on the two-lane highway. The Chevys, the Fords, and the Plymouths were easy. There were some new ones that weren't so easy.

"That's a Kaiser," I shouted.

"You're making that up," Terry proclaimed. "There's no such thing, is there, Dad?"

"Yep. There is, Terry. There's a new garage at home, Hudson Motors. They sell Kaiser-Fraiser cars," Dad said, validating my claim.

"And Henry J too," I added, which was one of America's first compact cars. With gas at less than twenty cents a gallon, the ugly Henry J didn't last long.

Approaching Minneapolis, Minnesota, Terry, in an advanced state of fatigue and frustration added:

"Are we home yet?"

We still had a long way to go.

Carl Linblad Andersson was Gramma Hulda's oldest brother, and had immigrated to the U.S. in August 1898 and settled in Minneapolis. I can only assume that Gramma was in contact with her brother and had planned to meet with him on our trip. Unfortunately, Carl died on September 8, 1947, just prior to our arrival in Minneapolis. I was extremely sick the night of our arrival so my primary focus was on my own health, but I believe that Dad and Gramma left our hotel to visit the Andersson family.

Through my cousin Jon Thunberg, whose grandmother was Hulda's sister Elin, I have numerous photographs of Carl. One, taken by M. L. Babcock in Pine City, Minnesota, is of Carl as a young man, possibly soon after he arrived in the U.S. Two others were taken by the C. L. Merryman Studio in Kerkhoven, Minnesota, and Carl, a very handsome man, appears to be about age 40. Another, also taken by Merryman, pictures Carl with his teenage son, whose family I haven't been able to locate. Finding an Andersson or Anderson in Minneapolis is a daunting task, but one that will be pursued.

With sadness we ended what was otherwise a fascinating trip.

CHAPTER 6: GROWING PAINS

AT MOST ELEMENTARY SCHOOLS reaching the sixth grade allows us, albeit for only a brief moment in time, to enjoy a position of prominence — to be "first fiddle" for the first time in our lives. We were now bigger, stronger, supposedly smarter and more comfortable within our surroundings and our friends that we had grown up with over the past five years. That didn't mean, however, that we didn't commit some personally insensitive blunders and cause some hair-raising moments.

Richard Williams was an alright kid. He was always well dressed. Most often he wore a suit and tie to school which, I would speculate, made it difficult for him to get into the down-and-dirty activities that we normally engaged in at recess or after school. He wasn't athletic. Most of us boys thought he didn't "fit in." He, to us, was a little strange. In the fifth grade we called him "queer," not knowing what the word implied to adults.

"Hey, it's 'queer,'" one of the guys yelled on the first day of school as Richard approached us in the schoolyard. There was a look of resolve on his face but Richard was conspicuously apprehensive as he confronted us.

"You are not to call me 'queer' anymore. My name is Richard Williams. Is that clear?" he said forcefully as though he had practiced those lines and prepared for this moment all summer.

"Geez, that's okay with me," I responded. "Hope you're not sore about it."

"No, I'm not sore about it but 'queer' is a bad word and you're not to call me that again," he emphasized.

We never did again.

I admired Richard's courage. It would be several years

before any of us knew what the word meant. We were older and wiser as sixth graders but our social skills were just beginning to develop in the school of "hard knocks."

There was a girl whom most of us avoided in class. Her clothes were soiled and threadworn, and rain or shine her snotty nose always seemed to be running. Worst of all, personal hygiene wasn't a priority on her mother's list since their home did not have a bath. She had bad BO. Most of our class didn't know of her plight. Patty Olson, her faithful friend, knew that she was one of seventeen children (the second youngest) in a family that was struggling just to survive. Insensitive to her needs, we should have supported rather than shunned her.

Patty, in addition to being one of the best hitters in our baseball games, was also a chum of mine.

"Buster, I've got a 'secret place' that's got all kinds of swell stuff in it. Do you want to see it?" Patty asked. Most of us, at one time or another, had a "secret place."

"Geez, that sounds swell. I'll tell my mom I'll be at your house tomorrow aft,' okay?"

There was a large old barn adjacent to Patty's house on Richardson Street. It was Patty's favorite place to hang out. Hopefully unobserved we entered the barn by lifting up two loose wall panels. Inside was a treasure trove of old things from someone's past, protected and covered by sheets and tarpaulins. Under one of those tarps was Patty's "secret place." I was marveling at this private inner sanctum when suddenly a booming voice shattered the silence.

"I know youse kids are in here! I saws youse sneak in. Come on out right aways!"

Terrified, Patty and I cuddled together for support. Heavy footsteps approached our tiny hiding place. We could visualize a menacing monster only a few feet away waiting to prevent our escape and, worst of all, grab us.

Minutes passed. The footsteps didn't go away. Minutes grew into a half hour. Then, an hour. The early fall darkness was encroaching on our hiding place.

"He must be gone," Patty reasoned as she whispered

in my ear.

"I'll take a peek out," I said quietly as I lifted the corner of the heavy tarpaulin.

The man with the monster voice appeared to have gone. Slowly, I stuck my head out into the dark and dusty barn. Patty followed. We crawled on our hands and knees groping to find our only known route to escape certain doom.

At last the loose wooden panels and freedom. We ran as fast as we could through the field to Patty's house, never looking back.

"Where in the world have you kids been?" Patty's mom asked. "Mrs. Quist has called and she's been out looking for you, Buster. You better call home right away."

I did, but it didn't matter. I got the "strap" anyways.

On the north side of our school near what was then kindergarten, there was a small grassed-in area that had a concrete structure that formed a skylight for the furnace room in the basement.

A heavy metal grate covered the top of the structure to prevent anyone from falling into the fifteen-foot hole below. The grate was set on a small ledge inset from the top of the structure. Water covered the bottom of the pit and provided a perfect environment for a colony of frogs. It also was an attractive curiosity for eleven-year-old boys looking for diversion during recess.

"Look at all the frogs down there," Jerry said, as we dropped small rocks on them through the grating.

"Hey guys, I bet we can lift this thing off and climb down there," I suggested to my classmates. "Get around the edge and pick this thing up."

With the help of four or five of my friends I was able to lift the cumbersome grate off the ledge. Suddenly, somebody let go of the other end. My fingers were enmeshed in the grate. Down went the grate to the bottom of the smelly pit.

Down I went with it!

I heard the unmistakable sound of breaking glass and the next moment I was lying in the coal bin in the furnace room.

"Holy Cow!" Mr. Duchateau, our janitor, called out as he raced to help me. He was a nice man but he hated chewing gum. He really scolded us if we were chewing gum. Good thing I didn't have any in my mouth that day.

"Buster! My goodness gracious. How in the world ... ?" Mr. Duchateau exclaimed as he pulled me out of the coal bin.

Hearing of the calamity, Miss Hetherington, our principal and my sixth-grade teacher, a large, heavy-set woman with dark rings around her eyes, came bursting into the furnace room.

"Is he alright Mr. Duchateau?" Miss Hetherington asked, as she searched for a towel to wipe off the coal dust that blackened my blonde hair and clothes.

"He's got a bump on his head but somehow he didn't get any cuts from the glass," the janitor said as he surveyed my arms and legs.

Miss Hetherington took me into her office and called my mom.

"Mrs. Quist? This is Jennie Hetherington over at Elmore School. Buster has been in an accident."

I could just picture Mom with a look of agony and concern on her face as she must have asked if I was injured.

"He's okay Mrs. Quist, but ... but he does look like 'Little Black Sambo.' He's covered with coal dust. He sure needs a bath," my principal said.

Visiting Elmore School recently I noticed that the grate had locks on it. A testimony to the fact that I left my hand print there.

The 1947 school year for me got off to an ominous start. For my friend Jack LaHaye, who lived west of us on Dousman Street across from the Jansens, it was tragic.

For some reason unknown to us, and maybe even to Jack's family, his mom committed suicide. One day when Jack went to school she closed up the house and turned on the gas stove. Jack found her when he came home from school. The entire neighborhood was in shock and disbelief. We did live and grow up in a perfect time and a perfect place, but even in an idyllic world bad things happened. It was as difficult to understand then as it is difficult to comprehend today.

Making certain that I was exposed to every activity and had an opportunity to learn all that I could learn, my parents encouraged me to sign up for Cub Scouts. I became a member of Pack number 6, headed up by John M. Walter, who was my Cub Master. Mom was our Den Mother and 1140 Dousman was the Den for our pack of wolves. Jim Jenkins, who was a year older and who lived on Division Street, was our Den Leader. Jim was also a member of Grace Lutheran Church, where we held a number of our meetings. Jim recalled this story.

"Mrs. Jenkins? This is Thelma Quist, Buster's Mom. The kids just left my house. I'm worried silly. I served the kids hot chocolate and I just discovered that the milk is bad. All the kids will probably get sick."

That was my mom. She called all the mothers and fretted over the spoiled milk. None of us got sick but she wanted to be a good mom — even if we were a pack of wolves, then bears, then lions. She was conscientious almost to a fault.

I can vividly recall having outings at Mr. Walter's home in DePere, located on the Fox River. His yard was so large and forested that we practiced cooking and camping at his home. My most memorable scouting experience, however, came when I went to Bear Paw Camp at Mountain, Wisconsin, my first summer after I graduated to the Boy Scouts. There was an elaborate ritualistic ceremony for those who were "called out" for the "Order of the Arrow."

Mr. Bob Bennett was the head of the Nicolet Area Council for the Boy Scouts, and he, along with all the adult volunteer staff, was decked out in authentic Indian headdress and full regalia to conduct this ceremony. I was "tapped," or chosen, by my fellow scouts to join the Order. As I stood by the shore of Bear Paw Lake, a line of flickering lights approached me in the dark moonless night. An eerie and frightening sight for the uninitiated. I was relieved to discover that the lights were lanterns floating on a canoe.

I boarded the canoe, destination unknown. My guide paddled to the other end of the lake. Armed with only a bedroll and no flashlight, I was left alone without a fire to spend the night in the woods. As the canoe left the shore and the last remnant of civilization faded into the mist, I realized that I was on my own for the first time in my life, in the wilderness.

The night was as long as it was sleepless. The silence was only pierced by the hooting of an owl and the echo of my own cough. I prayed for the morning light and that a hungry bear wouldn't discover my presence. Staring blankly into the starlit heavens I pondered: Where does the sky end? Are there worlds like ours out there? This scary night was probably my first encounter with an unknown that would fascinate me all my life.

The rising sun brought my guide and the canoe to the shoreline. I was humbled but safe.

The prolonged ceremony continued. Mr. Bennett, poised and standing rigidly in front of me like an Indian Chief in the presence of the members of the "Order," raised one arm high above his head. Then with a descending blow he brought his hand down hard on my shoulder. If I would have flinched I would have failed my final test of courage. I staunchly resisted the inclination to cushion the blow and passed the test. I was accepted into the "Order of the Arrow."

Joanie began her junior year at West High School, while Terry started second grade at Elmore. We were apparently obstacles to her "interpersonal and social" development.

"Joanie? Your dad and I are going to a party at the Roeders' house this evening. You'll have to stay home and keep an eye on the boys," Mom said.

"Oh Mom! Darn it! I've got a date tonight to go to Bay Beach. I hardly ever get to go out on a date. I don't want to sit with Buster and Terry. They're mean. They're monsters. They never do anything I tell them to do anyways," Joanie said pleading to get out of her date with hell.

"We can't find anyone else this late. You'll just have to call your date and tell him you can't go."

It seemed that Mom always found a job for Joanie when she had plans to go out. To Joanie it wasn't a coincidence. It was a devious scheme to keep her from dating. Mom's objective was to protect her daughter from the boys "who only wanted one thing."

"Quit fighting youse guys or I'll lock you in your room," Joanie, losing her temper, warned us.

"Just you try," Terry hollered back. "I double dare you."

"Okay, you asked for it."

Armed with Dad's shaving strap Joanie backed us into our bedroom and, true to her word, locked the door from the outside. There was a second door leading to our parents' bedroom and she locked that one too before we could escape.

Terry and I played football on our knees in our bed, with the bedposts acting as the goalposts. We often battled each other for yardage when we were supposed to be sleeping. Mom would yell at us, "Quit rutting around!" I never knew what that word meant but one day I looked it up. I wondered then if she knew what it really meant.

Our football game ended in a tie so Terry and I decided to duke it out with our pillows. In the melee one pillow burst and feathers flew all over the place. Soon a second split, filling the air with more feathers. Just as we started picking up the tiny, white things, Joanie unlocked our door.

"Geez n' plutz!" she screamed. "Mom and Dad will be home in a few minutes. If you don't get all those feathers picked up, Dad will tan your hides darn good."

We beat the deadline but had a hard time 'splaining why the pillows were ripped.

Now that the War was over our attention turned to other games. One of our favorites was "kick the can." We put a tin can on the sidewalk in front of our house and one of us was "it." The person who was "it" had to find all the other kids who were hiding in the bushes or behind the trees; once identifying them the race was on to the can. If you beat the person back and kicked the can you got to be "it."

Pam Rondou, our next door neighbor who was about four years old, and her brother Robert, who was six, loved to play hopscotch on the sidewalk in front of their house. Pam, despite her young age, was very proficient at the game, often beating us and her older peers. Unbeknownst to Lee and Virgil, her dad and mom, at this point in time, Pam was dyslexic, unable to recognize words or letters (which she later overcame and became a special needs education teacher).

Also unbeknownst to our mom and dad, Terry had a condition that is now called ADD — Attention Deficit Disorder. He was hyperactive and always getting into trouble in the neighborhood. Nothing really serious, but he seemed to find mischief everywhere he went without consideration of other people's reaction or fear of punishment.

After one particular incident, Pam overheard her parents talking.

"Lee. That Buster is such a nice, well behaved kid. But that Terry. He's a 'stinker.' How can those two brothers be so different?"

Professionals now know, of course, that ADD can be hereditary or caused by brain damage during pregnancy. In the 1940's behavior such as Terry's was exhausting and frustrating to parents, as well as those with whom an afflicted child came in contact. Mom, for some reason, blamed herself for Terry's condition, which greatly impacted my brother's early years.

———

Thanksgiving 1947 brought our two grandmothers, Uncle Bob, Larry and our family together to our house for one of Mom's lavish feasts. BMA, Dad's employer, provided the turkey. The event is preserved on film, unfortunately without the desired conversation, as the technology we take for granted today to marry sight and sound was still years away. Conspicuously recorded was Mom's innate desire to serve everyone as she hustled back and forth between the kitchen and the dining room, making certain that all her guests were taken care of. There isn't a single piece of film footage showing her sitting at the dining room table. She usually ate after everyone was finished. I often wondered if both our grandmothers preceded Mom in the same practice.

"When I say run laps I mean run!" Bob Coppens, our coach, who was a West High School student, lashed out at our basketball squad as we practiced. For good measure he took aim and fired the basketball at us to emphasize he meant business. We got the message, and it paid off.

Pictured in the *Press-Gazette* is a photograph of the West Side Sixth Grade Basketball League Champions. We had a perfect six win, no loss record. Our team consisted of Calvin Whiting, Billy Anderson, John Farr, Harry and Jerry Proctor, Bob Boguski and myself. Remarkably Billy, John and Bob were fifth graders.

Fort Howard, led by my buddy Otie Foster, was second place with a 5-1 record, followed by Norwood, Lincoln, Tank and our "B" team. No single incident or individual performance sticks out in my mind. I believe that we simply exhibited what seven young boys could accomplish with learned skills and teamwork. To me, I was also creating a desire to win.

Mom made an unusual observation.

"Buz, I think your playing the piano has helped your basketball. I think your fingers are better coordinated and it helps you handle the basketball."

I thought that was a pretty dumb statement at the time but who knows, maybe she was right. Following my sister, I took piano for several years, despite the fear that my buddies might regard me as a "sissy." I have in my possession two piano recital programs from 1947 and 1948, held at the Allouez Community House on East Walnut Street. My teacher was Miss Ethel Wilquet.

In 1947 I must have wowed the audience with my rendition of "Little Tarantelle." A year later I preformed a duet with my friend from Cub Scouts, Harvey Anderson, and we played "The Tortoise and the Hare." I also performed a solo piece. My favorite was Tchaikovsky's

Concerto #1 as I became more proficient in my third year. 1948 was also Terry's introduction to a public performance as he played "The Burly Bear."

My significant musical breakthrough, however, came on May 11, 1948, at Miss June Anutta's May Festival, as part of The West Youth Chorus. It featured, according to a May 10, 1948 feature article in the *Press-Gazette*, "about 115 of the best singers in the fifth and sixth grades of Elmore, Lincoln, Norwood, Tank, Jackson and Chappell schools ...." Along with the article is a large picture of Don Haupt, my classmate, and me singing "The Arkansas Traveler." *I must have impressed Dave Evjue, who attended Lincoln. Fifty-six years later he remembered my role in the event.*

Unfortunately this event, with the end of puberty, marked the demise of my singing career. Thirty years later I would appear in two major musical stage productions, "The Man of LaMancha" and Steven Sondheim's "A Little Night Music." Tellingly, I had the only non-singing roles in both productions!

Little did I know at this stage in my life that there would be a Van Cliburn finalist concert pianist in my family, in the person of a determined and diminutive young lady. A talent, however, for which I could not genetically claim any responsibility. You'll meet her in Book Three.

Ruth Sorenson and Miss Jennie Hetherington each taught our sixth grade class one-half day. On my report card for each of the three reporting periods under the heading "YOUR CHILD DOES HIS BEST WORK IN:" both teachers emphasized art as my number one skill, and reading as number two. Physical education was number three.

Miss Hetherington also wrote on my report card, "Is capable of splendid things." What was it to be? Was I to be an artist like my sister Joanie? A student of history as Miss Ferslev predicted? An athlete, as I struggled to learn the skills that would make me competitive? Only time would tell, of course, but it must have reinforced our teachers' devotion to their chosen profession to witness that some of us would, indeed, "do splendid things."

Paying this tribute to those who shaped our lives should qualify as one of those.

Jennie Hetherington gave me a note to take home to my mother as the door to my wonderful experience at Elmore School came to a close:

... you and your mom and dad have done so many gracious things. You have surely made me a very happy teacher (I gave her a corsage). I trust you will all have a lovely summer and truly enjoy your cottage ... keep on being the grand fellow you are.

> *Sincerely,*
> *Jennie Hetherington*

We all were good kids, despite the fact that our friends at Annunciation called us "Elmorans." We retaliated by referring to our Catholic friends as "mackerelsnappers" because they all ate fish on Friday. Nevertheless, despite the clearly defined religious partition between Protestants and Catholics, we as kids bridged the divide with ease.

As Miss Hetherington alluded to in her cordial note, our parents supported our teachers and our school 100%. Our parents wanted us to have what they didn't or couldn't have when they were our age. Mom and Dad exposed me to every activity that was available. Like seeds, some of these activities bore fruit as we matured.

Simultaneous to my success as a member of our winning basketball team at Elmore, I made the Leader's team at the Y with the older and taller boys. Otie Foster and I were the only eleven-year-olds to make the team. As I recall, we didn't get to play much, but we gained valuable experience. Otie had a secret passion that he shared with me.

"Let's eat some lunch here at the Y and go see Roy Rogers at the Packer (Theater)," I suggested to Otie after we finished our swim class.

"Ah geez, no. You gotta go to Chili John's and try their chili," Otie responded.

"Where's that? Never heard of the place," I replied.

"Just a couple of blocks on Pine Street."

"Okay. I'll go for it," I said, accommodating my friend, as we arrived shivering in the cold.

"You can order the hot or the medium or the regular," Otie said as we entered the small, spartanly furnished restaurant. I can't say it was a Mexican restaurant, but the chili was darn sure different from what I was accustomed to.

"I get hot when it's cold like today," Otie suggested with a slight grin on his face.

We each got the "hot" bowl of chili and dug in.

"Son of a biscuit!" I shouted as the inside of my mouth erupted like a volcano. Tears came to my eyes and my lips felt like I had just kissed a fire-breathing dragon.

"Heh, heh," Otie laughed slapping his legs with both hands.

"Holy cow! How can you eat this stuff?" I yelled, trying to wash away the burning sensation with a glass of water.

"Geez, I love it," Otie, still rocking with laughter, said.

"Judas priest .... Now I know why you're so darn small. This stuff burns out your stomach!"

We both laughed while I ordered the "regular." I went to Dehn's and got a malt, and sloshed the cold, creamy ice cream around in my mouth to extinguish the flames. We then went to the Packer Theater. Otie kept cutting farts. Strong stuff that chili.

I liked Roy Rogers and Hopalong Cassidy, but I thought Gene Autry was a "wuss." He wasn't tough enough, in my book, to be a cowboy. Then again, I had never seen a real live, honest-to-goodness cowboy, even in Montana. But the icon of the old west would soon ride into my future.

I finished the 1947-1948 Y year in first place in my age class in the Letterman's Club Competition. I had 1,391 points, beating my friend Norm Kroening by a mere two points. The top point-getter for the year was Tommy Rand, who had an incredible 2,607 points despite the fact that he was one year younger. A couple of events stick out, however, in my mind.

An article in the April 23, 1948 *Press-Gazette* sports

section featured Blair Mathews, who won the first annual free throw contest. Blair was a star on the West High School Basketball team and one of the older boys that I idolized. He sank an incredible 86 out of 100 free throws and was tied by Gene Crooks, who lost to Blair in a playoff. I won the Cadet division with 56 out of 100. I vividly remember that I did exceptionally well until I got to 70 or 80. Just turning twelve in April, I was so exhausted I could barely get the last ten throws to the rim. I missed every one of them.

John Scovell devised an unusual race that he called something like "three box potato race." The "potatoes" were round wooden pegs that would fit in your fist. The boxes were atop a wooden stand spaced about five yards apart. The object was to place, as fast as possible, all three potatoes — one in each box, one at a time — and then reverse the procedure without dropping a potato or knocking over the stand. Kinda like a cowboy barrel race without a horse. I had a good run.

Twenty-six years later I visited the Y with my mother, wife, son and a niece. I hadn't seen Johnny for almost twenty years. As I entered the lobby, who should come around the corner in a hurry, as he always was? It was my mentor, now in his mid-seventies and working his last year before retirement. Before I could say a word he took one look at me and said:

"Buster Quist!"

I couldn't believe it. Neither could Mom, who adored this wonderful man who, to me, didn't look much different then than he did thirty years prior. But Johnny, then in his forties, looked like he was 65 with his craggy face and grey hair.

We renewed our acquaintance. He said my son, then age ten, looked just like the Junior Leader that he knew long ago. He was almost a carbon copy of his dad except, unknown at the time, my son had an extra "X" chromosome. What part did a condition now known as Klinefelter's syndrome play in his life? Considerable, as you will learn in Book Three.

"Come here once," Johnny said with his arm around me, using an old Green Bay expression. "Got to show you something."

We walked into the gym where I had labored with love in the pursuit of excellence in my youth. He pointed to the large board on the wall in the main gym that listed all the records in all the Achievement Tests going back to the 1930's.

"See there," Johnny said. "Your record still stands."

I was still the top "potato runner." That event probably was discontinued but Johnny, as always, wanted me to feel good about myself as he did with all the boys.

I asked my mentor and teacher:

"Johnny? Could you tell when I was a youngster that I would become a pretty good athlete?"

He laughed as his head rocked backward.

"Buster. You were one of the hardest working and most determined kids I ever saw. You weren't a natural athlete but boy, were you aggressive. I betcha that's what made you a winner."

A pretty honest assessment from someone who mentored thousands of kids. Maybe the Viking aggressive nature _was_ in my genes.

On my most recent visit to the Y the record board was gone, a victim of the modernization process, along with the marks made so long ago. We now live in a generation which focuses on the here-and-now and what-have-you-done-for-me-lately. My mentor and the teacher to thousands of Green Bay boys died in 1994 at the age of 81. May Rediscovering America! be, in part, a tribute to this wonderful man.

"We gotta a new car! We gotta new car!" Terry said as he burst into the living room where I was reading the Press-Gazette. Joanie and I ran out the front door to witness what was in those days a major event.

"Jeepers, creepers — it's yellow," Joanie gasped.

"Eee gads, it's ugly," I proclaimed, as I viewed this large strange-looking car that resembled an inverted bath tub.

"I think it looks great," Dad said, reinforcing his decision to buy this obnoxious and gaudy automobile.

Dad had traded the 1946 Nash Ambassador for this new 1948 Nash that I suspect the garage couldn't sell. No one had yellow cars. Not since the flashy days of Stutz-Bearcats did anyone own a yellow car. But, we had one.

"But, it has a bed in the back," Dad said somewhat apologetically.

"A bed? Why would we need a bed in our car?" I asked.

A good question. No answer.

Expectations were high for our Fisk Park Softball team. We were the defending city champs. Practices were spirited and fun. We had discovered that winning was a lot more fun than losing. The season was about to start when:

"Mom? Mom? Guess what? Jerry (DeGroot) is sick. Someone said he caught polio," I announced as Dickie and I returned from practice.

"Oh my Lord," Mom said as she sat down on a dining room chair to catch her breath.

Scattered cases of polio had occurred the past two summers but the devastating virus had largely missed our community. Until now.

"What is polio?" I asked my mother, who was obviously greatly impacted by the gathering storm that was now blanketing the entire country.

"It's a disease that causes paralysis. Children who get it often can't walk or ..." Mom couldn't finish the sentence as tears welled in her eyes. The virus crippled my friend.

We had a family meeting and we prayed for Jerry.

Jerry was crippled by the polio but our prayers were answered. He survived, became a priest and now is the head of St. Norbert's College in DePere. Jerry overcame his handicap.

"Don't drink any water from any of the fountains at the park, kids," Mom said. "And, don't drink Cokes from anyone else's bottle and don't get real close to your friends," Mom continued.

"How can we play ball if we can't get close to our teammates, Mom?" was my obvious question.

We couldn't of course. The disease, also known as infantile paralysis, was spreading panic over the entire land like a smallpox epidemic. I recall that the city parks soon were closed. No one went to the movies or the beach. Our neighbor Molly Hannen also was infected, but fortunately hers wasn't serious. Almost everyone became a prisoner in their own home. But, we had a refuge from the insidious and debilitating virus. Sand Bay.

By the summer of 1948 our cottage at Sand Bay was not complete but it was livable. Still no electricity, so we used kerosene lamps. No indoor plumbing, so we used the "outhouse." And no refrigerator, so we used an "ice box." But, we were seemingly safe, away from crowds and had our very own beach to ourselves. Out of danger.

Until —

"Hub? They say that mosquitos carry the polio virus," Mom, with that worried look on her face, said.

Sand Bay was a breeding ground for the pesky insect. Behind our cottage and across Snake Island Road was a low swampy and marshy area. In the early evening just as the sun was setting the mosquitos, forming a visible black cloud, would rise from their native environment with their easily audible and distinctive droning "buzz." Terry and I, armed with cherry bombs and two- and four-inchers (fire crackers), would bombard the mosquito squadrons with these hand grenades and the percussion would knock them (temporarily) from the summer sky into the marsh. Now, we couldn't even torment our tormentors for fear of being bitten.

During the day the three of us literally lived in the water out of danger from the flying menace. We looked like wrinkled prunes at the end of the day. At night, we played ping-pong in our large screened-in porch that we called a breezeway, or we made a smokey bonfire on the beach. While fishing, we doused ourselves in a new product called "insect repellent," and used hats with netting that kept the critters from our necks.

The polio epidemic continued to plague the country for

six more years, until a microbiologist by the name of Jonas Salk discovered a vaccine that immunized children, as well as adults, against poliomyelitis. By 1960 new infections had decreased by 96%.

"Buster? We're out of ice. Go over to Johnson's and get a block, okay? And, take Terry with you," Mom said, probably to get some relief from her two "tigers."

Pulling my little red wagon (I think it was an American Flyer) Terry and I took the road to Johnson's store. We couldn't pull the wagon through the soft sand, so we had to take the long way to the store. On the way we stopped at the old Haines, now Brandes, property. Earlier we had made an amazing discovery. The basement of the old house had a large room filled with sawdust. That was where Mr. Haines had kept his ice during the summer. He would, during the winter, drive out onto the frozen bay and cut blocks of ice, and store them in this area in the basement. The ice, buried in the sawdust, would not melt and would last during the entire summer. Now, however, the sawdust had become a perfect haven for, SNAKES. Seemingly, hundreds and hundreds of green and brown snakes.

The flooring above the basement was removed and the former ice room was open to us above. Patiently we sat on the concrete ledge above the pit — the snake pit. As one of the slimy critters slithered out of his hole,

POW!

"You gottum!" Terry shouted.

My Red Ryder BB Gun, purchased by my dad as a Christmas present, found its mark. I handed my weapon to my ten-year-old brother.

POW! Another devil bit the dust. Terry had already become a good shot.

In the Army he would become a Marksman.

Now wary, the insidious colony of snakes retreated to their tunnel-laden lair. We continued on to get the ice.

"Hi Mr. Johnson," I said, as we entered the only store within miles. "We need some ice."

"That'll be ten cents a block," Mr. Johnson said as we

each dipped into the freezer for a drumstick (ice cream). Mr. Johnson had electricity and he had the only well at Sand Bay. He probably didn't want the county to extend the line to make our life a little easier. We hurried home so the ice wouldn't melt.

Not long after, Terry made another amazing discovery in a land that was an everyday adventure for any boy.

"Daddy! Daddy! There's a monster fish on our beach. He's bigger than I am," Terry exclaimed.

Skeptical but curious, Dad followed Terry down to the beach. It was, indeed, a monstrous fish. A "lunker."

"Well, I'll be darned," Dad said. "It's a Muskie. I didn't know there were Muskies in Green Bay."

"How big is he?" Terry wondered.

"He's got to be over five feet I guess," Dad surmised. "You know, these Muskies can swallow small ducks whole."

"Geez louise," I said, as I started to envision meeting up with this monster while swimming. Fortunately, this one was dead and the seagulls were already having a feast on the carcass.

"Some day we'll go fishing for Muskies," Dad said.

And we did, which I will relate to you shortly. As it turned out, according to Dale and Bill Stroschein, who now occupy the former area where Johnson's store once stood, a record Muskellunge was caught in 2000 in Sand Bay. It was over six feet in length but it was an "illegal catch." A term unheard of in the 1940's.

My friend Dickie was suffering from "cabin fever," mostly confined to his house. I invited him to spend several days at Sand Bay. He jumped at the chance.

"There's some real small streams on the other side of the road, Dickie. I've seen some real large fish in them," I relayed to my buddie.

"That's swell. Let's go to find out if they're still there," he replied.

Soaked in insect repellent, with long sleeved shirts and long pants tied at the ankles, we headed toward the marsh. I grabbed Dad's fishing net knowing that we would be in a pretty tight area.

"Look out for snakes," I warned Dickie as he began to waffle.

"I don't like it in these weeds, Buz. They're too tall. I won't be able to see the snakes," Dickie said haltingly with apprehension.

"Aw, they're not poisonous. Don't worry," I reassured my friend, who hadn't spent much time in the "woods."

We found a little, quiet stream that was only a couple of feet wide. "Shush," I said pressing my finger to my mouth.

"Look! A lunker!"

"What's a lunker?" Dickie asked, puzzled.

"It's a monster fish," I responded as I dipped the net into the shallow stream trapping the large fish.

"You got 'im! You got 'im, Buz," Dickie cried out. "Whew, what a monster."

Pleased as punch, Dickie and I took off running towards the cottage with our prize catch trapped in the net. Dad was standing in the driveway.

"Look what I caught, Dad."

"You caught him with the net?" Dad asked as he examined our two-foot-long prize.

"It's a Northern. And, it's not a him. It's a her. She is spawning — laying her eggs. You're going to kill all those baby fish if you don't get her back in the water right away. Go! Now!"

Deflated and concerned for the welfare of the mother pike, we carefully returned the lunker to her chosen spot.

Despite our misadventure, Dickie thought Sand Bay was swell.

We returned to Green Bay for a significant celebration. The State of Wisconsin was 100 years old. The Centennial Celebration. Movie film captures me and Sharon Bookmeier in the parade on a float that recognized all of those who had served as members of the Safety Patrol, or what is known today as Crossing Guards. We took our job seriously, which is now, I believe, entrusted to adults. Phyllis Kessler is prominent in the film as the leader of the parade and Larry, as expected, was following her every move. And, Phyllis had good "moves."

Our cottage in Sand Bay was much larger than our home in Green Bay. Mom had at last a spacious kitchen that opened up into a great living room, which was open to a rafted ceiling featuring an enormous clear-span window looking out onto the bay. Appropriately, it was called a "bay window."

Yet unfinished was a massive, native-rock fireplace. Preserved on film are the stonemasons completing their job during the summer of 1948. We had three large bedrooms downstairs, and an open yet unfinished kind of dormitory upstairs that could house a small army. What is so readily memorable is that the entire interior was finished in knotty pine that matched the massive pine log structural beams. We even had a garage. I suspect since no mortgage was ever filed of record that Dad paid cash for the entire project. He had reasons to be proud, and when finished the next summer it would be a showcase.

On a visit to Sand Bay in July 2003, I again walked down Snake Island Road, attempting to reframe a picture of 1949 from the modern up-to-date homes that now graced this popular area. I proceeded up the driveway that once greeted the Quists' arrival at this cherished spot. The new spacious home was a far cry from what was, in comparison, our modest cottage, but as I surveyed the pristine home a familiarity suddenly occurred to me. I rang the doorbell and explained to the owners, John and Leslie Denis, that this once was our most revered place. I was graciously invited inside. I couldn't believe what I saw! The west end of the Denis home was almost exactly as I remembered it from over fifty years past! The knotty pine paneling, the loft, the rafters that once sported the unfortunate seagulls, Terry's and my bedroom and the large panoramic bay window that allowed us to peer out onto God's magnificent creation. As I had just experienced visiting our old home on Dousman in Green Bay, I was home again. The Denis family had purchased the cottage in 1998 and the previous owners had remodeled and greatly expanded the cottage leaving most of the original home intact.

On this same return to my roots in 2003, I had just finished a game of golf at Horeshoe Bay with Harry Proctor and my cousin Gerry Barlament. The three of us were recalling those good 'ole days. I asked Harry:

"What was your favorite radio program after school?"

Without hesitation Harry jumped to his feet and bellowed out, "With his faithful Indian Companion Tonto, the daring and resourceful Masked Rider of the plain led the fight for law and order in the early western United States. Nowhere in the pages of history can one find a greater champion of Justice. Return with us now to those thrilling days of yesteryear. From out of the past come the thundering hoof beats of the great horse Silver. The Lone Ranger Rides again — Hi Ho Silver, Away!"

Proof again that our heroes were deeply ingrained in our psyche.

"Buster? How would you like to go fishing for Muskies?" Dad asked.

"Boy oh boy! That would be swell. Where are we going?"

"It's a lake near Hayward. It's a long ways. It will take us most of a day to get there," Dad informed me.

Geez, it was a long ways but the excitement of seeing and catching a Muskie sustained both of us. Dad had a friend of one of his BMA agents in Hayward that arranged for the boat, tackle and everything we needed. There was an unexpected surprise, however.

"Yuh can't take yer kid out on tha lake. He's too small," the grizzly old codger running the dock at Grindstone Lake said. "These lunkers will jerk him outta that boat as easy as fallin' off a log."

"How about if he doesn't fish?" Dad suggested.

"Guess that'll be okays," the old-timer agreed.

Dad had to get all new equipment. He needed a stronger casting rod and thirty pound test line with a steel wire leader in order to reel in these lunkers. I was awed by the pictures of the Muskies in the tackle shop at the lake.

Dad's friend knew the lake and the spots but we didn't

have any luck. It was getting close to noon when there was little chance that the Muskies would bite. We were drifting with the motor off. I had rigged a line with a bobber and, not having a pole, the line was attached to a small wooden peg that I held in my hand.

"Dad? I'm hungry. Can I get a sandwich and a coke?"

"Sure, help yourself to the cooler," Dad replied.

I wedged the wooden peg into the rail on the side of the boat so I would have both hands free to eat. I opened the coke and tossed the cap overboard. Leaning against the side of the boat I watched the shiny, silver bottle cap float towards the bottom. Suddenly out from under the boat a huge black shape of a fish appeared pursuing the shiny cap.

"Daddy!" I yelled. "Look! A Muskie!"

Both my dad and his friend moved to my side of the boat, tipping it precariously close to the water. While they were fumbling with their rods the Muskie grabbed my line and headed towards the lily pads. My line, stuck in the railing of the boat, tipped the boat even further. As the boat was being pulled by the Muskie water rushed in over the side. We were being swamped!

Everybody was yelling. We were going to sink!

Suddenly my line snapped! The boat righted itself. We didn't capsize but we were ankle deep in water. Gosh, what an experience. But, the big one got away.

I discovered that fishing was like flying. Hours and hours of boredom mixed with moments of excitement. Dad caught a few two- or three-footers but we failed to land a lunker.

Fast forward to the year 2001. I've been invited by Tom Noble from Minneapolis on a fishing trip to Reindeer Lake in Saskatchewan, Canada, which is very close to the Arctic Circle. I'm with a group of six very experienced anglers from Minneapolis. Their quest is for Northern Pike — a close cousin to the Muskie. It was July 1st and 36° when we arrived at the Arctic Lodge (by airplane, since there were no roads in this part of the "outback").

Accompanied by an Indian guide, Terry Dunlay and I

headed out on the massive lake on a rainy, cold and misty day. I tried to recall all the fundamentals taught to me so many years ago by my father, but snarls and backlashes in my reel caused considerable down time. Despite my fumbling and bumbling using barbless hooks, I caught eleven pikes and one lake trout. All around 36 inches but no lunkers. One of the guys in our party caught a trophy pike — 46 inches. A "keeper." All the others were catch and release.

"Fish on," the guide yelled as one of us got a "hit."

"Fish off," he said when I would lose my catch.

The Northern Pike are very aggressive fish endowed with razor sharp teeth. Our Indian guide, equipped with heavy gloves, removed the hooks, allowing us to keep all our fingers. On one occasion Terry brought a small pike up alongside our boat and before the guide could capture the exhausted fish in the net a monstrous comrade attacked and bit off almost one-half of the smaller fish! His own brother at that! Experts say that the pike can catch and eat prey up to half its size because of their massive hinged jaw.

In three days I had managed to land 38 fish, all larger than any I had ever caught back in the old days in Door County. We had a pool with a money prize going to the fisherman who caught the biggest lunker. We were down to the last few hours of this magnificent experience and Terry and I were physically running out of gas. "One more spot," the guide suggested.

Our guide maneuvered the boat into a small cove in shallow water on a dark overcast day. We cast our lines towards the reeds and the bank of the shoreline. Under the tutorship of my friend Terry I had learned how to begin reeling in my line before my lure hit the water so it wouldn't snag on the bottom. I chose a "red eye wiggler," which was a bright, shiny, stainless steel lure that prominently featured two large, glass, red eyes on each side. Smart choice.

I deftly cast my line towards the bank. Suddenly out of the still waters a massive creature soared, attacking the lure before it hit the water! The battle was on.

"Fish on!" the guide yelled.

"Keep your line as tight as a bull's ass at fly time," Terry

202

joked. "Ya got a keeper."

Feet braced against the sides of our 16' aluminum Lund boat I steadied myself for the confrontation of a lifetime. Mr. Pike ran and headed for deeper water under the boat. He twisted and turned trying to chew through the steel wire leader. My right arm began to cramp from four days of casting.

"Terry? I don't think I can get him in," I said, sort of pleading for help.

"He's all yours. You can get 'im," Terry reassured me.

Fifteen dramatic and exhausting minutes passed, filled with excitement and potential pride. Finally, Mr. Pike succumbed to the battle as I pulled him alongside the boat.

"Keep that line tight!" Terry yelled. "He's probably playing possum."

I had lost a lunker the day before by relaxing too soon. These guys were clever, experienced fighters.

Adroitly, our guide slipped the net under Mr. Pike and lifted the lunker into the boat. I was exhausted but victorious. The catch of the day measured 47½ inches and the guide estimated that he weighed over 30 pounds! The "rookie" won the pool. On the ground at the Winnipeg airport I called my wife.

"Hon, UPS will be delivering a long, six-foot box in a day or so. Be sure to take it down to the grocery store and keep it in the freezer, okay?"

"Oh no," she replied, at the thought of a ghastly trophy adorning her contemporary home.

April fool!

I released the lunker and kept the photograph to prove that my fish story wasn't just a fish story. It wasn't a Muskie but Dad would have been proud. Dad was always proud of me.

———————

Just prior to the start of school, Dad had a proposition for me.

"Buster? There's a paper route available in our neighborhood. Would you like a job as a paper boy?"

"Ah geez, that would be neat, Dad. What do I have to

203

do to get it?" I asked.

"You have to buy the route from the boy who has it now," he relayed to me. "It's $75.00."

"Buy it?"

"Yep. I'll put up the money and you can pay me back, but you've got to be certain that this is something you want to do. Like the mail, come rain or come shine, the paper has to be delivered. Do you understand?" Dad warned me.

Like most kids my age I saw the opportunity and didn't hear the warning. This would be my first honest-to-goodness job. Dad paid me for cutting the lawn and washing his car, but this was a real job. Little did I know how difficult it would be.

"This is how you fold it," the paper boy who sold me the route instructed me, as I began my three-day training program. "It has to be real tight so it doesn't come apart when it hits the ground or the porch, you know," he added.

There weren't any rubber bands to tie the newspaper. Nor were there any plastic bags to keep the paper together and dry from the inevitable rain and soon-to-fall snow.

There were seventy-seven customers on this route, which was north of Bond Street and west of Gray, and extended all the way to Velp Avenue (which was out in the country in those days).

"Pack all the folded papers in the bag like this and then use the straps to warp around your handlebars on your bike like this," he instructed me. "Then you'll be able to pick 'em out of the bag as you ride along and throw them onto the porch. I'll show you when we get to the route. It's real easy when you get the hang of it."

With the bag loaded and resting on his handlebars and me on my Schwin, we rode out past Elmore School to the route. My instructor tossed the paper with great skill backhand across his body on to the porches. Some missed but he hit most of them.

"That's all there is to it," my experienced trainer said in a nonchalant manner. "'Cept," he said, "watch out for the old crotchety fart that lives in that house. He's mean sometimes."

The next day my mentor showed me how to do the bookkeeping after I made my collections. He did have one last piece of advice, however.

"Watch out for Joey. He's a shyster."

I didn't quite know what he meant, but I soon found out.

The *Press-Gazette* truck dropped our papers off at Rondou's Store, just a few blocks east of Annunciation School on Bond Street; it was owned by two great aunts of Robert and Pam Rondou, our next-door neighbors. Each bundle of papers had the correct number of newspapers (77) plus a couple of extras. There were about ten paper boys at this station. The guy in charge was an older boy named Joey. Joey wasn't a shyster. He was a "schmuck."

Joey was out of high school, or never finished. He looked like a punk, with a cigarette always hanging out of the corner of his mouth. One day in my first week I missed the drop-off of my papers by a few minutes.

"Hey guys? Any of you seen my papers?" I asked.

No one answered. A few guys snickered.

Joey came walking out of the store puffing on a cigarette. When he didn't have one in his mouth he had one stuck above his ear. A real tough-looking guy. Much taller than I was but he was real skinny.

"Joey? My papers aren't here," I asked.

"Oh geez, doze guys must of forgot to leave 'em," Joey said with a tell-tale smirk on his face. Some of the paper boys laughed. Joey jumped on his motorcycle and left. All the other kids soon left except one.

"You can't tell on me Buster," the last remaining paper boy said. "Joey hid your papers but if you tell he'll beat me up."

"I won't tell, I promise."

"They're under the store in the back," my friend in need said as he hurriedly got on his bike and left.

Sure 'nuf. My papers were scattered in a crawl space at the back of the store. It was dirty and smelly under the old store and it took me a long time to get them together and folded. People expected their papers to be on time. Joey knew that I would incur the wrath of my customers for being late.

The old crotchety man was waiting for me as I neared the end of my route just south of Velp Avenue.

"Listen kid. Let me tell you how the cow ate the cabbage," the old man said. I didn't know what he meant, but I was about to find out.

"My paper's gotta be on time, ya hear? An' when its rainin' or snowin' I want the paper in between the storm door and the door, ya hear? If not, I ain't goin' to pay ya, ya hear?"

"Yes sir," I said meekly. I heard what he said.

Riding my bike on Velp Avenue to get to my last customer's house was very risky. The road to Duck Creek was extremely narrow for a major highway and the gravel shoulder was not suitable for bikes. The gravel was actually not what you would normally expect (pea-sized) alongside the road. Small, sharply-edged rocks would be a more accurate description. It was darned near impossible to ride on the shoulder. I had to walk my bike over the rocks.

"Don't you ever ride your bike on Velp Avenue," Mom warned me several times. She had good reason to be wary.

My cousin Gerry Barlament, who lived in Duck Creek, rode his bike on Velp one evening on his way home from Green Bay. A driver, probably unable to see the cyclist or drunk, hit Gerry with such force that the bike and its rider catapulted into the ditch out of sight from the unlit highway. Gerry, knocked unconscious and desperately in need of medical care, was left there to die.

A neighbor happened to be outside his home at the time of the accident. He thought he heard the sound of the crash which made him search his field along the highway. He heard a faint cry.

"Help me ... help me," the muffled voice repeated.

The good samaritan discovered the young boy, loaded him into his truck and got him to the hospital. My cousin had multiple injuries but his life was spared.

The driver was never identified.

Riding the bike with a full load, with only one hand on the handle bars, and throwing the paper accurately was a lot tougher than most anyone would think. Add to that a pesky dog yapping and snapping at your heels. It wasn't easy, but, the hard part was about to come.

SNOW TIME!

With the sidewalks packed with snow or ice my bike was inoperable. Often I loaded my bag on my sled and walked. Daylight vanished quickly in the winter and I wouldn't get home until after everyone else had eaten supper. When the weather got severe, Dad drove the car while I ran and placed the paper in each door. Rain or shine, the paper had to be delivered. The radio and I were the only source of the news. A big responsibility for a twelve-year-old kid. I took my job seriously.

Each paper sold for five cents. A weekly subscription, that I collected once a week, was 35¢. I retained 8.5¢ per customer for my earnings. As I recall, I made approximately seven dollars per week if all my customers paid their account. Some (seemingly) were never home. Some had difficulty paying. It was a real course in Business 101. My friend Dickie soon bought a route and every day we packed our papers together.

As I adjusted to the rigors of my new job, I also opened another door in my life: Junior High School. The old artifact of a school that looked like a fort was as ominous and unfriendly as the hard-nosed commandant that ruled it with an iron fist. I got the message the very first day that this intimidating place wasn't warm and fuzzy like Elmore School.

"Buster? Is that your real name?" the person registering me at Franklin Junior High asked coolly.

"Well no. But I've been called Buster all my life," I responded.

"Miss McMahon does not permit the use of nicknames at Franklin. What is your given name?"

"It's Herbert, but I don't like Herbert," I relayed to my

inquisitor.

"That's unfortunate. What is your middle name," she asked.

"It's Larry but ..."

"Then Larry it will be. And remember, you are not to use the name Buster anywhere in school, and tell your friends not to call you Buster," the registrar, who was more of a drill sergeant, demanded.

"Yes ma'am," I replied meekly and respectfully.

I met up with Jerry and Harry Proctor, Calvin Whiting and a couple other "Elmorons" as we filed into the assembly hall for "indoctrination." I introduced my friends to Otie, my fire-eating friend, who came to Franklin from Fort Howard School. We were all milling around talking about our summer exploits when a loud, bellicose voice echoed throughout the hall.

"Sit down and stop talking! Right now!" the short, heavy-set woman with grey-blue hair bellowed out. That was our first introduction to Miss Margaret McMahon, the commandant and chief executioner of Franklin Junior High.

"When I come into the room you are all to stand at attention and stop talking immediately. There is one thing you new seventh graders need to know as the eighth and ninth graders will tell you. I'm the boss around here and I make all the decisions. If you remember that one rule, you'll get along at Franklin just fine," the lady, whose deep voice sounded more like a man's, laid out in plain simple English. My mom had warned me about Miss McMahon. My cousin Larry had also warned me about Miss McMahon. Joanie had warned me too, but until I witnessed her in the flesh, standing on the stage looking down on me possessed with the presence of a general, I couldn't appreciate how intimidating this person could be. Her reputation was well-founded, as we were about to discover.

We were given a list of Miss McMahon's rules. One, in particular, was as unfathomable as it was impracticable:

"NO MALE STUDENT SHALL USE THE GIRLS'

STAIRWAY."

"NO FEMALE STUDENT SHALL USE THE BOYS' STAIRWAY."

It didn't take Jerry Proctor long to determine that a rule was a rule and there was a Ruler. Given permission to retrieve something from his locker on the first floor, Jerry was at one end of the long hallway and the boys' stairway was at the other. As he surveyed the calm and quiet of the hallway and peered down the stairs he thought to himself, "Heck there's no one around. No one will see me if I take the girls' stairway."

WRONG!

No sooner had Jerry hit the bottom step when out of nowhere popped the formidable form of Miss McMahon.

"Stop!" she shouted, her voice echoing in the vacant, chamber-like hallway, undoubtedly finding its way into the nearby classrooms for equal effect.

Jerry froze in his tracks and he turned slowly to meet the most hellacious hall monitor of all hall monitors face-to-face. Silence. Not another word was spoken. Only a slight nod of Miss McMahon's head — her nose pointing to the top of the stairs. Jerry quickly retreated taking two steps at a time. He muttered to himself, "Where did she come from? Where ...?"

Miss McMahon, affectionately and surreptitiously referred to by her students as "Mickey," was everywhere. She looked and moved like a Sherman tank equipped with modern stealth technology.

Billy La Fave was a pretty tough kid from the south side of town near Broadway. I shared a locker with him for a short time in P.E. class. He also sat in front of me in study hall. We sat in old wrought-iron and wooden desks with ink wells in the top right hand corner of the desk. A teacher sat at a desk perched on the stage overlooking the students in the study hall. A "click" from the closing of the rings on your notebook was cause for expulsion from study hall and, worst of all, a visit to THE principal's office. The room was absolutely silent. Not a creature was stirring, not even a ...

Billy had a large geography book propped up on his desk to demonstrate to the teacher in front of him that he was reading his assignment. Hidden, out of sight, in the text book was a Superman Comic Book. The ruse worked well until —

I sensed the presence of someone lurking over my shoulder. Ah geez! It was Miss McMahon! I shuttered. My sphincter puckered up.

Without a word and without warning the mighty Miss McMahon grabbed Billy by his shirt and flat lifted him out of his seat! With the miscreant's upper torso wedged in a headlock Mickey proceeded to drag Billy out the swinging glass door to the "tower." Then, for everyone's edification, Mickey left the intercom in the "open" position so we could benefit from the prisoner's fate. Dave Evjue, one of my new friends, told me that the exact same fate befell Don Paschen, who was also caught red-handed reading a comic book. A misdeed of gigantic proportions.

Lest the reader think that I'm prone to hyperbole, current testimony from a teacher who served in this woman's army validates my story.

Ralph Swartz came to Franklin as a social studies teacher in this year, 1948. He will be remembered for his natty attire and omnipresent bow tie. Hearing that there might be an opening at Franklin Junior High, Mr. Swartz called upon the Superintendent of Schools, Mr. Denman. He quickly learned that:

"If you're interested in a position at Franklin, the person you have to see is Miss McMahon."

Ralph passed the litmus test — initially.

All teachers were required to pick up their mail in the principal's office every day before classes started. No exceptions. One day Ralph was one minute late. Standing in a commanding position at the mail station was, you guessed it, the irrecusable Miss McMahon.

Not a word was said. Mickey pointed to her watch. Ralph was never late again. In Mickey's defense, Ralph said, "She ran a tight ship. She was a good administrator." Many generals are.

So the buxom and burly Miss McMahon had the students and her teachers intimidated and timorous. Surely some of the parents met her head-on when their children were verbally or physically abused? Oh yeah?

A vice president of the Wisconsin Public Service (WPS) complained to the chairman of the board of WPS that his son had been humiliated and banged around in the principal's office. The vice president imposed upon his boss, one of the most influential and powerful businessmen in the community, to intercede in his son's behalf to put an end to this absurd treatment.

"Miss McMahon? You will not treat the children of my employees in this way. Do you hear me?" the chairman forcibly said in unmistakable terms on the telephone.

"But I did!" was the terse reply. End of conversation.

My cousin Merlin Barlament preceded me to these hallowed halls by fifteen years. "Mickey" was then about age 43. Merlin, a ninth grader, was a good-sized, athletic kid. He writes in his memoir:

The principal was Margaret McMahon, a large, buxom woman given to wearing purple dresses and in possession of a very short fuse. I was summoned to her office in my second year there (Franklin). We had been assigned lockers to be shared with another student and two different times were scheduled to meet. My good partner did not show up for either meeting so I put a lock on it. He reported that I had failed to show and had locked him out. I suppose, since his name was Farley, she placed more credence to his story. I told her that was a lie and she swung at me with no warning. Despite the surprise attack, my reflexes were fast enough that I jumped back and caused her to miss. In doing so though, I fell through the doors of the bookcase.

Her assistant principal (Miss Schweger) rushed in with the crash and told Maggie not to hit me again. To ease her mind I said, "Aw, she missed me." From then on I was not her favorite.

Franklin Junior High was adjacent and connected to West High School. My "shop" class was taught by Ed Boguski, who was Bob's (my teammate at Elmore School) father, and was in West High. Joanie was now a senior but I avoided her because she always introduced me as "her little brother." According to my chart from the Y I was now 5'6" tall and weighed 124 pounds. I was bigger than my sister. So, "nah, nah, nah, nah, nah."

Orville Hays also began his first year at Franklin in 1948. He was my P.E. teacher. I'll never forget one of the first days in class.

"Larry? (That was me.) You are obviously having trouble seeing the eye chart. You need to see a doctor for glasses."

"Aw geez. The guys are going to call me 'four eyes,'" I said. Reluctantly, I got fitted for glasses but wore them sparingly, and at least on one occasion "toyed" with them.

Mr. Boguski, my shop teacher, was apparently also near-sighted. Like many people often do he let his glasses slide down on the bridge of his nose while he was addressing and looking at the class. I must have thought he looked odd. I lowered my glasses to the tip of my nose. My classmates snickered.

"Larry? Are you trying to be funny?" Mr. Boguski asked me.

"No sir," I responded respectfully.

"You're trying to be a wiseacre, aren't you?" he continued, obviously irritated. "You're mimicking me, aren't you?"

"No sir. My glasses just slipped," was my feeble excuse.

"Maybe you would like to put on a little demonstration for Miss McMahon, huh?" my teacher said as he approached me and grabbed me by my arm.

"Aw geez, not the principal's office," I thought to myself as Mr. Boguski led me out of the class.

Portents of doom surrounded me like an enveloping cloud. Would Miss McMahon beat me up? Would I have to write "I will not cut up in class" 1,000 times on the blackboard? What would be my fate? I was worried as I entered the principal's office, aka "the tower."

I dodged a bullet. The commandant and chief executioner was out of the office! Miss Schweger, the assistant principal, who was short, rather plump and much less intimidating than her mentor, scurried me off to an ante room and told me to stand facing the corner of the room.

Not one word was said to me. "I must be getting the silent treatment," I thought. One hour passed. Then two. I desperately had to take a pee but I didn't dare say a word. I was about to go in my pants when another bell rang. The last bell of the day.

"You can go now," Miss Schweger said curtly.

I was literally saved by the bell.

Changing teachers for every class was new to all of us and one of our biggest adjustments to Junior High, but most were pleasant experiences. Like history class with Miss Shaunessy, a young, very attractive lady probably teaching her first year.

Sally Frisch, a good looking girl sitting next to me, whispered, "Miss Shaunessy is getting married. The paper said she is marrying Robert E. Lee."

Being in history class I thought that information was pretty significant. I raised my hand.

"Miss Shaunessy? I understand that you are marrying a famous character, Robert E. Lee."

Taken by surprise my teacher replied, "We won't discuss that."

And, we didn't.

Getting married was an occupational hazard, particularly working in Mickey's domain. After class Sally said, ignoring one of Mickey's rules:

"Buster, I can't believe that you asked her that. You're pretty bold, you know that?"

"Geez, I thought that was swell. She's so darned pretty. I can see why she would get asked. Every guy in class is in love with her," I relayed to my new friend.

I was also bold enough to ask Sally for a date. She

accepted. Cousin Larry took us to a movie in Dad's Nash and picked us up. Sally and Sharon Bookmeier would soon become the best of friends. They must have compared notes. I probably passed muster. I remained friends with both of them for a long time.

After school was out many of us guys would go across the street to Fisk Park to watch the West High varsity football team practice. My cousin Larry was on the team. So was Dick Proctor, Harry and Jerry's brother. I took a few moments before I went to get my papers.

At practice I could see the stars, those players I idolized, up close: Blair Mathews, whom I knew at the Y; Bob Coppens, who coached our basketball team at Elmore the year prior; Bob Markham and Whitey Stuiber, my cousin's buddies who took Dad's car on the joyride to Chicago; Doug Lier, one of my sister's friends; and Lyle Tobin, who was one of Joanie's boyfriends. And, of course, Floyd Rathburn, the star halfback for the Wildcats. So prominent in the mind of a twelve-year-old were these heroes that I can put faces and names together over fifty years later. These years were impressionable.

"Frosty" Ferzacca, the head coach of the Wildcats (who was allowed to use his nickname because he was out of Mickey's jurisdiction), was a wizard of the T-formation. He had high hopes for the 1948 team but the season fizzled and West High had only a 4 win, 3 loss record going into THE game, the East-West War. This game was equal to the Marinette-Menominee matchup in Dad's day, which I chronicled earlier. There was no Fox River Conference title at stake, only the bragging rights to the city championship — but that was more than enough incentive.

The Wildcats totally outplayed the East High Red Devils and won 13-0. They led in first downs 18 to 5 and in total yards gained 241 to 98. Ken Woosencraft kicked two field goals and Floyd Rathburn, the 175-pound bruising running back, ran for 103 yards and one touchdown. It was, however, the riot after the game that made this year, 1948, memorable. The lead line in the November 8th *Press-Gazette* said:

Whether Green Bay's half-century-old East-West

game will be discontinued hung in the balance today, as police and school authorities pondered the reasons for the worst demonstration — Major Olejniczak denied that it was a riot — in the city's history and how to prevent its repetition.

The melee touched us personally.

"Someone has taken my briefcase!" Dad exclaimed as we returned to our car after the game. "Why would someone steal my briefcase?"

Dad had just written hundreds of insurance applications on employees at Kraft Foods, and most of that paperwork was still in the car on the weekend. He was forced to write them over again, which took days and days of work. He, like most of the Bayites, never locked his car no matter where it was parked. It was one of the few times that I witnessed anger in my easy-going father.

Hundreds of rambunctious students had blocked traffic on the Walnut Street Bridge. According to reports, one car, a late 1930's Chevy or Ford two-door coupe, which was as stubby and pugnacious-looking as its occupants, belonged to our celebrated principal, Margaret McMahon, and her roommate and assistant principal Miss Schweger. Some say that our cars are an extension of ourselves. Mickey's car was indeed, her.

Rumors running rampant at Franklin on Monday morning told a story that our classmate, the tough guy Billy La Fave, was one of the ring leaders of the riot. He, according to reports, brandishing a sledge hammer or a pick axe, was planting the weapon into the hoods of a few of the parked cars stranded on the bridge. One such car was Miss McMahon's! She had no difficulty identifying the culprit.

Time may have embellished this story but one thing is certain: there was an emergency assembly on Monday in the West High auditorium, and an irate and angry Miss McMahon delivered an unforgettable tirade on "hooliganism" and how our generation was going to hell in a handbasket! So, something significant happened to Miss McMahon that weekend.

Some of my friends don't remember Billy La Fave. No

215

wonder. I suspect that his tenure at Franklin could have been terminated after this incident. But Dave Evjue remembers him quite well from Lincoln when he was kicked out of Chappel School. Yes, I have a vivid imagination, but I can't believe that the basic tenets of this story are not true.

On some Friday afternoons during the football season, after delivering my papers, I rode my bike to Annunciation School to watch Dickie play against the other Catholic schools. He kept his paper route even when he started to play ball. Seventh graders at Annunciation could play tackle football, and as I watched the action through rolling clouds of dust and dirt I was frothing at the bit to play. At Franklin, I couldn't participate until I was in the ninth grade.

Father Kiernan, who was head of Annunciation School, always attended the games. He looked unapproachable dressed in his cassock, but I desperately wanted to play football and I wasn't too keen about Franklin Junior High so —

"Father Kiernan?" I asked, looking up at this stately, dignified-looking man.

"Yes, my son," he replied.

"I'm Dickie Maierle's best friend. Can I come to Annunciation?" I implored.

"Well son, are you Catholic?" Father Kiernan replied.

"Ah, ah — no," I replied. I go to Grace Lutheran Church," I confessed.

Father Kiernan, with a broad smile on his face chuckled a bit.

"Well son," he continued, "I would suggest that you discuss this with your parents."

That was as close as I came to conversion to Catholicism until a beautiful Catholic girl came into my life eleven years later. Imponderable as it seemed at that time, fifty years later the two prominent churches would be discussing reunification and the forgiveness of Martin Luther's transgression. Given then what we know today, maybe Father Kiernan would have said in answer to my inquiry,

"Certainly son. We'd love to have you attend Annunciation."
Gosh! I could have played football in the seventh grade.

As dark and rigid as Franklin was there were rays of sunshine in the form of the opposite sex. Sharon Bookmeier was still at the top of the list, but new girls like Sally Frisch, Marsha Liedeka, Charlotte Fisk, Helen Ward, Nan Eliason and others were "ooh, la, la." A trim, lithesome blonde by the name of Joy Randoph particularly caught my eye.

As one could imagine given separate staircases, there weren't too many boy-girl activities at Franklin. Frequently, however, there were dances at the Young Women's Christian Association (YWCA, we called the YW) and our friends' houses. Mom and Dad would drop me off and pick me up. What happened in the two intervening hours was a mystery. I remember that the dances were upstairs at the YW.

Making eye contact with Joy across the room I smiled.

She smiled.

I waved my hand.

She giggled and deferred to her friends. Then she gave me a little wave.

I gradually worked my way across the crowded room and summoned up enough nerve to speak to her.

"I'm B — oh Larry," catching myself, I said.

"I know who you are. Your friends call you Buster, don't they?" the beautiful blonde with an angelic face and flawless complexion replied.

"It's a nice dance, huh?" I asked awkwardly, trying to break the ice while the jukebox played "To Each His Own" by Eddie Howard. I couldn't admit to Joy that I didn't know how to dance. She probably would think I was a "putz." So, we talked.

I was fortunate to be invited to parties on Friday nights at the homes of my newfound friends. Junior High widened our social circle. Charlotte Fisk, whose family I always assumed at one time had once owned the land that we knew as Fisk Park, hosted several parties. The boys usually were Duke Merdinger, Bob Greiser, Dave Fischer,

Dave Evjue and others. The girls were Helen Ward, Marsha Liedeka, Nan Eliason, Amy Stewart and others. Amy was an interesting and courageous young lady. She was a small person — a midget.

A popular game was "pin the tail on the donkey," which was always good for laughs. "Musical chairs" was another. Faced with a limited number in our group I was compelled to try to learn how to dance. We even got a little "creative." Rather than facing each other someone (it was probably Duke, who was considerably "faster" than the rest of us boys) suggested that the boys face the back of the girl with our left hand on our partner's waist and the right hand extended outward. We thought this new technique was swell until:

"For crying out loud," Charlotte's mother said as she came down to the basement to check on us. "That's not the correct way to dance. Where do you kids get these crazy ideas?"

We quickly conformed. Left alone again to our own devices it was time to play "spin the bottle." Aligned in a circle alternating boy-girl, boy-girl, a coke bottle was spun by one of the kids and the person in the middle would kiss the person of the opposite sex that the bottle pointed to when it stopped spinning. A peck on the lips was usually followed by giggles and screeches. Finally, I was the "spinner." The bottle stopped. It pointed straight at Amy.

I paused. I felt strange. I knew that everyone's eyes were on me. Kissing any of the other girls would be swell. Kissing Amy would be different. After all, she was different. Very different. I slowly made my way across the circle. On my knees I was as tall as Amy. I paused again.

"You don't have to kiss me if you don't want to Buster. I understand," she said softly so no one could hear.

Despite the fact that I was having a difficult time assessing the situation, I said, "I want to kiss you."

And, I did. Everyone cheered.

The irony, of course, is that Amy had a better sense of who she was than we had of ourselves as "normal" people. Privately she may have had her bad moments, but with her peers, she was determined to live and to compete in a big

218

person's world. I always admired the way she handled herself. Unfortunately, Amy died at a young age.

It was difficult for me to understand why approaching a girl posed such a quandary that it made my palms sweat. At Elmore School we played baseball and kickball with the girls and Sharon, who could run just as fast as I could, was just, well, one of the guys. Somehow, things were different now, and that wasn't the only thing I observed. Intuitively, music, which I paid little attention to previously, was arousing my senses, as it was also affecting my friends.

Joanie, my sister, bought a new album called "South Pacific." She played it over and over again. Soon, I discovered that I knew the words of all the songs and would sing along with the record that she played on her portable record player. Strangely, I now could recall the old war songs like "I'll Be Seeing You," "We'll Meet Again," and "The White Cliffs of Dover," and responded energetically to Glenn Miller's upbeat tempo of "In The Mood" (despite the fact that I couldn't dance very well, much less jitterbug). I wasn't unique. I think all of us were moved by the sounds that we absorbed.

After the turn of the century, a research team at Dartmouth (College) Center for Cognitive Neuroscience made a significant discovery. Using functional magnetic resonance imaging, the researchers found that the ability to recognize and retain music is found in the rostromedial prefrontal cortex of the brain, which also plays a key role in learning and the response and control of emotions.[1] What does this have to do with this memoir or anything at all?

Virtually all eras are defined with certain types of music. Music, more than any other sensory stimulus, has a profound impact on young people in particular, and can change their attitudes, behavior, values and their entire lives, as we'll soon discover. For certain, it changed mine. But, that was still a few years away.

Winter and ice-skating provided a breakthrough as far as my bashfulness was concerned. Though I couldn't dance well I was an accomplished skater, and the rink at

Fisk Park at night was the perfect setting for "getting acquainted." Joy and I skated to the music of "Peg O' My Heart," "Deep Purple" and other sort-of romantic songs. On solid ice and more confident of my footing we breezed around the large, crowded rink with our friends. Plus, at 25° and with heavy mittens, Joy wouldn't know that I had sweaty palms.

"Crack the whip!" Jerry Proctor yelled out as the mood and tempo of the music changed. We all formed up in a line extending from the light pole in the middle of the rink to the snow bank at the outer end of the circular ice pond. The speed of the line grew faster and faster with those on the outer end racing to keep up and keep in a straight line. Then, when those on the outside reached top speed those on the inside nearest the middle of the rink stopped. Three or four skaters, like someone on the end of a line of a water-ski boat crossing the wake, were forced to let go, sending them out of control towards the snow bank.

They were "whipped!"

Great fun, and I finally got comfortable with Joy.

Amongst all the photographs at the Y is one of our 1948-1949 Leaders Basketball Team. Paul Zimmerman was three or four inches taller than I and was our "big man" at about 5'10." Tommy Rand was already demonstrating the skills that would make him an outstanding high school and college player, following in his brother's footsteps. Norm Kroening was absent for the picture, but he was a strong player. Otie, by now, was a whiz at handling the ball. Today, he would be a point guard. Tommy Watts, David Murray and a couple others completed our team. I have a write-up from one of our games. The headline in the *Press-Gazette* read:

JUNIOR LEADERS WIN
OPENING CAGE CONTEST
Opening games in the YMCA Intermediate Basketball League saw the Junior Leaders take a 25 to 13 win over the Washington Junior High-Y.... Buster Quist and Norm Kroening paced the Leaders' attack in the second game....

I have no idea who scored the most points, but in those days it didn't really matter to us. We played to have fun, but we also played to win.

Fifty years later Otie recalled to me as we played a round of golf together:

"You were really aggressive, Buster. You hustled all the time and came up with the loose balls and rebounds. We sure could have used you at West (High School)."

It was nice of Otie to say that. It reaffirmed my contention that I had to play hard at basketball to overcome my lack of a natural affinity for the game. My vertical jump was 17" at age 12 (measured at the Y), which was certainly nothing to write home about, but meaningful enough to mention for the sake of posterity. We didn't know then that white boys couldn't jump.

At age twelve-and-a-half I probably was struggling with growing pains. I finished the year with 1299 points; third place in my age group, and far below Dick Tahlier's 2166 points (who led all the intermediate class competitors). This year at the Y was more memorable for what happened outside the gym, however.

January 8, 1949, was Parents' Night. It was a formal dinner rather than a demonstration as in years past. It started at 6:00 p.m. according to the written program. Dressed in a new suit and tie Mom bought me for Christmas, I had been dropped off late in the afternoon, prior to the dinner. I had time to kill. But, time there almost killed me.

Otie, Tommy Rand and some of my friends were playing fooseball and other games in the lobby. Some of the older boys were playing table pool directly adjacent to us. An argument broke out amongst the players over whose turn it was for the table.

Words led to pushing and shoving.

Shoving led to a fistfight.

The confrontation escalated. My friends and I tried to get out of the way of the bigger boys. One of the protagonists grabbed a pool cue by the narrow end and took a prodigious swing at his adversary. He ducked. I

221

didn't!

THWACK!

Turning away from the action the cue caught me square in the back of my head. My lights went out for the second or third time. The blow opened a large gash on my skull.

"He's bleeding!" yelled one of the kids.

John Scovell and Lee Prodehl came running to my rescue. Blood was streaming down my neck and onto my new suit. I woke to find a large pack of ice on my head. My parents arrived and took me to the Bellin Hospital emergency room. Mom was worried about me. I was worried about my new suit.

I missed the banquet. I missed David Murray's invocation. I missed Paul Zimmerman's and Otie's speeches and Jimmy Ladwig's closing prayer. I just wished that guy with the pool cue had missed me.

A pattern of calamity was developing here. And, Jane wasn't the victim.

My cousin Larry's athletic career at West High was more an exercise in frustration than it was of competition. Larry was a member of the 1948 varsity football team but saw limited action. As he had done his previous two years, he tried out for the basketball team but failed to make the "cut." Commiserating with his buddies who suffered the same fate as a flock of chickens, an idea was hatched.

"Hey youse guys. Why don't we make up our own team?" Larry suggested.

"Geez n' plutz, Larry that's a swell idea," Lyle Tobin said.

"Let's talk to John Scovell at the Y and see if we can play there," Larry added.

And so, the West All Stars were born. All the team members were boys who had been cut and left off the West High School team. Along with Larry were Lyle Tobin, Ken Woosencraft, Chuck Alt, Forrest Clothier and Whitey Stuiber. Lo and behold this team of guys that "couldn't make it" found out that they could, and they won the

Green Bay City Championship. Then to top if off, the All Stars journeyed south to Madison, Wisconsin, in Dad's yellow Nash, and defeated the Madison City All Stars. Believe it or not, they were the state champs! Quite an accomplishment for six guys that couldn't make their own high school team. But, that's not the end of the story.

"I bet we can beat West," Larry suggested.

"Shoot, they'd never play us guys," Whitey retorted.

"If we needle 'em enough, I bet they will," Larry opined.

Sure enough, it worked. The West High varsity agreed to play the team that "couldn't make it" at the Y. Pat Malone, the Wildcats' coach, was not supposed to be in attendance, but apparently curiosity (befitting a cat) got the best of him. To Coach Malone's chagrin, the boys that didn't meet his muster, beat his best. Given that his team had just finished last in the Fox River Valley Conference, Coach Malone probably should have taken a closer look at those he rejected.

Larry and his teammates found vindication in their victory and a claim to fame.

————

It was late winter of 1949. All of us were anxious to see and feel the first signs of spring. When Dad said we were going to the cottage we naturally thought spring was in the air and summer would soon follow. We had no idea what was in store as we quickly loaded the "yellow bath tub" and headed north. I got a friend to deliver my route.

"Ice is threatening our cottage," Dad said, obviously concerned as we started out to Sand Bay.

"An ice storm?" Mom asked.

"No, Alex called and said it was an 'ice shove,'" Dad replied. "He said ice was piling up on the shoreline and had already taken out several cottages. Just flattened them."

"Geez. Did it hurt our house?" I asked, trying to picture in my mind what was happening. It was impossible to visualize. What was an "ice shove"?

"I don't know. Keep your fingers crossed, kids," Dad

continued with a decided look of concern on his face. "Here we're just about finished building our cottage and now this."

The roads off highway 57 were covered with snow and packed. It took twice the time to get to Sand Bay. We stopped and put on chains, which wasn't any fun. I crawled under the car to line them up with the tires as dirty slush dripped in my face.

We inched our car towards Johnson's Store. It was a sight to behold! A mountain of ice stood majestically but dangerously between us and our cottage and the bay. Unlike a glacier the ice had moved uphill relentlessly towards the store and had demolished Mr. Johnson's cabin like a blade of a bulldozer.

What about our cottage? The suspense was stretched like a rubber band.

Abandoning our car, which was about as reliable in the snow and ice as a drunk on skates, we headed west on foot over the Brandes property towards our cottage, holding our breath. Our birch trees near the beach had disappeared under the onslaught of ice. Terry and I, scrambling up the jagged teeth of the ice floe, finally got sight of our cottage.

"It's okay! It's okay!" Terry yelled, as he was the first to reach the top of the mountain of ice.

"Thank God!" Mom said as she tried to climb the slippery slope.

Dad returned to catch one of the rarest weather events known to man on film. It was, now knowing our home was safe, great fun to climb to the crest, and Terry and I hammed it up for posterity.

We had the good fortune or luck to build our home about 200 feet or more from the beach.

Numerous theories abound as to the cause of an "ice shove," but certain conditions are necessary to create this "perfect storm." The "shoves" normally occur in the early spring, when the ice begins to melt in the shallow water along the bay shore. For some inexplicable reason the water level drops dramatically, but it goes largely unnoticed due to the cover of ice. Suddenly, accompanied by high winds out of the north, the water rises and literally lifts and shoves or carries the ice towards the shoreline with such force and speed that it folds up like an accordion against the beach, taking anything in its wake with it. Bill Stroschein, who bought the Johnson Store in 1961, maintains that Sand Bay had a rocky beach until this "ice shove" occurred. If that is the case, this phenomenon that happened in 1948 was, indeed, a perfect storm.

Reaching age thirteen ushered in a plethora of changes in not only my life but in the lives of almost every young man. We weren't boys any more. We no longer played softball. We were old enough to play baseball, which we appropriately called "hardball." In Orville Hays' P.E. class we were introduced to track and field, as we ostensibly had the stamina and maturity now to run a mile. Most importantly, perhaps, we observed in the shower room that most of us were growing pubic hair and we were no longer embarrassed by the minuscule size of our penis, compared to the older boys. The code word for our private part was "mandrake," taken presumably from the cartoon "Mandrake the Magician."

In gym class I asked my new locker mate Wayne Zimmerman, "Billy told me he 'made' this girl. What does 'made' mean?"

"Ah, he's saying he had sex with her."

"Geez, awe schucks! Do you believe him?" I asked, my curiosity rising along with my testosterone to a new level.

"Aw, you know Billy. You can't believe half of what he says," Wayne responded.

Locker room talk at Franklin and at the Y was my introduction to the education so essential but elusive to all of us boys. As we huddled together in a booth at Dehn's Ice Cream Shop, one of the boys produced a comic-like book that when you quickly flipped the pages with your thumb, the nudes would simulate having sex. There certainly weren't any sex education classes at Franklin, nor were our parents forthcoming, so we learned what we

225

could "on the fly."

While the boys were grappling with their transformation, the girls also had a problem in their P.E. class.

"Jeepers, Mickey insists that we wear these old fashioned bloomers, for crying out loud," Marsha Liedeka said to her friends.

The "bloomers" were a throwback to the turn of the century. Our mothers wore them in P.E. class. Miss McMahon was indeed from another era, and nothing was about to change until she was gone. And, by the mid-fifties changes did, indeed, occur.

"Listen here youse guys," Joanie said addressing Terry and me firmly. "My date is coming to pick me up tonight and I don't want any monkey business out of either of you. This is a special date and I don't want you to embarrass me ... again."

Our sister didn't have many dates in high school, and when she did apparently her two "bothers" would discourage the boys from ever returning. This night however, was a special one. It was the Senior Prom.

Lyle Tobin was a tall, wiry, fun-loving red head who doodled in class drawing cartoons. In one, several guys are vying for Joanie's company while skating at Fisk Park. A caption above Joanie's head says:

"I'm sorry you handsome men but I promised this one to 'Varmit.'"

"Varmit" was Lyle's nickname.

In another, "Doan Doan" (Joanie's nickname) says:

"Besides Varmit is going to pick me up in his <u>new Nash</u> and when I get home I'm going to show my brother Terry how to play football."

If Joanie ever played football with Terry she would have been a tackling dummy.

Lyle and Joanie dated off and on during her senior year. Most of the time however she "hung out" with her girlfriends at Dehn's, Bay Beach, the Blue Jay games and the movies. Her friends were Mary Ellen Docter (Tom's sister, whom everyone called "Doc"), Jo Ann Krezien

(Johnny), Mary Feller (Janer), Jo Ann Secord (Zeke), and Mary Jane Renard and Pat Luzerne (who, fortunately or unfortunately, weren't saddled with nicknames). Boys and dating weren't that important to Joanie and her "gang," and the prospect of having sex was as remote as Joanie teaching Terry how to play football.

The theme of the *West Hi-Way 1949* (the yearbook) was the "49ers" of 100 years past. Cowboys and cacti project a western motif, which the yearbook's artists must have gathered from the westerns at the Strand Theater or library research of the old west. Little did Joanie or any of us know that we would all soon be living in the landscape pictured in the *Hi-Way*.

Our next-door neighbor Larry Fitchett came over to our house one evening after I finished my route.

"Buster? How would you like to be the bat boy for the team I manage?"

"Wow! That would be terrific. What team is it?" I asked anxiously.

"I will manage the Green Bay Junior American Legion Team. These are high school boys. Some of them that go to West I'm sure you know. We play teams all over the Fox River Valley. It will really help you learn the game," Larry detailed for me.

A picture appearing in the *Press-Gazette* in the early summer of 1949 featured the team. My high school heroes Roger Bookmeier (Sharon's brother), Floyd Rathburn (West High's star halfback), Blair Mathews (a Leader from the Y and free-throw champion), and others starred on this team.

After one of the team's games, Floyd, who played catcher, removed his protective cup and laid it on the bench.

"What's this thing for?" I asked.

Everyone laughed.

"I don't get it," I added, not knowing what was so funny.

Finally Larry offered an explanation, "It's only a water

cup."

The laughter was even louder. I finally got the "drift." Fortunately, I didn't use the cup to get a drink of water.

After the games, we seemed to always find an A&W Root Beer Stand. Larry and Lewis Morgan, the American Legion Post Athletic Chairman, would always dig into their pockets and come up with money for our celebratory treat. I think that the team may have won the state tournament. Little did I know then that baseball and the American Legion would play a pivotal role in my athletic career. Larry Fitchett heightened my interest in the game.

"Hub, I'm going to the Blue Jays' game tonight. Do you want me to take the boys?" our next door neighbor offered.

"Oh geez, they would love to go," Dad responded.

And we went to the game. Often I would go with my cousin Larry to the Blue Jay games. We would sit with the "Knot Hole Gang" along the third base line with our friends. The Blue Jays were a professional farm league team, and my stint at batboy and watching the young pros piqued my interest to a new level in baseball. My coach at Fisk Park suspected that my place was on the mound. He was right. I discovered that I had a strong right arm. With a heavy schedule of baseball, plus our family's desire to spend as much time as possible at Sand Bay, I sold my paper route. Dad recouped his investment and I didn't have to battle another winter.

Peddling papers was an incomparable experience. Being responsible to many different adults other than my parents imposed and ingrained a conscientiousness within me that I retained all my life in my profession. People were counting on this kid for information that they couldn't get any other way other than listening to their radio, which didn't fully satisfy their needs. Being counted on as a financial advisor, later in life, took on the same responsibility.

1. Paul Recer, Associated Press, *The Arizona Republic* (January 3, 2003).

CHAPTER 7: FIRST LOVE

THE "ICE SHOVE" HAD RETREATED, leaving a remarkable series of sand bars extending two or three hundred yards off shore. At certain times the water would only be ankle deep way out in the bay. It was great fun to be so far from the bay shore.

The cottage was, at last, finished. It looked pretty "spiffy." Dad's manager, Gilbert Diehl, had a meeting for all of BMA's agents in the state at the Edgewater Beach Hotel in Ephraim. When the meeting disbanded, most of his entourage came to Sand Bay for a day. Captured on film are a spirited (if that's possible) game of horseshoes, those catching rays on the beach or trying to reel in a bass in the lily pads, and most of the group enjoying smoked perch and beer on the beach. Mom appears to be enjoying her responsibility as hostess while Gil's wife Ellie, handicapped with a broken arm, can't fully fulfill her role as the manager's wife.

Dad and Gil were devout fishing buddies. One film clip shows Gil in chest high waders fly fishing in the Poppel River. Gil still is dressed in white shirt and tie! Presumably, Dad and Gil were on a sales call together and found time after the meeting to try to land some browns or rainbows, and they didn't want to take the time to change clothes.

Joanie wasn't able to enjoy the cottage much this summer because she was working. So memorable was her fun experience at the Alpine Inn in 1945 when WWII ended that she returned to Egg Harbor to work as a waitress for the Bertschingers. Most of the summer help were teenagers, and Joanie's first extensive time away from home and on her own was "swell." She would return again in 1950, somewhat reminiscent of Mom's summer at the Grand Hotel at Mackinac Island almost thirty years prior. My turn to carry on a summer tradition would soon follow.

Captured on the same film is one of the most memorable days in my young life. Dad had purchased a large yellow and blue plastic beach ball. Terry and I were diving onto the resilient sphere in the shallow water, repelling us off into the air like a missile launched from a pad. After Dad and his ever-present camera had departed, leaving us at the main beach by Johnson's Store, a beautiful young girl approached me.

"You guys are having a heck of a lot of fun with that ball. Can I join in?" she asked.

Astonished, I stared at this older and magnificent creature for a moment and then replied:

"Oh, oh sure."

"I'm Karen," she said. "I live up the beach."

"My name is Buster. That's my brother Terry. We live in the big cottage over there," I said pointing in a southwesterly direction.

"Oh, I've walked down there in front of your house while it was going up. It's neat," she said, as Terry interrupted our one-on-one exchange.

We must have played with the beach ball for a couple of hours.

"I best be going home," Karen said. "Are you going to be here tomorrow?"

"Sure, sure. Will you?"

"See ya," Karen said playfully, and she bounded off down the beach. Transfixed, my eyes followed this vivacious girl until she faded into the surf and sand.

Karen was obviously older than I was. A lot older. She had a beautiful wide, engaging smile but it was her curvaceous body that captured my eye. Terry didn't pay much attention to her. I wouldn't have at his age either. My interests were dramatically changing.

I managed to escape from Terry the next day. I think he went fishing to Snake Island with Dad. I had Karen to myself.

"How about a drumstick or a coke?" I asked the beautiful girl from up the beach.

"Geez, that would be neat," she purred in a sort of mature way that I was certainly unaccustomed to. Karen had a feline-like mystique about her.

We spent several hours talking. Karen was 15 and would be a sophomore at Lincoln High School in Manitowoc, a town southeast of Green Bay.

"Do your folks have a cottage here?" I asked nervously opening a dialogue.

"Yeah. My parents and four other families bought our property up the beach just after the War. We're all from Manitowoc," the perky brunette said.

"That's about the same time that my parents bought ours. The cottage is just now finished. It has taken a long time to get it built," I replied, starting to feel a little at ease with this older and much more sophisticated girl. "We always used to come up to Door County in the summer time. We used to rent a cottage at Fish Creek before we built here."

"Geez. We've been coming to Door County since I was real little. We used to camp out at Peninsula State Park in a tent," Karen added as she giggled a little bit.

"Hey, we did that too. I was pretty small then but I remember Nicolet Bay and our trips to Ephraim. I don't think we had a tent, though. I remember looking up at the stars before I went to sleep."

"My dad and all his friends built the cabins by hand. Dad tore down an old chicken coop and silo at home and trucked all the lumber up here to build our cabin. It took us quite a while too. Other than Terry, do you have any other brothers and sisters?" Karen asked changing the subject almost mid-sentence.

"I have a sister. She's a senior at West High this year. How about you?"

"Well ... I had an older sister, Beth, but she died when I was only two. She caught pneumonia," Karen relayed to me somewhat reluctantly.

"Geez. I'm sorry. A friend of mine drowned at Fish

Creek. I sure felt bad about that. It must have been real awful to lose your sister."

"Yeah, it was. I'd prefer not to talk about her though," Karen added as her peppy demeanor seemed to dim. "I guess I better go. Why don't you come up to our place one of these days. Come with me once and I'll show you which cabin is ours."

Although Karen was only two when her sister died, the death had a profound impact on her relationship with her parents. Rather than devote more attention and express more affection to their remaining daughter, Karen's parents withdrew and denied her the love that every child needs. Violet Markwardt would later in life reveal to her daughter that it hurt too much to be close to her child. She feared that she might lose Karen also. Her father, Lester, of German extraction, lost his job at a bank when it closed during The Depression, furthering the feeling of loss that permeated Karen's early years. Karen cried every time she thought of Beth.

"Buzzie's got a girlfriend," Terry revealed to Mom while she was fixing a fresh catch for dinner.

"Oh? Did you meet a girl, Buz?" Mom asked.

"Yeh. She sure is nice. She's from Manitowoc."

"She's got boobies, too," Terry said, embellishing on his faux pax.

"Oh?" Mom, now keenly interested, responded. "How old is your girlfriend, Buz?"

"Mom, she's not a girlfriend. She's just a friend. She's nice to talk to. She's a year or so older," I said as I fudged on Karen's age.

"Why don't you invite her to the cottage. I'd like to meet her," Mom inquired with an obvious interest in my female friend.

Several days passed. It was the Fourth of July. Karen came over to help us set off our firecrackers. She went over with a BANG!

"This is my friend Karen," I said as I introduced the Manitowoc girl to my mom.

"Oh ... hello," Mom said coolly as she fidgeted

nervously and found something to do in the kitchen.

Years later when I introduced my second fiancée to my mother she turned her back on us and left the room in an obvious act of rejection. This event wasn't nearly as bad, but even at 13 I knew something wasn't right with my mom as far as girlfriends were concerned.

"Mom? Karen is going to stay for dinner and fireworks after, okay?"

"That's okay. Dad is going to light the charcoal. You can fix your own burgers on the grill when you're ready to eat," she replied with her back to us.

"Mrs. Quist? I've got my slacks, sweatshirt and stuff. Where would you like me to put them so I can change out of my suit later?" Karen inquired.

"Leave them in Joanie's room," Mom said as she made a little effort to be hospitable. My sister had the middle bedroom on the first floor, but she was working in Egg Harbor.

We took off to the beach where Terry was busy building forts in the sand.

"Whatcha doin'?" Karen asked my brother who would soon turn eleven years old.

"I'm building a big fort so we can blow it up with cherry bombs," Terry informed my friend, who probably wasn't too up-to-date on the play habits of younger boys.

Karen, now in our world, joined in. We built a massive fort using old coffee cans as molds for the fine, wet sand. Finally the massive structure was ready for demolition.

Cherry bombs, for the uninitiated, are hard, round, red firecrackers, larger than a cherry, loaded with gun powder or whatever, with a long fuse. When ignited they set off one heck of an explosion.

We set several bombs in critical areas that supported roofs, second stories and turrets of the fort.

"When I count to three light the fuses," Terry, who was in charge of the demolition, ordered. We all retreated to a safe spot.

BOOM ... BOOM ... BOOM!

Almost in unison the bombs went off and sand filled

the sky just like in the war movies.

"WOW!" Karen exclaimed. "That was scary," she effused, apparently getting into this boys' stuff.

"Hey Karen? We've got two-inchers and four-inchers too," Terry added.

The four-inchers were like a small, red stick of dynamite. They had awesome destructive power.

"Watch, Karen," Terry said, as he grabbed a large Hills Brothers coffee can and placed it firmly in the sand with a four-incher under it. Terry lit the fuse.

KA-BOOM!

The explosion had a kind of muffled, deep-throated sound but the coffee can soared into the air like a rocket, punching out the seams.

"WOW!" Karen shrieked, delighted with the display. "This is fun," she added, as she seemed to be having a great time.

"The cherry bombs even go off in the water," I interjected wanting to keep the enthusiasm percolating.

I lit the fuse of the cherry bomb. Suddenly as I was drawing my arm back to toss the explosive device into the bay the fuse ignited with a burst of flame and consumed the whole length of the fuse. Panicked, I let it go!

BOOM!

It exploded just beyond my finger tips.

"Ouch!" I yelled.

"What happened?" Karen asked as she ran to my side.

"It went off too quick! My fingers are tingling."

A very close call. I got a blood blister on my right index finger. Our enthusiasm, tempered by this almost near-life-altering experience, caused us to switch our focus. My future would have dramatically changed had I lost one or two fingers on my right hand.

The sun was setting and it was getting dusk. That meant the loathsome mosquitos would be merging from their swamp-like environment and would be attacking us in droves. The joke in northern Wisconsin was that often these pesky insects would land at an airport and the fixed based operators would refuel a few of them before they realized that they were not airplanes. They were big, but not quite that big.

"Hey, let's go to the house and play ping-pong," I suggested to Karen, hoping that Terry wouldn't want to play. We had a "breezeway" between the cottage and our garage which was screened in to protect us from those blood-thirsty pests. We were still concerned about catching polio from these critters.

Karen changed into more conservative apparel which must have met with Mom's approval.

It took Karen a little while to catch onto the game.

"Ha! I gotcha," Karen boasted, as she made another point.

It was time to turn the tables on my erstwhile non-competitive fun match. I got a high, soft return.

SLAM!

I drilled a shot past Karen that she never saw coming.

"What was that?" she said in disbelief.

"You were getting a little too cocky," I said, as I let her know that just 'cuz I was only 13 I wasn't a wimp. She was impressed, I thought.

We adjourned to the living room waiting for the last rays of light to disappear. The real fireworks needed a pitch black night to really create the desired effect. In northern Wisconsin in July, darkness didn't come until after 9:00 p.m.

There was a *LIFE* magazine on the coffee table and it had a picture of the *USS Arizona* sinking in Pearl Harbor (which I have used on this cover).

"Karen? What do you remember about the War?" I asked, recalling those memorable days just four years past.

"Geez, I remember all the things we did at school to raise money and bring all the rubber and cans to school and all that stuff, but most of all I remember the submarines."

"The submarines?" I asked, excited that Karen knew something about subs.

"Yeah. They were made in Manitowoc during the War.

We got out of school every time one was launched. We called them 'fresh water submarines.'"

"Holy cow! I read a book on subs. I would have given anything to see one launched." I was amazed. We shared so many interests in common.

About that time Terry burst into the room.

"It's dark enough now. Let's shoot 'em off," Terry shouted, and hurriedly ran out the door with his box of fireworks. We each had our own favorites.

Dad supervised the pyrotechnics. We used the large, fat sparklers with a long stem to light the fuses. We had roman candles and rockets that burst open in blues, greens and reds high over our heads; spin wheels that we attached to a tree; Mount Vesuvius that spewed forth multifarious colors; and Terry's favorites, stink bombs and smoke bombs. I didn't like them, but they helped keep the mosquitos away.

"Hey, it's late. I better get on home," Karen stated somewhat reluctantly. I walked her down to the main beach by Johnson's Store.

"That was really fun, Buster. Thanks for having me over."

Karen gave me a big smile, then turned and faded away into the night. I had lied when I told Mom that Karen was a friend. She was, in my mind at least, my first real girlfriend.

Later that evening I was in the bathroom which was adjacent to the kitchen. Mom and Dad thought I was in bed out of earshot.

"Hub? That girl that your son brought here is in high school. Heavens to Betsy, she's darned near as old as Joanie," Mom said.

"Well, I don't see anything wrong with that," Dad said, sounding unconcerned.

"She looks like a 'floozie' to me, Hub."

"Geez, Thelma. You're always saying that. I thought she was a nice girl, and those people from Manitowoc up the beach are real nice folks. What's the problem?" Dad asked.

"She could take advantage of Buz. She's been around. I can tell. He's just a young, innocent boy. He's only thirteen. She's fifteen," Mom continued.

They finally dropped the subject. I didn't know how Karen would "take advantage" of me, but I thought I'd sure like to find out.

Amongst a treasure trove of pictures is one with Karen and me on the beach (which adorns the cover). I'm lying in the sand next to her, with Terry adjacent. Karen's friend and neighbor Jinny Kluth is next to her, and our neighbor Gordy Ware is also in the original picture.

Another is in the driveway of our cottage. Karen's new (to her) 1929 Model A Ford that she acquired in June 1949 is in the background, adjacent to Dad's 1950 beige Packard. Karen and I posed together with Jinny and my brother Terry, who appears not to be enjoying the moment. Dad took the picture. He thought Karen was "cute."

I accepted Karen's invite and went to her cabin one evening for a bonfire and cookout. All of her neighbors, mostly from Manitowoc, built a huge bonfire with billowing columns of smoke to ward off the mosquitos. We had hot dogs roasted on the fire, marshmallows and watermelon. What a picnic. But, all of that was simply a sideshow to one of nature's greatest theatrical productions — the "Northern Lights."

As we sat on the beach, eyes cast to the heavens, the sky became a kaleidoscope of various hues of blues, greys, greens and subtle silvers, known as the Aurora Borealis. Charged particles in a magnetic field created luminous flashes of light that held us spellbound. Karen's touch to my hand and her unforgettable smile made the moment even more magical. I had witnessed this phenomenon before but now I saw this wonder through more sensitive eyes.

"Buster? I've got a 'secret place' that Jinny and I go to. Would you like to see it?"

"Heck, yes. Where is it," I replied eagerly as I burned my marshmallow to a crisp. My focus had withdrawn from the fire to the warmth of the person beside me.

"Can't tell you. It's a secret," Karen said in a sort of flippant manner, as I had discovered was her trait. "If you can bring your boat up here tomorrow, I'll show you the neatest place in the whole wide world."

I couldn't sleep thinking what the next day might reveal. Past summers it was hard to find new things to do. Now, a whole new universe opened up to me at Sand Bay, and I had someone to share it with.

Karen, in a two-piece swim suit which revealed her curvaceous body, was waiting for me on the beach as I cut the motor and glided into the shoreline. Karen's dog, a Springer Spaniel whom she named Skipper, was also anxious to get into the boat, wagging his tail wildly and barking up a storm.

"We're going to the creek," Karen announced. The creek was only a short distance from her cabin. I didn't even know it was there. It <u>was</u> a secret place.

The water was too low. A sand bar blocked the boat's entry into the creek, so we waded up the shallow inlet to the almost invisible sanctuary so cherished by my friend, who by now thought enough of me that she could share her secret place.

"Let's search the bank for turtle eggs, Buster. Sometimes you can see the tops sticking out in the sand. They're like little ping-pong balls. Look out for the big live ones though. They're snappers," Karen warned.

"Geez, this is really a neat place. Skipper likes it. Look at him jumping through the weeds."

"Yeah he loves it here. I only have him for the summer. Mom and Dad won't let me keep him at home," Karen, obviously dismayed by that thought, revealed.

Strange, I thought. Who would only have a dog for the summer?

"Dad always gives me things and then takes them away. It's his way of punishing me for things he thinks I did wrong," Karen said reluctantly, as she caught a good-sized frog and held it softly while calming the little creature's fear.

"Hey! There's snakes in the water too," I declared as

one swam between my legs.

"Yeah. And what's really neat are the smelt that run in early summer. You can just reach into the water and catch them in your hands. They're delicious, you know?"

"Yep, we've had them," I countered.

We returned to Karen's cabin after our morning at her secret place. I met Mr. and Mrs. Markwardt for the first time, and they certainly were a lot more gracious to me than my mother was to Karen. The knotty pine interior and the large fireplace reminded me of our cottage, but given what Karen had disclosed to me earlier, there was an imperfection or a flaw in both of our houses. Like the knotty pine paneling, it served well as an ornamental veneer but its structural strength was flawed by the knots.

Another and this time more magnificent summer was coming to an end. Karen invited me up to her cabin. I think her folks were in Sturgeon Bay. After a fun-filled summer together we were alone.

"Do you like to dance, Buster?" Karen asked as we sat in front of her cabin taking in a romantic view of the bay.

"I'm not very good at it, Karen, I'm sorry to say."

"Well then, I'll teach you," she offered. We went inside the cabin and turned on her portable radio which was just like Joanie's. Awkward at first, I began to feel the rhythm of the music and gathered a sense of the emerging moment. I was just a little taller than Karen and we were eye to eye. We were both in swim togs. Karen was in her two-piece suit. She was the most beautiful girl I had ever seen and now we were as close as bees on a flower. Our skin and the beads of sand rubbed lightly together warming our touch. I felt a tingly feeling as goosebumps popped out on my arms and legs. I was being carried away on a swift and churning current with a destination unknown, oblivious to any consequence.

I wanted to kiss her. Could I embolden enough courage to do it? I had only given a girl a peck on the lips when we played "spin the bottle." This was far more meaningful. My palms were sweating. I was only a breath away from Karen's luscious lips. For the first time in my life, Mandrake performed his magic in the presence of a girl. I was spellbound. I closed my eyes and made the momentous move....

"No! No you can't kiss me," Karen said in a kind of flippant manner.

"Why?" I asked stunned by her reply.

"Cuz ... I'm not sixteen yet! I won't kiss a boy until I'm sweet sixteen," she laughed.

That would be near Christmas time.

I didn't know if I was disappointed or relieved.

Suddenly Karen broke away from our embrace and ran to the door of the cabin.

"Hi Mom, hi Dad," she said, as her parents pulled up in their car in back of the cottage. I was so enveloped by the ecstacy of the moment that I didn't even hear the car pull up. The most delightful and intriguing moment in my life came to an abrupt end.

Mr. and Mrs. Markwardt were, as Dad said, good folks. They were a little surprised that we were alone. We visited a while and then I headed back to our cottage. I looked back several times to catch one last glimpse of this beautiful, and as I had just experienced, sensual, but flirtatious young woman. The hot sun-baked sand between the cabin and the cooler, wet sand near the Bay shore never singed my toes. Euphoric and flying, I never touched the sizzling silicone.

"Did you have fun at Karen's?" Mom asked inquisitively.

"Oh yeah, same old stuff," I replied, smart enough to allay my mother's worst fears.

I didn't know what love was at this time in my life, but this must have been it.

Tuesday, Joanie was off to Oshkosh State Teacher's College. Terry was entering Miss Ferslev's fifth-grade class at Elmore School, and I returned to face "Mickey" McMahon's hard-nosed, intimidating tactics at Franklin Junior High.

As I rode my bike down Dousman Street a new breeze of confidence flew in my face. That air of apprehension that I felt when opening that door to the seventh grade a year ago had subsided like a worn out wind. Emboldened by my new sense of manhood I found the mettle to bear up to whatever danger "Mickey" could muster. My new-found conviction was tested early.

"Didja hear what happened to Jerome DeMille?" Dave Evjue asked in my first class.

"No. What happened?"

"'Smokey' (Jerome) came to school today with a Mohawk haircut. You know, his whole head was shaved except for a strip down the middle," Dave said.

"Holy cow! What happened then?" I asked.

"Mickey came into his class and kicked him out of school until his hair grows back. Geez, he's going to miss a month of school, eh?" Dave said.

Eighth grade was off to a predictable start, but all the talk in P.E. class was about the new boy in school. A real big kid with the reputation of starting (and finishing) a lot of fights. His name was Richard Campbell. He was secretly known as "Soup." I wanted to know this guy. I wanted to be his friend.

"What school did you come from, Richard?" I asked sizing up this red-headed kid, who was probably six feet tall and weighed over 160 pounds.

"Saint Pat's. The priest said I was incorrigible. He told my mom that I was hopeless. I'd never amount to anything," Soup lamented seemingly demoralized by the experience. "Hey, call me 'Soup,' okay?"

"Geez. You got kicked out of a Catholic school? I guess that you've heard of 'Mickey,' our principal?"

"Yeah. Already had a meeting with her," Soup, rolling his eyes, said.

"What did she say?" I asked anxiously.

"She said she knew all about me and my reputation. She said she was the boss and made all the rules and as long as I followed her rules she and I would get along just fine. She also told me that if I was good I could play football with the ninth graders," Soup relayed to me and several of the guys who had huddled around us in the

241

gym.

"Geez. I wish that I could play," I lamented.

Obviously Soup was big and tough enough to play with the ninth graders. Hell, he could have played with the West High varsity team, but his size wasn't the only reason he was playing. Miss McMahon and the assistant football coach, Ralph Swartz, figured that if they let Soup play it would occupy his time and he would work off his pent-up hostility on the playing field rather than in the classroom. It worked! Soup and "Mickey" avoided conflict and the former trouble-maker went on to become an outstanding high school, college and professional football player. There was an upside to the tough and rigid discipline at Franklin. There were many success stories. I was also one of them. "Tough Love," if that is what it was, didn't harm any of us. In fact, it made us stronger.

Despite the excitement of the new year Karen was foremost on my mind. I fondly embraced my pillow each night as I continued to dance to "Some Enchanted Evening," and the other songs we heard. I was anxious to get back to Sand Bay to see her. Fortunately, Dad wanted to return to the spot where he had discovered a school of Northern Pike. Early Saturday the four of us headed north to find an extension to a summer that was fading fast.

"I'm going to Karen's," I announced to my parents as we rolled up in the driveway at our cottage.

"Take a sweatshirt," Mom advised, as there was a "chill" in the early morning air.

The exhilaration of my expectation and the aerobic stimulus of my near-mile sprint up the beach made the sweatshirt an unnecessary drag on its purpose. Breathing hard, I knocked on the door of the Markwardt cabin.

There was no reply. Their car was not there. The cabin seemed to be vacated for the winter. Maybe Karen would not be there anymore. I was crestfallen. I turned and retreated slowly from the place that had just a week before fueled a flame of infatuation.

On the beach where the sand had previously quickened my step, I found time to linger and gather my thoughts. Karen never said she wouldn't be back. Why didn't she tell me? I sat down on a log near where bonfires had just recently ignited the summer dark and focused my attention away from the place that hosted my first romance. I looked longingly out on to the bay.

The sky was no longer bright and blinding to the eye. It was as if a massive translucent curtain had dropped to the horizon's edge casting a greyness to the blue. At the end of every summer season in Door County I felt a sense of sadness that this time of joy and a precious period of my youth had passed forever. This summer I felt a deeper loss.

This year, the summer of '49, provoked a deeper response from within me. Would I ever see and feel the warmth of this person again? Was she as intrigued with me as I was with her? Or, was I just a summer fling, to be toyed with? A young, innocent kid, who as Mom had said, "would be taken advantage of." Considerable time would pass before these painful questions would be answered.

"How come you're back so fast," Mom asked.

"Karen and her parents must be gone for the season," I said, unable to disguise my disappointment.

"Just as well," Mom said, obviously pleased by the fact that the "floozie" would no longer be tempting or corrupting my innocence. "She's too old for you anyways," Mom added.

Unknown at this point in time, Karen and I had a more significant familial fact in common other than our similar introduction to Door County. Karen's mom was Czech and her family roots were in Bohemia. Violet Markwardt attended the Moravian Church. Had our mothers and grandmothers known that at this point in time, there probably would have been little resistance to our relationship — despite the age gap. Karen wouldn't have been a "floozie" in my mother's eyes. Our grandmothers would have been ecstatic — probably promoting a "match" as grandmothers are prone to do.

Fast forward to the year 2002. I was sitting in my office

243

in Phoenix, Arizona, when I received a message from Dave Kroll, an assistant manager of our company. This story achieves a high rating in the "small world" category.

"Buster, I want you to take a moment and visit with a gentleman from Wisconsin who is thinking about joining our company. His name is David Columb."

"Sure, anytime," I responded to Dave, who himself was born and raised in the Dairy State and who often summered at Gill's Rock in Door County.

Mr. Columb and I shook hands.

"I understand that you grew up in Door County, David? Where?" I asked.

"Oh, it's a very small town. You've never heard of it, I'm sure," David replied.

"Try me," I said as I laughed, making David feel at ease.

"I was born and raised on a farm near Little Sturgeon," he revealed.

"I know exactly where that is. It's only a couple of miles from Sand Bay." I said.

"Geez, how do you know that area?" David asked, his face lighting up like a Christmas tree. As soon as he said "geez," I knew our roots were entwined.

"I was born and raised in Green Bay but we had a summer home in Sand Bay. It was and still is one of my most cherished places in the whole wide world," I revealed to my guest, who was ecstatic.

We shared our mutual experiences for the better part of an hour. David revealed to me that his great aunt Josie Wautlet, had written a history of her grandfather (entitled Francois) who emigrated to the U.S. from Belgium in 1856 as a seven-year-old boy. It is a marvelous history, written by a granddaughter mostly in narrative (as I have done) to preserve the memories of the Le Grave family and the Walloon-speaking Belgians who settled this area around Brussels, Wisconsin, buying land at $.50 to $1.50 per acre.

Josie effectively related the story of Kermiss (the celebration of harvest) in the fall of 1871. October 8, 1871 — the very day of the great Peshtigo Fire that I related in Chapter 2. Josie describes the critical moment that meant *certain death or survival for the Le Grave family: "It was a tornado of winds, fire, a hell that beat mercilessly, devouring everything in its way. There was no place to go. 'Run for the well! Run for the well!' Eloi Meunier shouted through the high-pitched whining of the wind and fire that fell all around."[1]*

Miraculously, the family was saved by finding refuge deep down in the well. (Some who also fled to wells died of carbon monoxide poisoning.) Unfortunately, many of their neighbors lost their lives and virtually all their homes, farms, buildings, and churches were destroyed. The survivors were all forced to start anew.

Francois Le Grave married Henriette Meunier. It was Alex Meunier's nephew Alex whom I've speculated knew my father well and was probably the one person responsible for selling Dad the lot at Sand Bay — thereby securing our circuitous connection with this marvelous pioneer family.

Back at school I must have been daydreaming, thinking wistfully about Karen and the summer that had slipped so quickly away when:

"Larry! Larry Quist! You're not paying attention to a word I've said," Miss Harker, my eighth-grade English teacher, barked at me.

"I'm sorry Miss Harker, I didn't hear what you just said," I replied, shaken and embarrassed.

"Do you have wax in your ears young man?" she asked. "Have you memorized the Preamble to *Evangeline?*"

"No. No. I'm sorry. We were out of town this past weekend and I didn't get to study," was my lame excuse. Sure glad she didn't know what the real reason was.

"You darn sure better wake up and smell the roses young man or else ..."

Not a good start, and Miss Harker hammered on me all year. I did learn the Preamble, as memorization seemed to come easy, but all I could muster was a "C" in her class.

Dave Evjue, who had become a good friend, and I went to Gussert's Shawano Drug Store across the street from school to get a sandwich and a Cherry Coke. We often went to the Big Dip on Shawano for a lunch time snack and a malted milk — with saltine crackers of course. We both had a soft spot for Wisconsin's favorite product, ice cream.

"Miss Bacon made me the editor of the *Purple Parakeet*, Buster. Isn't that swell?" Dave informed me.

"Geez, that is swell Dave. That should make your chances pretty good to be on the staff of the *Parrott* at West, huh?"

"Yeah, I hope so. You'll have to write something for the paper, okay?" Dave suggested.

"Sure. Just as long as Miss Harker doesn't get to grade it," I said as we both laughed.

Dave was a good student and never got in trouble. He had no choice. His dad, Glen, was head of the biology and science department at West. I had enough smarts to align myself with the right kids.

It was duck hunting time. Sand Bay would be a perfect place for a hunting trip, so my cousin Larry and his buddies figured. Loaded up with ammunition and tons of beer Larry, Jack Coonahan, Floyd Rathburn, Bob Markham, Whitey Stuiber, and another carload of the boys headed for the Quist cottage for a weekend.

The ducks had already abandoned the friendly confines of Sand Bay. That didn't prevent Larry and his buddies from bagging their limit however. Somehow Mom and Dad caught wind of the fact that there was a hunting party camped out at the cottage. Sunday morning after church, we headed north. Our unexpected entrance revealed an unforgettable sight. The exhausted and inebriated hunters were semi-comatose, sprawled all over the living room, the bedrooms and the loft. Mom's immaculate cottage was a mess. Hanging from the rafters were the trophies — seagulls! Unable to find their intended game the hunters bagged the unsuspecting and innocent white gulls.

Typical of Dad's demeanor, he simply said, "Clean her up boys and leave everything as you found it. And — please bury the gulls."

1. Josie Wautlet, *Francois* (Algoma, Wis.: Zebra Enterprises, 1990), p. 34.

CHAPTER 8: ANOTHER CHANGE

THANKSGIVING 1949 WAS A DAY that will be remembered as one of the, if not the most, defining moments in the lives of our branch of the Quist family. As defining as the moment was when Knut and Clara and Sam and Hulda made their decision to leave their beloved country of Sweden almost half a century earlier. Dad's announcement to us dramatically changed all of our lives.

"Kids, your dad has been offered a new job. A promotion. I've been offered the position of branch manager for BMA. We have the choice of moving to Flint, Michigan, or Albuquerque, New Mexico."

"Albu ... what?" I asked.

"Albuquerque. It's in New Mexico," Dad, not sure of the spelling, said.

"Do we have to leave Green Bay?" Terry asked.

"No, we don't have to leave, but this is a great opportunity for your dad. I don't really want to turn it down, you see."

Almost immediately, I went to find my geography book. Terry and I had absolutely no idea where New Mexico was, other than it sounded like it was far, far away. We knew of Michigan, of course, even though our familiarity was with the Upper Peninsula, and we could picture that environment. New Mexico was a blank, and much of it actually was.

I was excited by the news because Dad was excited. He was beaming with pride. But, as I began to reflect on what leaving Green Bay would mean, misgivings, enhanced by flashbacks of prior events in my life in this perfect place, started building in my mind.

What about my friends with whom I enjoyed and

shared so many common interests and values? What about my future at West High and the YMCA, where I wanted to replicate the feats of my heroes? And what about our most cherished spot, Sand Bay? Why leave now when we were all comfortable and successful in just about every aspect of our lives? Especially Dad. His business was thriving. He was one of the most respected men in his profession in Green Bay.

"Thelma, Gerry (Tritch, a vice president of BMA) says that I'll receive a guaranteed salary of $24,000 per year plus all expenses, and with bonuses I could probably make $40,000 per year," Dad said as I was all ears. "That's more than twice as much as I make now."

I didn't have to "create" my father's comment to Mom. I remember it verbatim. $24,000 was a substantial income in 1949.

"Hub, I hate to leave Green Bay. Now that Larry is going into the service Mamma is going to be alone. And, you've got such a good business here. I don't like the idea of starting up new in a place so different as New Mexico," Mom opined.

"I'm going to meet with Gil in Milwaukee on Monday and see what he says," Dad offered, as it appeared that his decision, as yet, wasn't final.

Having firsthand insight into my dad's career in years to come, I suspect that the essence of Gil's conversation with Dad went something like this:

"Hub, you're a terrific salesman. You've built an excellent clientele in and around Green Bay. The folks in northern Wisconsin know you and trust you. It takes years to gain people's trust and confidence. Your business will grow to the point where you'll make the same amount of money in Green Bay as you will in New Mexico, plus you won't have the headaches as a manager like I do. You'll be out of sales. You'll have to recruit, train and motivate men and deal with their problems and frankly, Hub, I've got to tell you as one of my best friends and fishing buddies, you're not the manager type. You're not tough enough and you've got to be firm with your agents."

Dad, of course, didn't agree. The lure of a big salary

clouded his vision. Gil didn't want to lose his number one producer but, hypothetically, his analysis of the situation was accurate.

It's almost an axiom that the best athletes don't make good coaches. Likewise, great salesmen usually make poor managers. Corporations, particularly in this era, had the propensity to try to force square pegs into round holes. Dad was a terrific salesman, but a square peg.

Mom, too, had her reservations, but another factor entered the picture.

"Mamma (Grandmother Anderson), I hate to leave Green Bay, but there is one thing positive about a move, you know?"

"What's that Telma?" Gramma asked. (For some reason she never could say the H in Thelma).

"It would get Hub away from that damn Mabel. He says that he's not having an affair with her but Edna (Rose) says she knows he is," Mom relayed to her mother. This topic had been covered many times.

"Well, maybe that will work but Hub always has had an eye for the ladies. I don't think a move from Green Bay will change that," Gramma said prophetically.

Just prior to Christmas, Cousin Larry drove my mom and dad to Albuquerque in their new 1950 Packard Sedan to look at the opportunity, the city and a home. Dad had traded the ugly yellow Nash for a 1949 Packard and, for some reason, then immediately traded it for the beige, handsome-looking new Packard, just off the assembly line. In Albuquerque he bought a 1948 Plymouth. We were now a two-car family. The decision to move to the southwest was made. Larry and Mom returned to Green Bay. Dad stayed in a new home they bought while in Albuquerque.

I regretfully announced to my friends and teachers that I was leaving Green Bay. I was overwhelmed with "going away" parties. Each occasion made it more difficult to leave.

January passed. We were still in Green Bay. February. We were still suffering through another winter, thinking about the warm deserts of New Mexico. Finally in March, our home on Dousman sold. The cottage sold in a New York minute in the middle of the winter. Mayflower loaded up our belongings and Mom and Dad packed us into the Packard and we were off.

Given the inordinate amount of time to sell our home, I had the time to assimilate my feelings for the loss of my friends and the extraction from my roots. We were departing a place in a time when Mom and Dad never had to worry about strangers that might harm us, and we could walk or ride our bikes anywhere without fear. This wonderful place by the bay was devoid of gangs and trouble-makers who could exert peer pressure on our innocent minds. Gone too was a community support system dedicated to the development of its youth. I had time to privately shed my tears but not my regrets, which lingered.

What was ahead? Would this dramatic change be for the good as our grandparents' was nearly a half-century before? How would we all adapt to the vastly different environment and culture in a land as foreign to us as a different country? Would Dad be able to replicate the success that he enjoyed in Green Bay and be able to provide for his family?

And, what about our sanctuary at Sand Bay? An ideal place for kids who were going to be growing up in the fifties. That quiet cove couldn't be replicated and, most importantly, I wouldn't be there in June when Karen returned for the summer. Would I ever see my first love again? We had just begun to know each other. Was there a future for us or was she lost forever? Un-imagined surprises loomed ahead. (Book Two)

Once our car had left the City by the Bay, I kept my eyes focused out the front window and to the future — 1800 miles away.

———

We made an important stop in Kansas City, Dad's home office. We got the tour of the tallest building we had ever been in and ate in the company cafeteria. Dad had shed his trappings as a salesman and was now "management" — ostensibly the critical cog in the company's machine.

We made a pit stop in Tucumcari, New Mexico.

"Look, look at that gas station," I yelled as we were about to pass a structure that was made to look like an Indian tee-pee. "The sign says 'Terrible Terry from Tucumcari.'"

Mom, Dad and I thought the play on words was humorous. Terry didn't. He felt that the sign was a direct reflection on him. He had a "conniption fit," as Mom said. He cried for thirty minutes and never erased the terrible memory from his mind. Dad's promise that a big surprise awaited him at the new house was salve to his wounded pride. True to Dad's claim, it was indeed a big surprise.

About an hour later, scanning the strange rock outcroppings on what appeared to us as a barren, desert landscape, I made an unexpected visual discovery.

"Dad what are those white peaks?" I said, as I looked north out the right rear window.

"That's snow. Those are mountains covered with snow," Dad informed us.

"Wow! I didn't think New Mexico had mountains like we had seen in Wyoming and in Canada," I said, surprised while marveling at this phenomena.

"Yep. People in Wisconsin think New Mexico is all a flat desert. It's not. You'll see when we get close to Albuquerque. I understand that there is great skiing right now real close to town."

As we drove through a little town by the name of Moriarity on Route 66, the sun was setting in a late March sky that was slowly transforming itself into an artist's landscape. There were various shades of red, orange and yellow painted on a canvas of various hues of blue and turquoise — a color that didn't exist on our palette or in our vocabulary. The montage was pierced by long, narrow, finger-like clouds. Peering over the back of the front seat, Terry and I were caught for the first time in the magic spell of the southwestern sky.

The brilliant show of colors quickly faded into darkness as we wound our way through the Sandia

Mountains. As we emerged from the narrows of Tijeras Canyon a sea of lights, like reflections off a mirrored lake, greeted and welcomed us to this unique place called Albuquerque.

Exhausted but revitalized Terry said, "Geez, it's pretty."

"That's why they call it 'The Land of Enchantment,'" Dad said laughing.

1.
Lars O. Lagerqvist, *A History of Sweden* (Stockholm, Sweden: The Swedish Institute, 2001), p. 7.

2. Ibid., p. 11.

3. Ibid., p. 18.

4. *"Vikings in the New World"* web site.

5. Lagerqvist, op.cit., p. 21.

6. Taken from the Vasa Museum brochures.

7. Lagerqvist, op. cit., p. 87.

8. Ibid., p. 87.

9. Ibid., p. 155.

10. The House of Immigrants Museum, Vaxjö, Sweden.

1. *The Great Peshtigo Fire* (The State Historical Society of Wisconsin, 1999), pp. 54-55.

2.
Robert G. Wells, *Embers of October* (Princeton, N.J.: Prentice-Hall, 1968).

3. Doris Kearns Goodwin, *No Ordinary Time, Franklin and Eleanor Roosevelt: The Home Front in World War II.* p. 283.

1. Herbert Romerstein and Eric Breindel, *The Venona*

Secrets: Exposing Soviet Espionage and America's Traitors, (Regnery Publishing Co.), p. 608.

1. Doris Kearns Goodwin, *No Ordinary Time: Franklin and Eleanor Roosevelt: The Home Front in World War II.* (New York: Touchtone, 1994), p. 339.

2. Ibid., p. 384.

3. Ibid., p. 394.

4. Brown County Central Library, Office of Price Stabilization.

5. Goodwin, op. cit., p. 340.

6. Ibid., p. 346.

7. Ibid., p. 344.

8. Ibid., p. 364.

9. M.A. Barlament, *Footprints in the Sands of Time*, p. 26.

10. Louis Gianetti, Flashback: A Brief History of Film, (Princeton, N.J.: Prentice Hall, 1986), p. 199.

11. Goodwin, op. cit., p. 598.

12. Ibid., p. 598.

13. Ibid., p. 602.

14. Ibid., p. 605.

15. Ibid., p. 610.

16. Ibid., p. 608.

17. Adam Zagorin, "Notebook," *Time*, March 3, 2003, p.

18. Goodwin, op. cit., p. 342.

19. R. J. Rummel, *Death by Government* (New Brunswick, N.J.: Transaction Publishers, 1994), p. 8.

20. Robert B. Stinnett, *Day of Deceit* (New York: Touchstone, 2000), p. 8.

21. Admiral Robert A. Theobald, *The Final Secret of Pearl Harbor* (New York: Devin-Adair, 1954), p. ix.

1. Paul Recer, Associated Press, *The Arizona Republic* (January 3, 2003).

1. Josie Wautlet, *Francois* (Algoma, Wis.: Zebra Enterprises, 1990), p. 34.

www.ingramcontent.com/pod-product-compliance
Lightning Source LLC
Chambersburg PA
CBHW020511100426

42813CB00030B/3197/J